GRIMM

"By the pricking of my thumbs,
something wicked this way comes."
-William Shakespeare, Macbeth

DYNAMITE®

Nick Barrucci, CEO / Publisher
Juan Collado, President / COO

Joe Rybandt, Executive Editor
Matt Idelson, Senior Editor
Anthony Marques, Associate Editor
Kevin Ketner, Editorial Assistant

Jason Ullmeyer, Art Director
Geoff Harkins, Senior Graphic Designer
Cathleen Heard, Graphic Designer
Alexis Persson, Production Artist

Chris Caniano, Digital Associate
Rachel Kilbury, Digital Assistant

Brandon Dante Primavera, V.P. of IT and Operations
Rich Young, Director of Business Development

Alan Payne, V.P. of Sales and Marketing
Keith Davidsen, Marketing Director
Pat O'Connell, Sales Manager

ISBN13: 978-1-5241-0326-2
ISBN10: 1-5241-0326-8

First Print
10 9 8 7 6 5 4 3 2 1

Online at www.DYNAMITE.com
On Facebook /Dynamitecomics
On Instagram /Dynamitecomics
On Tumblr dynamitecomics.tumblr.com
On Twitter @dynamitecomics
On YouTube /Dynamitecomics

NBC

For three-plus years, Portland policeman Nick Burkhardt has fought crime both traditional and monstrous in his role of a Grimm, hunter of hidden fantastical beasts among us known as wesen. Unknown by Nick or anyone else, his longstanding love, Juliette Silverton has recently been transformed into a wesen as well...specifically a hexenbiest, possessor of great powers that come with the potential corruption of her soul. How long can she keep her secret, especially when she finds herself in more than a little danger?

Story by
Caitlin Kittredge

Art by
Maria Sanapo (#1-3, 4 pg.1-11, 5)
German Erramouspe (#4 pg.12-22)

Color by
Chris O'Halloran

Letters by
Tom Napolitano

Senior Editor
Matt Idelson

Associate Editor
Anthony Marques

Editorial Assistant
Kevin Ketner

Collection Design
Alexis Persson

Special Thanks to
Jason McNaughton and Liz Umeda

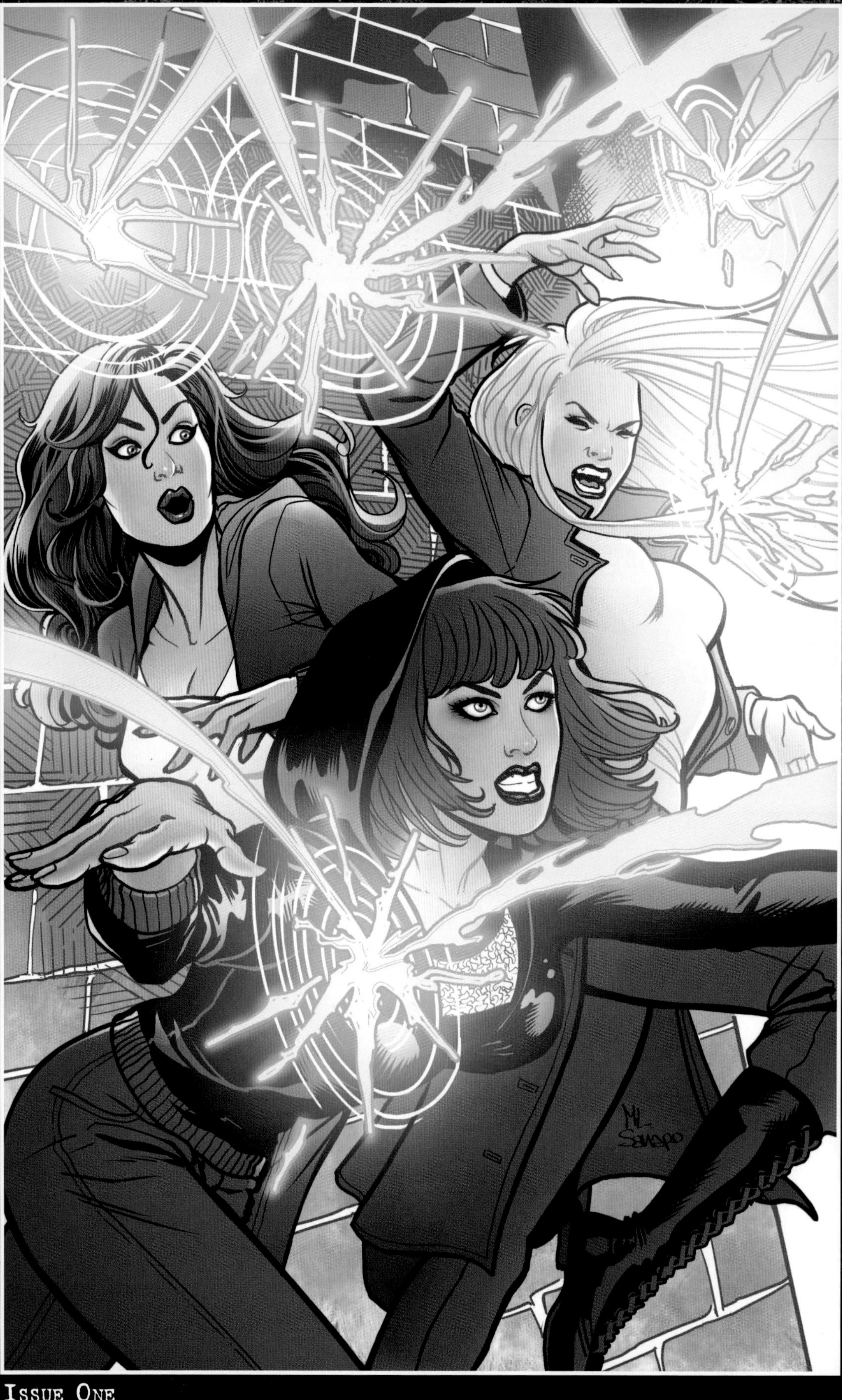

Issue One

Art by Maria Sanapo | Colors by June Chung

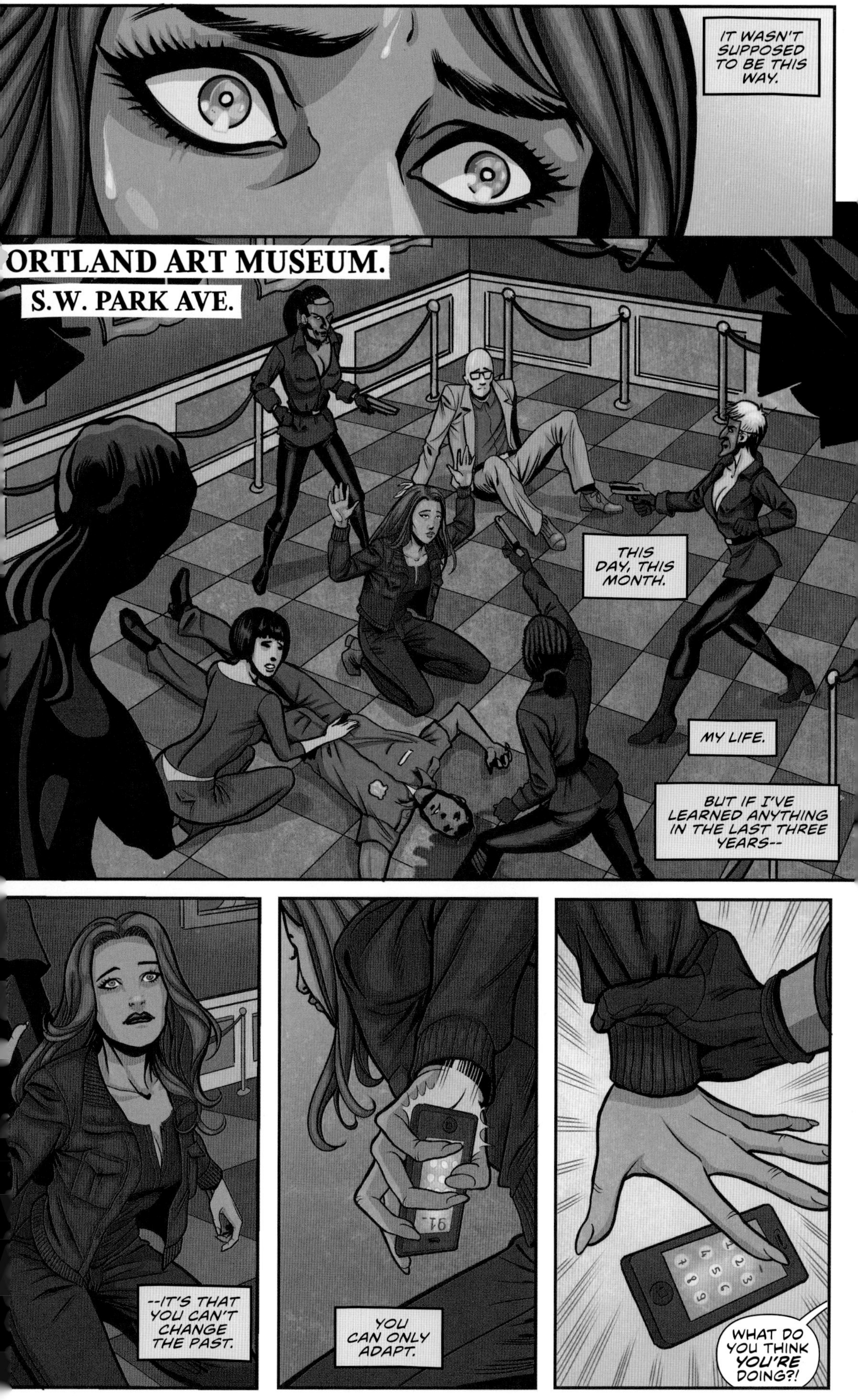
IT WASN'T SUPPOSED TO BE THIS WAY.
ORTLAND ART MUSEUM.
S.W. PARK AVE.
THIS DAY, THIS MONTH.
MY LIFE.
BUT IF I'VE LEARNED ANYTHING IN THE LAST THREE YEARS--
--IT'S THAT YOU CAN'T CHANGE THE PAST.
YOU CAN ONLY ADAPT.
WHAT DO YOU THINK YOU'RE DOING?!

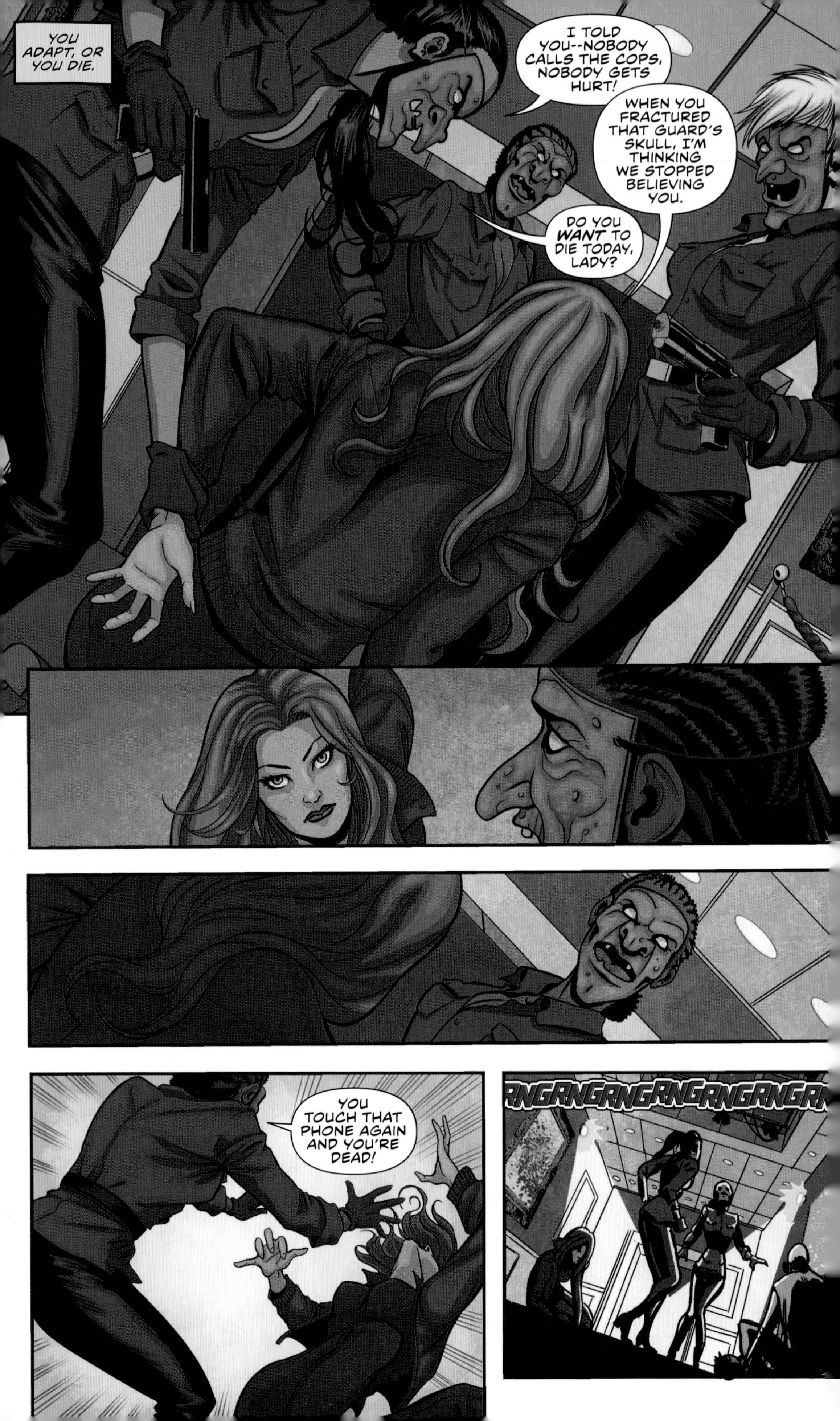
YOU ADAPT, OR YOU DIE.
I TOLD YOU--NOBODY CALLS THE COPS, NOBODY GETS HURT!
WHEN YOU FRACTURED THAT GUARD'S SKULL, I'M THINKING WE STOPPED BELIEVING YOU.
DO YOU WANT TO DIE TODAY, LADY?
YOU TOUCH THAT PHONE AGAIN AND YOU'RE DEAD!
RNGRNGRNGRNGRNGRNGRNGR

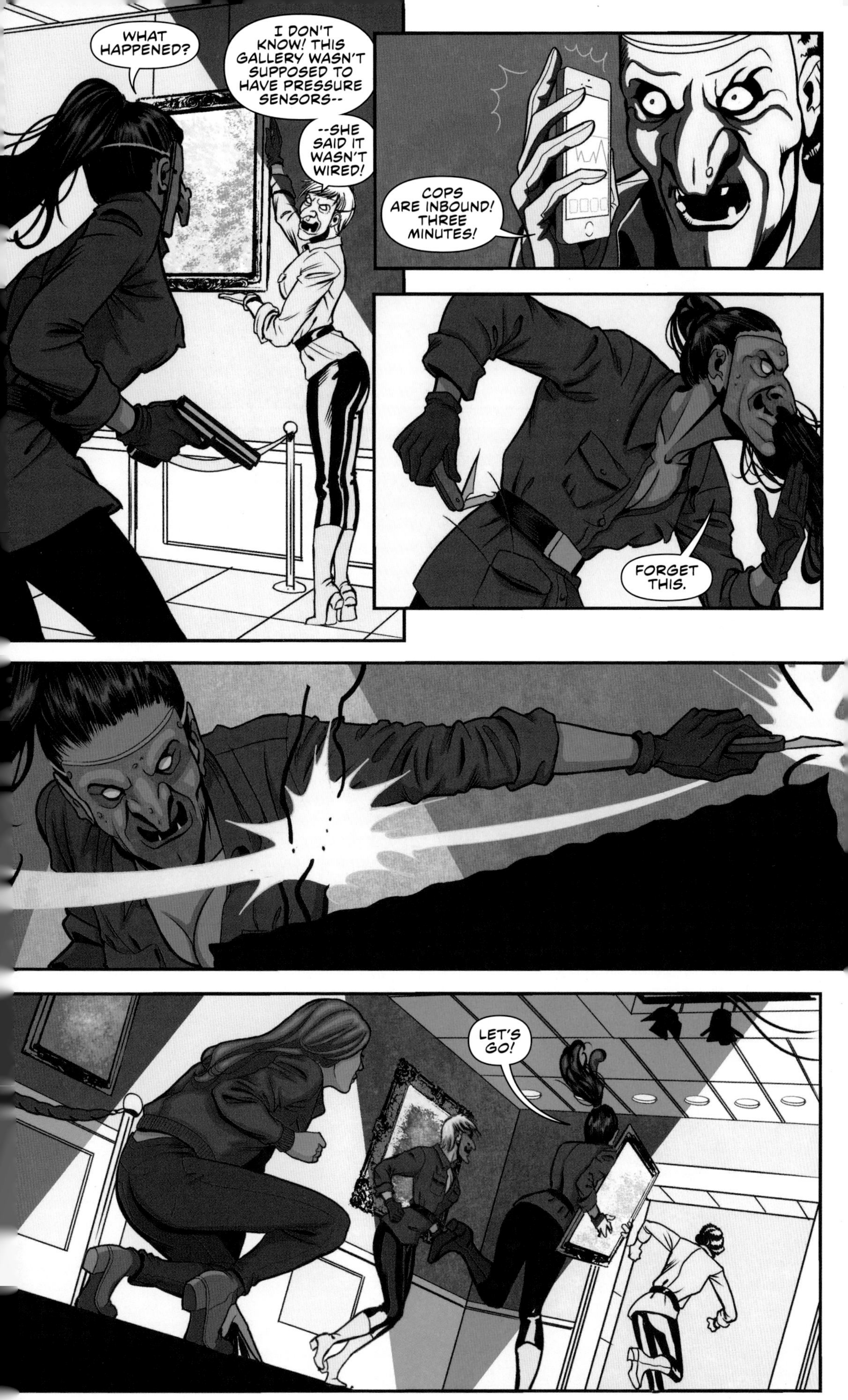
WHAT HAPPENED?
I DON'T KNOW! THIS GALLERY WASN'T SUPPOSED TO HAVE PRESSURE SENSORS--
--SHE SAID IT WASN'T WIRED!
COPS ARE INBOUND! THREE MINUTES!
FORGET THIS.
LET'S GO!

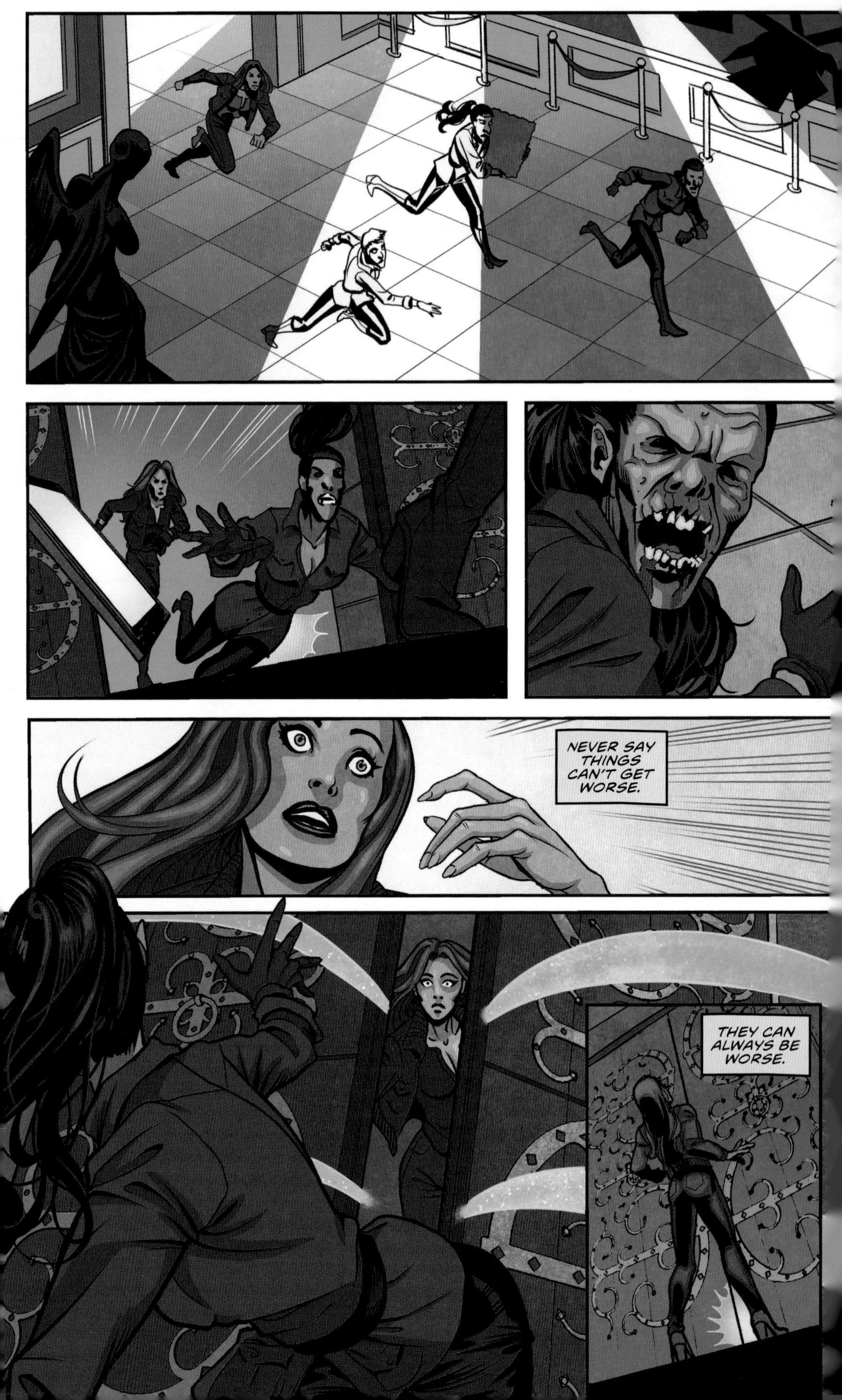
NEVER SAY THINGS CAN'T GET WORSE.
THEY CAN ALWAYS BE WORSE.

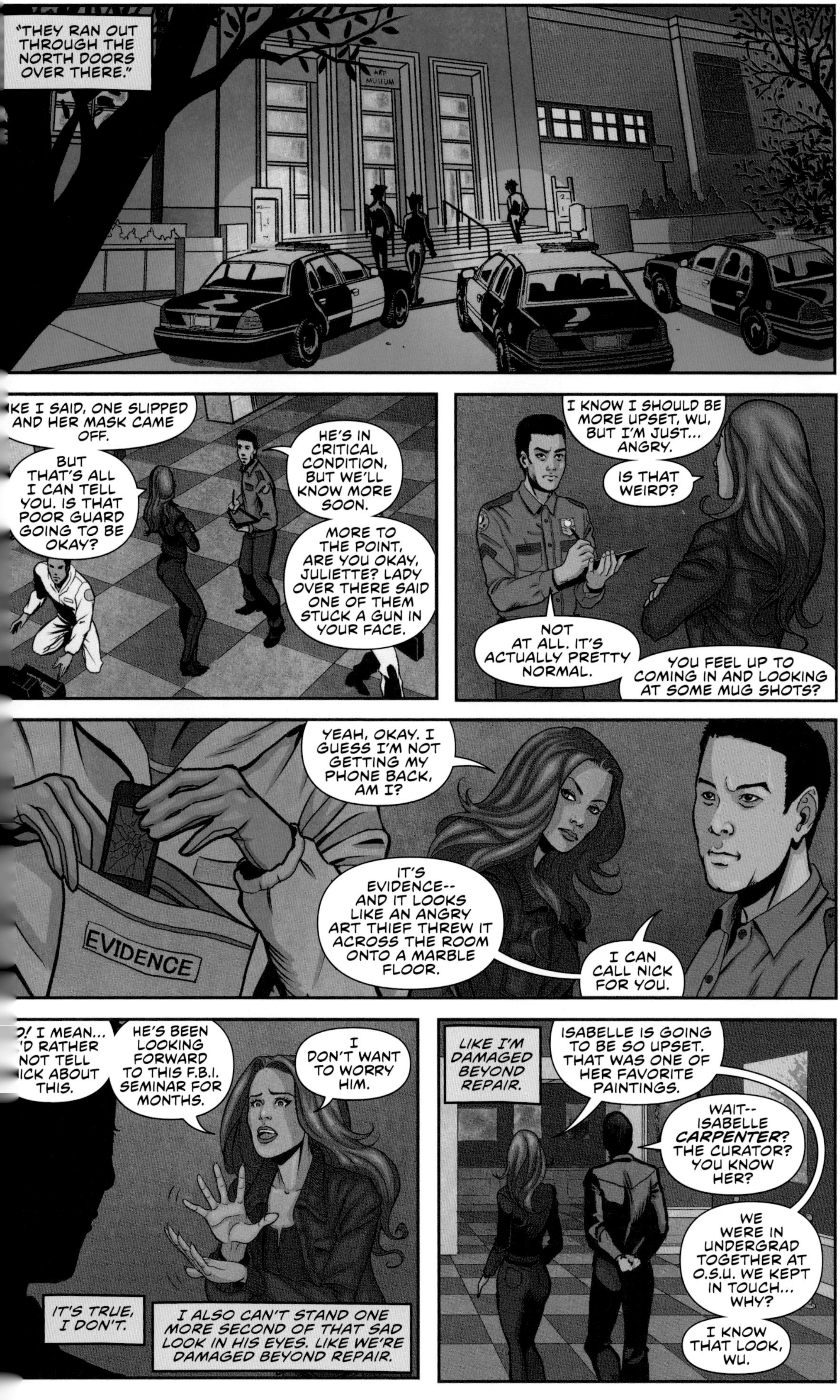

"THEY RAN OUT THROUGH THE NORTH DOORS OVER THERE."
ART MUSEUM
KE I SAID, ONE SLIPPED AND HER MASK CAME OFF.
BUT THAT'S ALL I CAN TELL YOU. IS THAT POOR GUARD GOING TO BE OKAY?
HE'S IN CRITICAL CONDITION, BUT WE'LL KNOW MORE SOON.
MORE TO THE POINT, ARE YOU OKAY, JULIETTE? LADY OVER THERE SAID ONE OF THEM STUCK A GUN IN YOUR FACE.
I KNOW I SHOULD BE MORE UPSET, WU, BUT I'M JUST... ANGRY.
IS THAT WEIRD?
NOT AT ALL. IT'S ACTUALLY PRETTY NORMAL.
YOU FEEL UP TO COMING IN AND LOOKING AT SOME MUG SHOTS?
YEAH, OKAY. I GUESS I'M NOT GETTING MY PHONE BACK, AM I?
EVIDENCE
IT'S EVIDENCE-- AND IT LOOKS LIKE AN ANGRY ART THIEF THREW IT ACROSS THE ROOM ONTO A MARBLE FLOOR.
I CAN CALL NICK FOR YOU.
O! I MEAN... 'D RATHER NOT TELL ICK ABOUT THIS.
HE'S BEEN LOOKING FORWARD TO THIS F.B.I. SEMINAR FOR MONTHS.
I DON'T WANT TO WORRY HIM.
IT'S TRUE, I DON'T.
I ALSO CAN'T STAND ONE MORE SECOND OF THAT SAD LOOK IN HIS EYES. LIKE WE'RE DAMAGED BEYOND REPAIR.
LIKE I'M DAMAGED BEYOND REPAIR.
ISABELLE IS GOING TO BE SO UPSET. THAT WAS ONE OF HER FAVORITE PAINTINGS.
WAIT-- ISABELLE CARPENTER? THE CURATOR? YOU KNOW HER?
WE WERE IN UNDERGRAD TOGETHER AT O.S.U. WE KEPT IN TOUCH... WHY?
I KNOW THAT LOOK, WU.

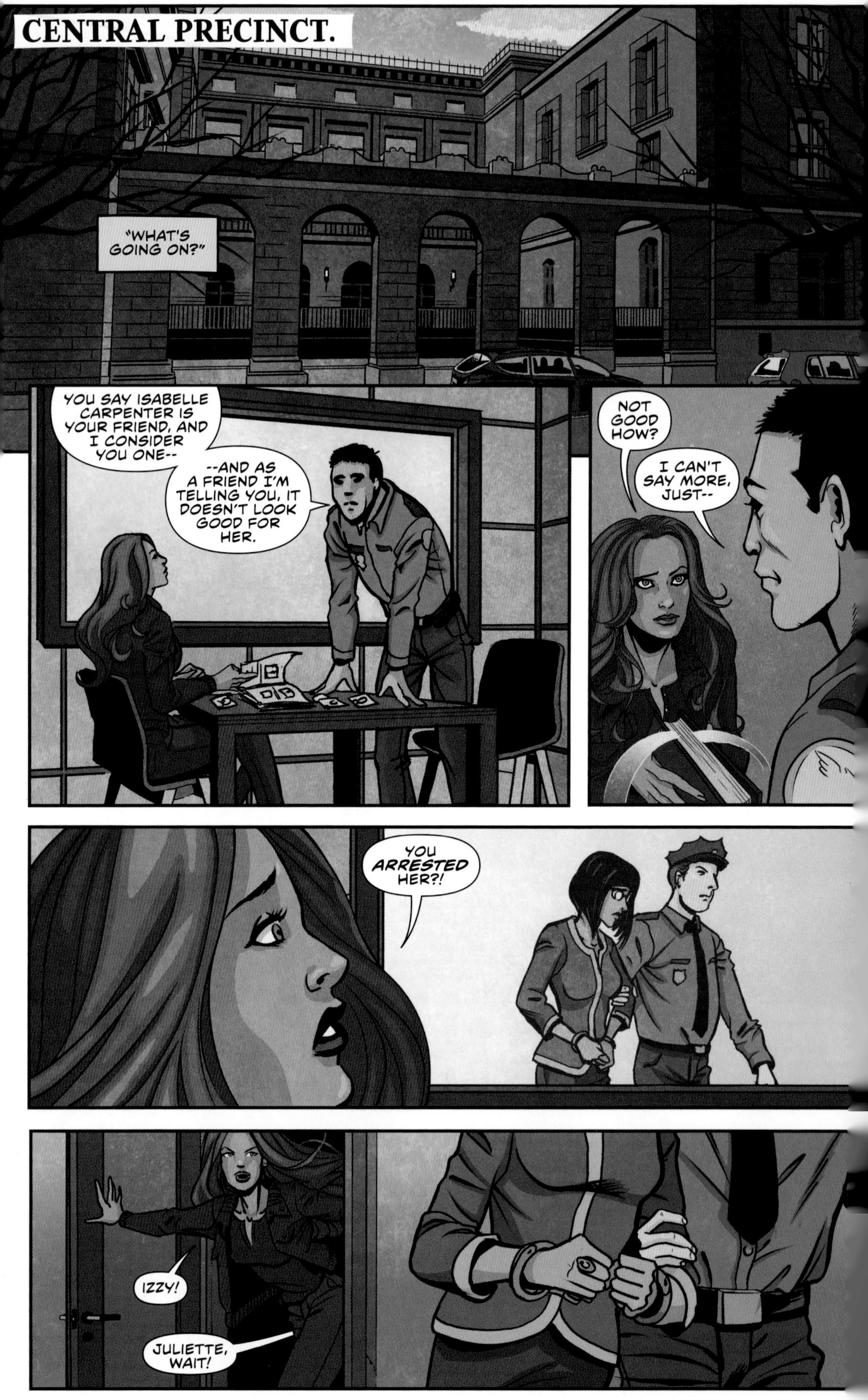
CENTRAL PRECINCT.
"WHAT'S GOING ON?"
YOU SAY ISABELLE CARPENTER IS YOUR FRIEND, AND I CONSIDER YOU ONE--
--AND AS A FRIEND I'M TELLING YOU, IT DOESN'T LOOK GOOD FOR HER.
NOT GOOD HOW?
I CAN'T SAY MORE, JUST--
YOU ARRESTED HER?!
IZZY!
JULIETTE, WAIT!

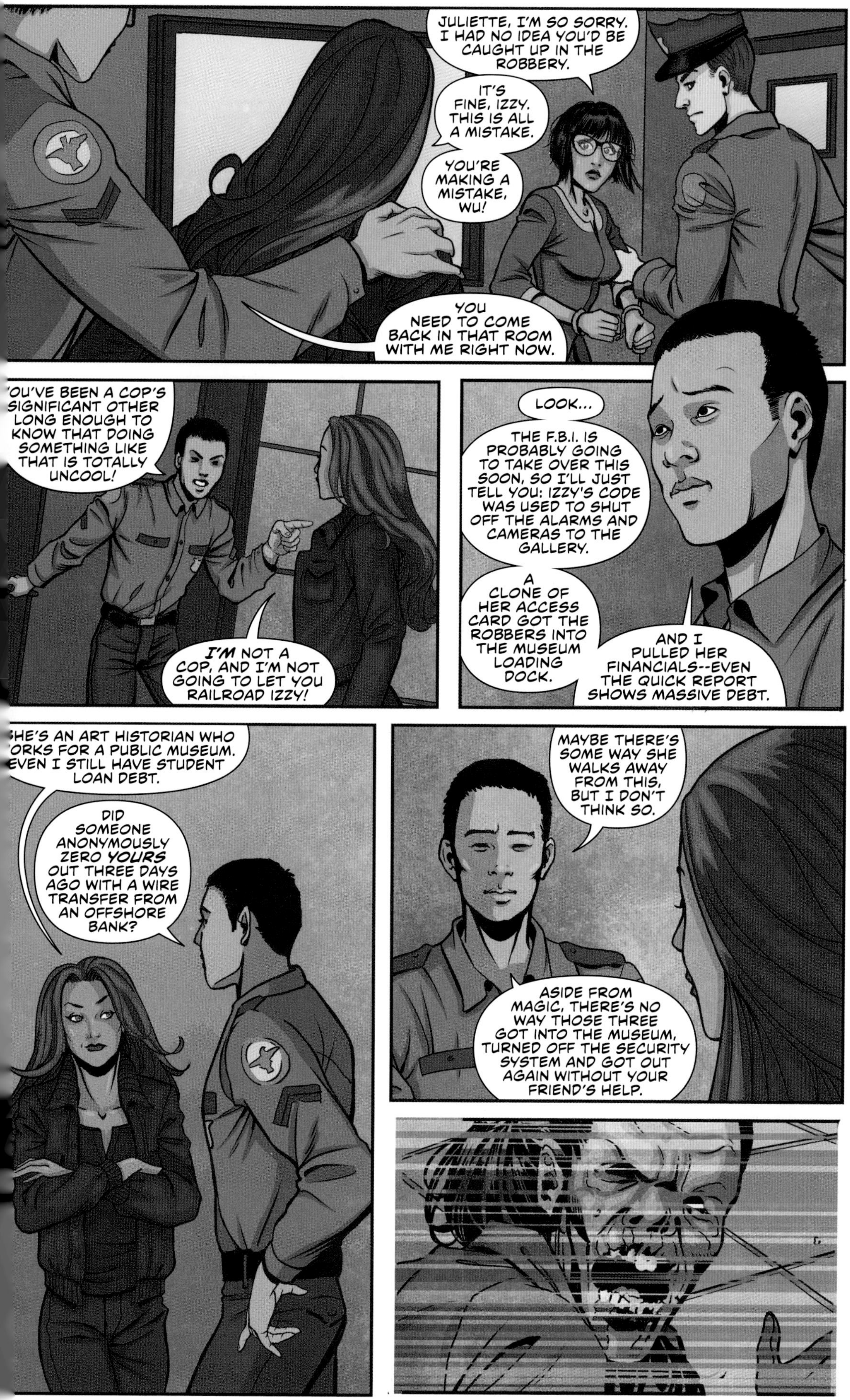
JULIETTE, I'M SO SORRY. I HAD NO IDEA YOU'D BE CAUGHT UP IN THE ROBBERY.
IT'S FINE, IZZY. THIS IS ALL A MISTAKE.
YOU'RE MAKING A MISTAKE, WU!
YOU NEED TO COME BACK IN THAT ROOM WITH ME RIGHT NOW.
YOU'VE BEEN A COP'S SIGNIFICANT OTHER LONG ENOUGH TO KNOW THAT DOING SOMETHING LIKE THAT IS TOTALLY UNCOOL!
I'M NOT A COP, AND I'M NOT GOING TO LET YOU RAILROAD IZZY!
LOOK...
THE F.B.I. IS PROBABLY GOING TO TAKE OVER THIS SOON, SO I'LL JUST TELL YOU: IZZY'S CODE WAS USED TO SHUT OFF THE ALARMS AND CAMERAS TO THE GALLERY.
A CLONE OF HER ACCESS CARD GOT THE ROBBERS INTO THE MUSEUM LOADING DOCK.
AND I PULLED HER FINANCIALS--EVEN THE QUICK REPORT SHOWS MASSIVE DEBT.
SHE'S AN ART HISTORIAN WHO WORKS FOR A PUBLIC MUSEUM. EVEN I STILL HAVE STUDENT LOAN DEBT.
DID SOMEONE ANONYMOUSLY ZERO *YOURS* OUT THREE DAYS AGO WITH A WIRE TRANSFER FROM AN OFFSHORE BANK?
MAYBE THERE'S SOME WAY SHE WALKS AWAY FROM THIS, BUT I DON'T THINK SO.
ASIDE FROM MAGIC, THERE'S NO WAY THOSE THREE GOT INTO THE MUSEUM, TURNED OFF THE SECURITY SYSTEM AND GOT OUT AGAIN WITHOUT YOUR FRIEND'S HELP.

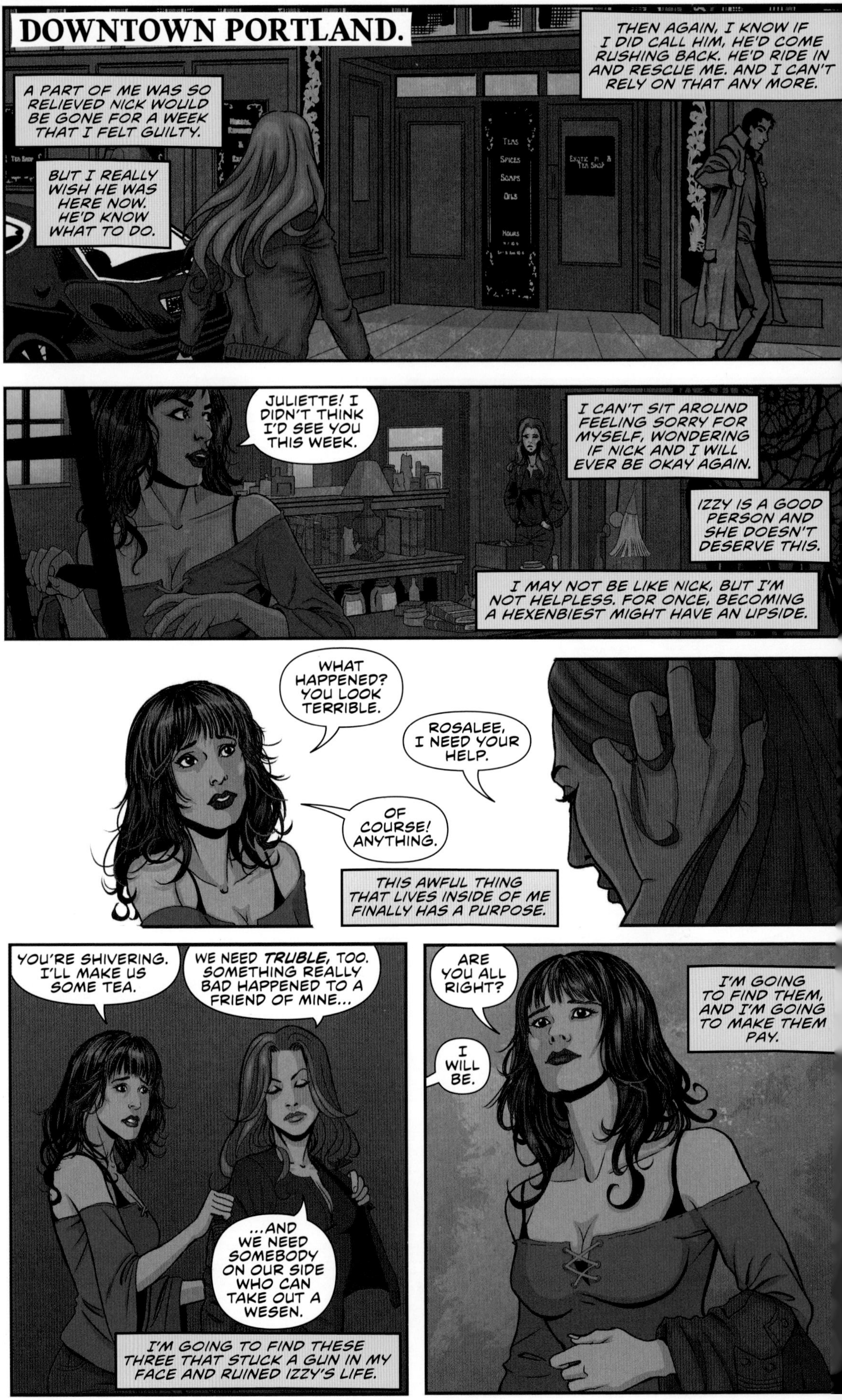
DOWNTOWN PORTLAND.
A PART OF ME WAS SO RELIEVED NICK WOULD BE GONE FOR A WEEK THAT I FELT GUILTY.
BUT I REALLY WISH HE WAS HERE NOW. HE'D KNOW WHAT TO DO.
THEN AGAIN, I KNOW IF I DID CALL HIM, HE'D COME RUSHING BACK. HE'D RIDE IN AND RESCUE ME. AND I CAN'T RELY ON THAT ANY MORE.
TEAS
SPICES
SOAPS
OILS
HOURS
EXOTIC SPICE & TEA SHOP
JULIETTE! I DIDN'T THINK I'D SEE YOU THIS WEEK.
I CAN'T SIT AROUND FEELING SORRY FOR MYSELF, WONDERING IF NICK AND I WILL EVER BE OKAY AGAIN.
IZZY IS A GOOD PERSON AND SHE DOESN'T DESERVE THIS.
I MAY NOT BE LIKE NICK, BUT I'M NOT HELPLESS. FOR ONCE, BECOMING A HEXENBIEST MIGHT HAVE AN UPSIDE.
WHAT HAPPENED? YOU LOOK TERRIBLE.
ROSALEE, I NEED YOUR HELP.
OF COURSE! ANYTHING.
THIS AWFUL THING THAT LIVES INSIDE OF ME FINALLY HAS A PURPOSE.
YOU'RE SHIVERING. I'LL MAKE US SOME TEA.
WE NEED TRUBLE, TOO. SOMETHING REALLY BAD HAPPENED TO A FRIEND OF MINE...
...AND WE NEED SOMEBODY ON OUR SIDE WHO CAN TAKE OUT A WESEN.
I'M GOING TO FIND THESE THREE THAT STUCK A GUN IN MY FACE AND RUINED IZZY'S LIFE.
ARE YOU ALL RIGHT?
I WILL BE.
I'M GOING TO FIND THEM, AND I'M GOING TO MAKE THEM PAY.

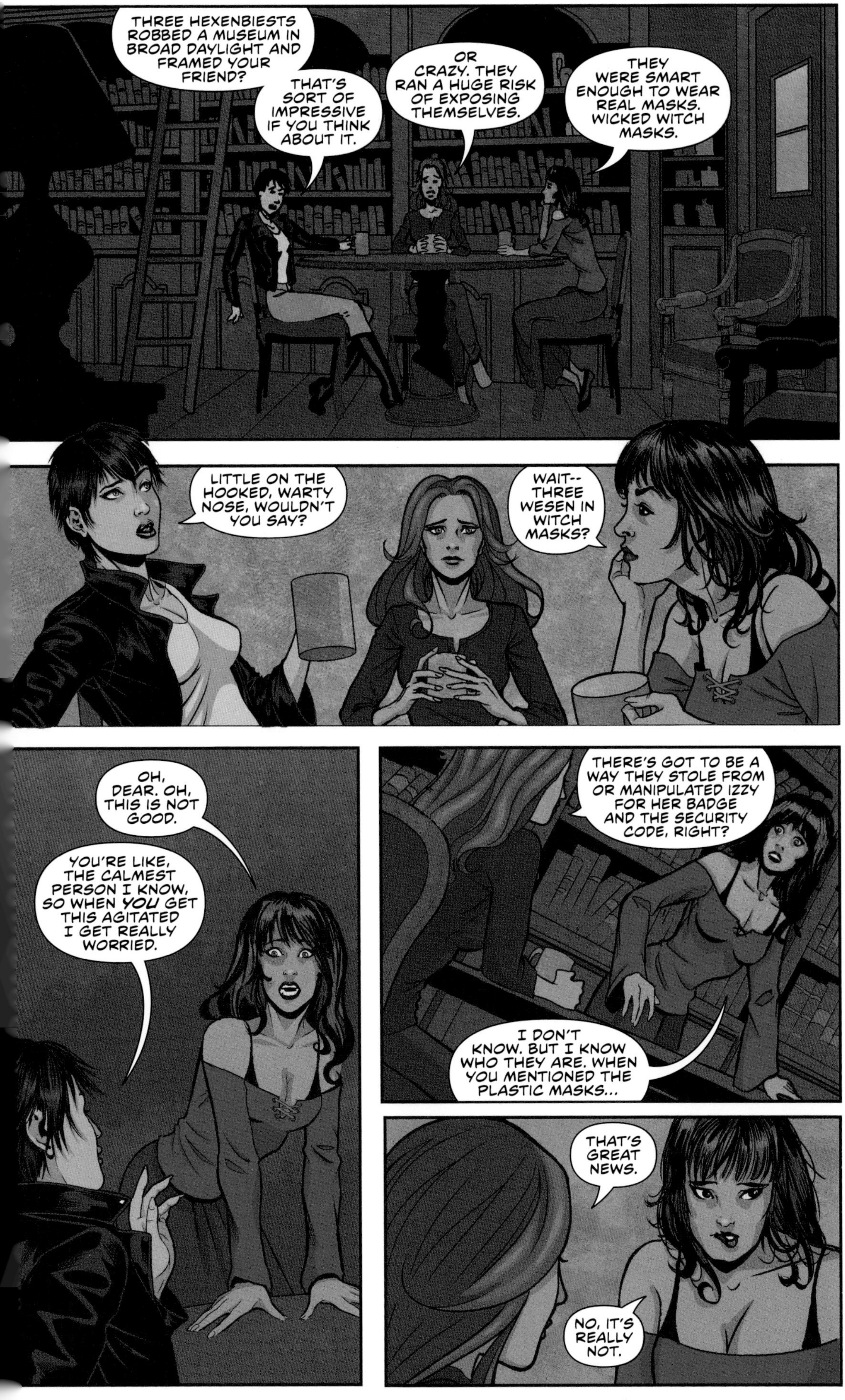
THREE HEXENBIESTS ROBBED A MUSEUM IN BROAD DAYLIGHT AND FRAMED YOUR FRIEND?
THAT'S SORT OF IMPRESSIVE IF YOU THINK ABOUT IT.
OR CRAZY. THEY RAN A HUGE RISK OF EXPOSING THEMSELVES.
THEY WERE SMART ENOUGH TO WEAR REAL MASKS. WICKED WITCH MASKS.
LITTLE ON THE HOOKED, WARTY NOSE, WOULDN'T YOU SAY?
WAIT-- THREE WESEN IN WITCH MASKS?
OH, DEAR. OH, THIS IS NOT GOOD.
YOU'RE LIKE, THE CALMEST PERSON I KNOW, SO WHEN *YOU* GET THIS AGITATED I GET REALLY WORRIED.
THERE'S GOT TO BE A WAY THEY STOLE FROM OR MANIPULATED IZZY FOR HER BADGE AND THE SECURITY CODE, RIGHT?
I DON'T KNOW. BUT I KNOW WHO THEY ARE. WHEN YOU MENTIONED THE PLASTIC MASKS...
THAT'S GREAT NEWS.
NO, IT'S REALLY NOT.

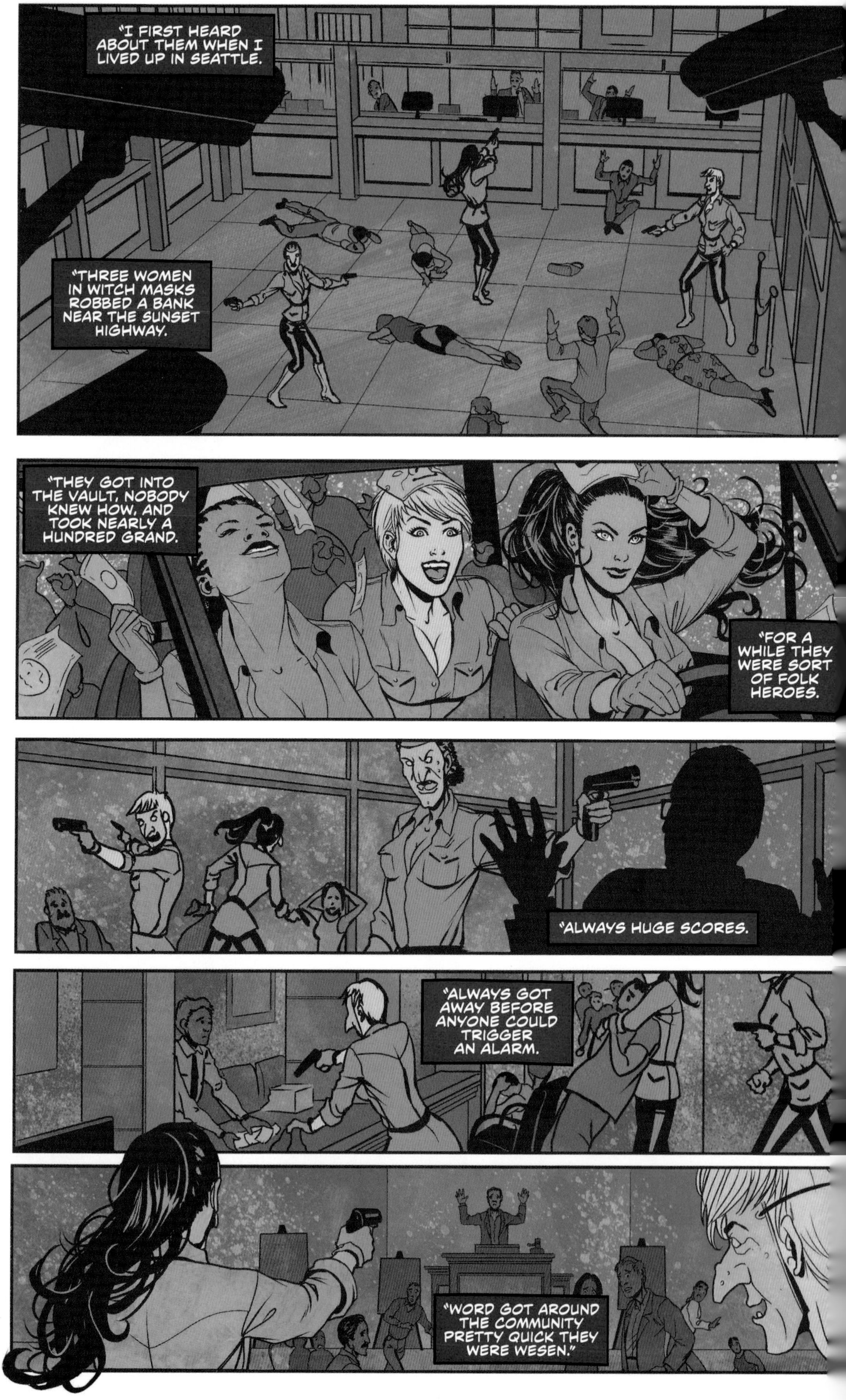
"I FIRST HEARD ABOUT THEM WHEN I LIVED UP IN SEATTLE.
"THREE WOMEN IN WITCH MASKS ROBBED A BANK NEAR THE SUNSET HIGHWAY.
"THEY GOT INTO THE VAULT, NOBODY KNEW HOW, AND TOOK NEARLY A HUNDRED GRAND.
"FOR A WHILE THEY WERE SORT OF FOLK HEROES.
"ALWAYS HUGE SCORES.
"ALWAYS GOT AWAY BEFORE ANYONE COULD TRIGGER AN ALARM.
"WORD GOT AROUND THE COMMUNITY PRETTY QUICK THEY WERE WESEN."

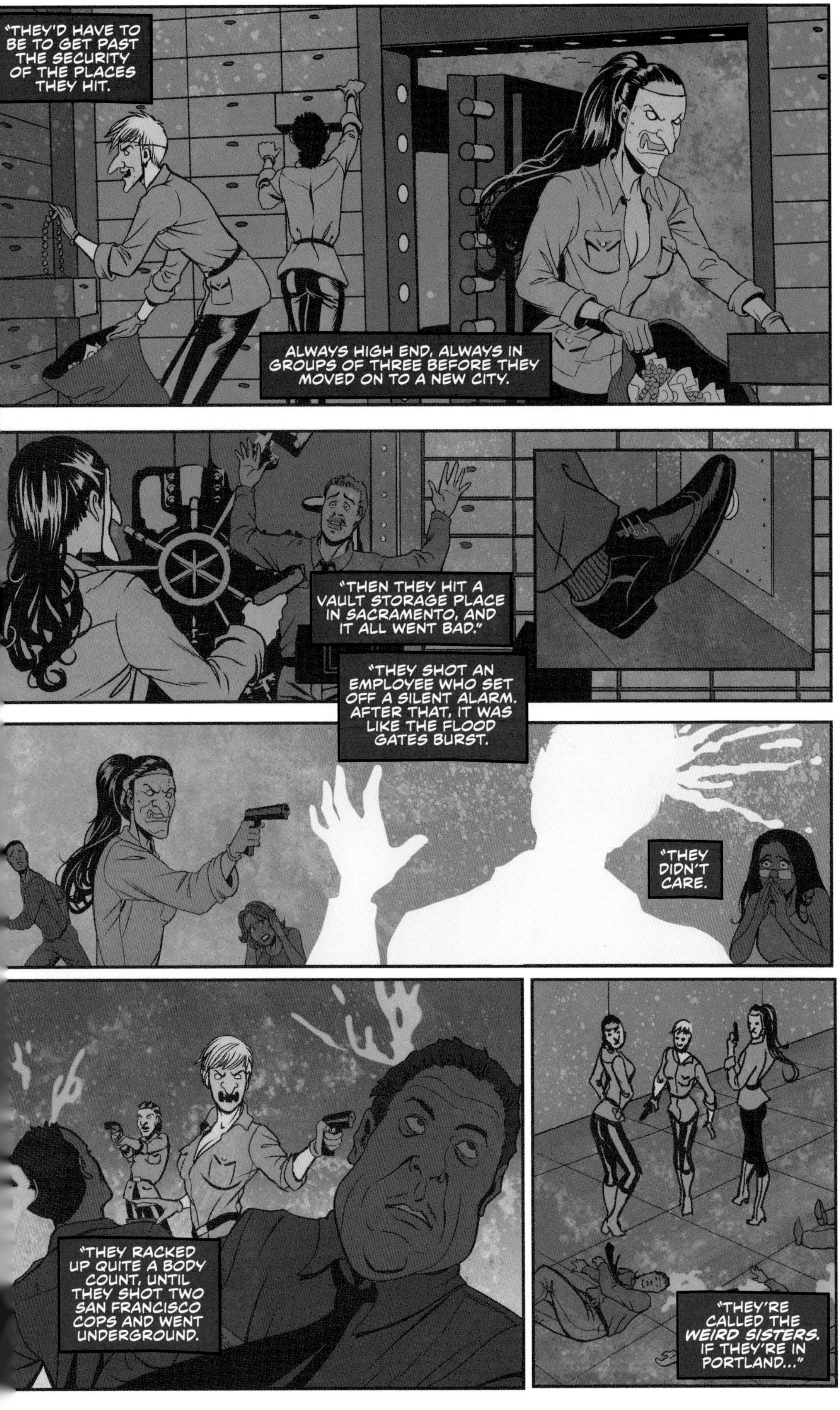
"THEY'D HAVE TO BE TO GET PAST THE SECURITY OF THE PLACES THEY HIT.
ALWAYS HIGH END, ALWAYS IN GROUPS OF THREE BEFORE THEY MOVED ON TO A NEW CITY.
"THEN THEY HIT A VAULT STORAGE PLACE IN SACRAMENTO, AND IT ALL WENT BAD."
"THEY SHOT AN EMPLOYEE WHO SET OFF A SILENT ALARM. AFTER THAT, IT WAS LIKE THE FLOOD GATES BURST.
"THEY DIDN'T CARE.
"THEY RACKED UP QUITE A BODY COUNT, UNTIL THEY SHOT TWO SAN FRANCISCO COPS AND WENT UNDERGROUND.
"THEY'RE CALLED THE *WEIRD SISTERS*. IF THEY'RE IN PORTLAND..."

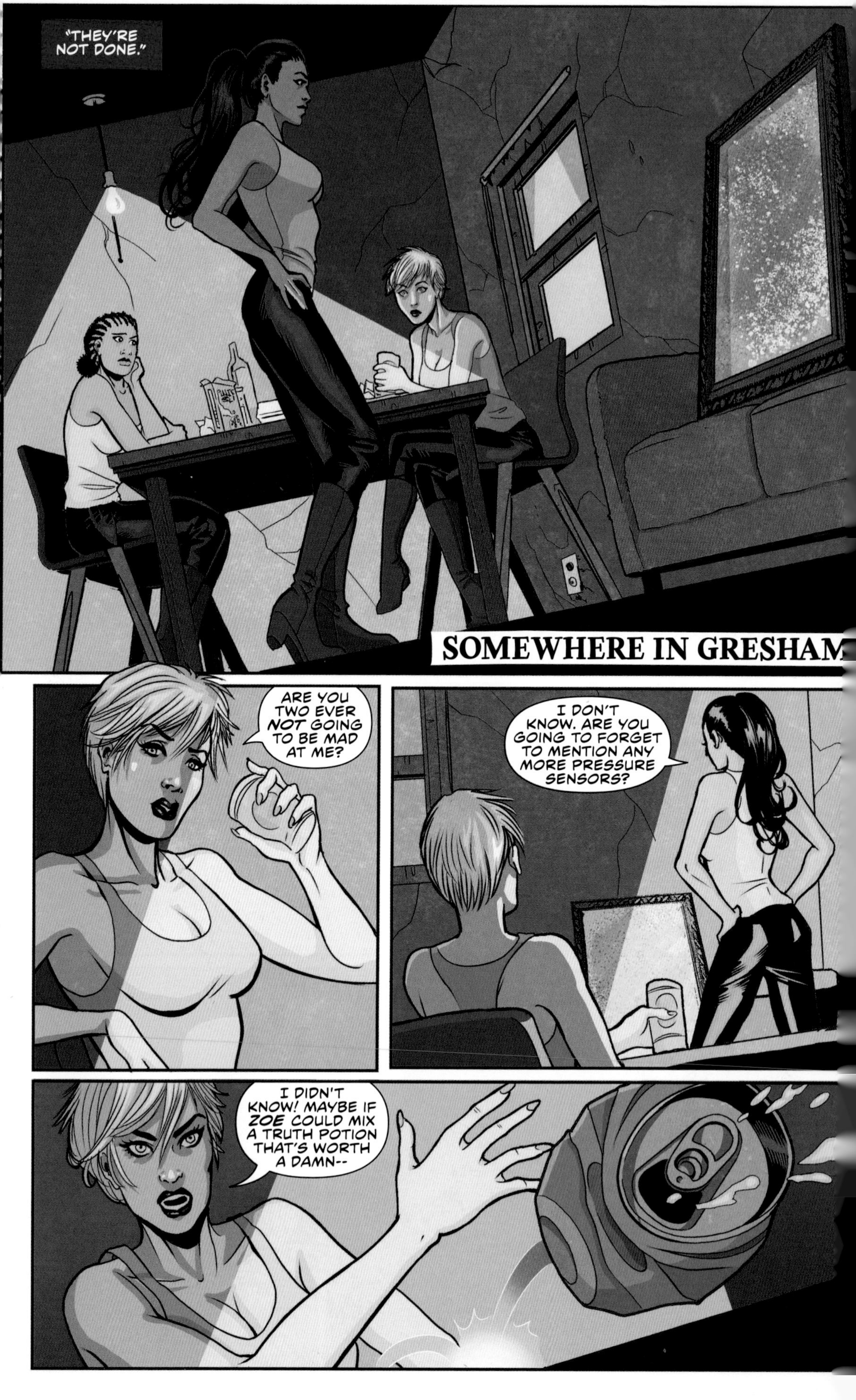

"THEY'RE NOT DONE."
SOMEWHERE IN GRESHAM
ARE YOU TWO EVER NOT GOING TO BE MAD AT ME?
I DON'T KNOW. ARE YOU GOING TO FORGET TO MENTION ANY MORE PRESSURE SENSORS?
I DIDN'T KNOW! MAYBE IF ZOE COULD MIX A TRUTH POTION THAT'S WORTH A DAMN--

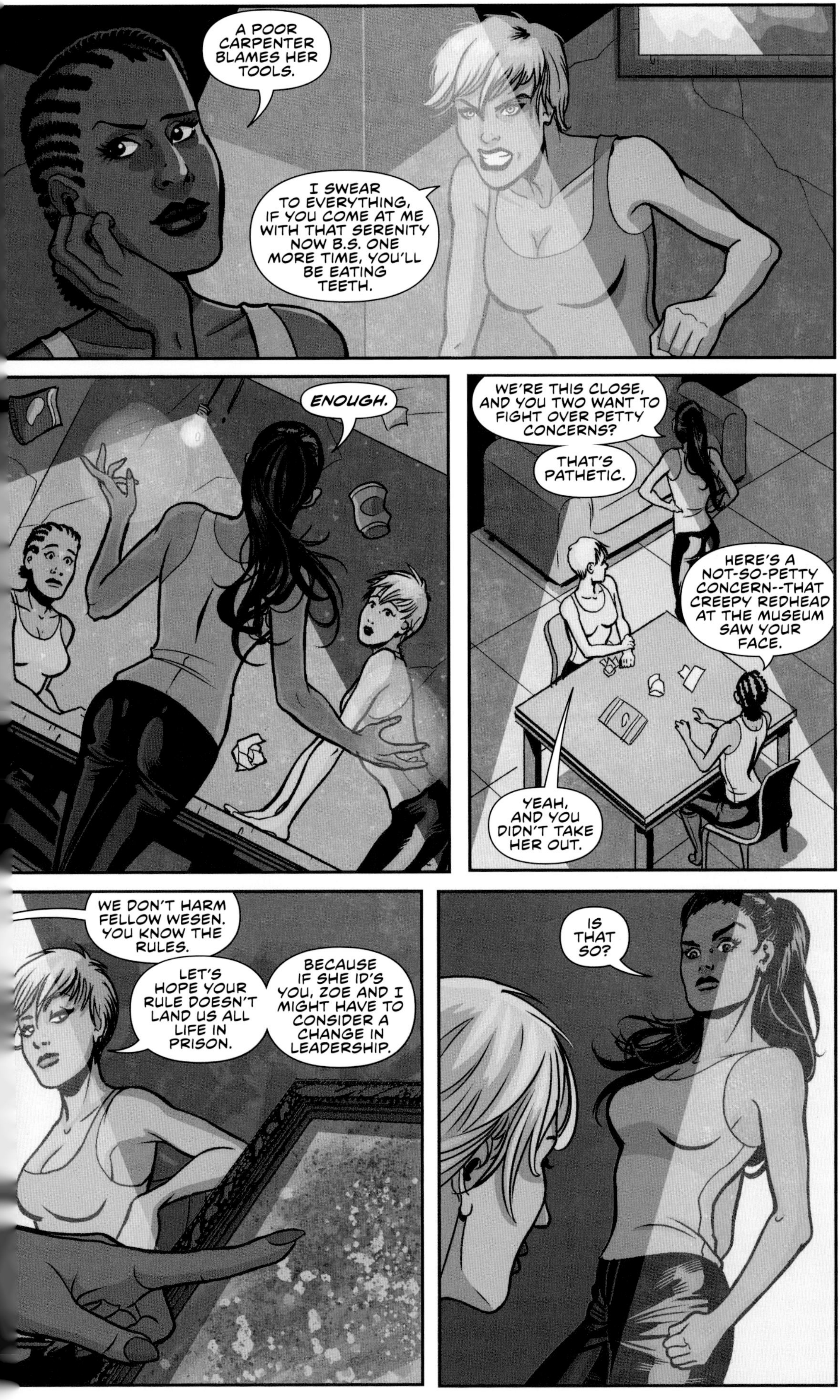
A POOR CARPENTER BLAMES HER TOOLS.
I SWEAR TO EVERYTHING, IF YOU COME AT ME WITH THAT SERENITY NOW B.S. ONE MORE TIME, YOU'LL BE EATING TEETH.
ENOUGH.
WE'RE THIS CLOSE, AND YOU TWO WANT TO FIGHT OVER PETTY CONCERNS?
THAT'S PATHETIC.
HERE'S A NOT-SO-PETTY CONCERN--THAT CREEPY REDHEAD AT THE MUSEUM SAW YOUR FACE.
YEAH, AND YOU DIDN'T TAKE HER OUT.
WE DON'T HARM FELLOW WESEN. YOU KNOW THE RULES.
LET'S HOPE YOUR RULE DOESN'T LAND US ALL LIFE IN PRISON.
BECAUSE IF SHE ID'S YOU, ZOE AND I MIGHT HAVE TO CONSIDER A CHANGE IN LEADERSHIP.
IS THAT SO?

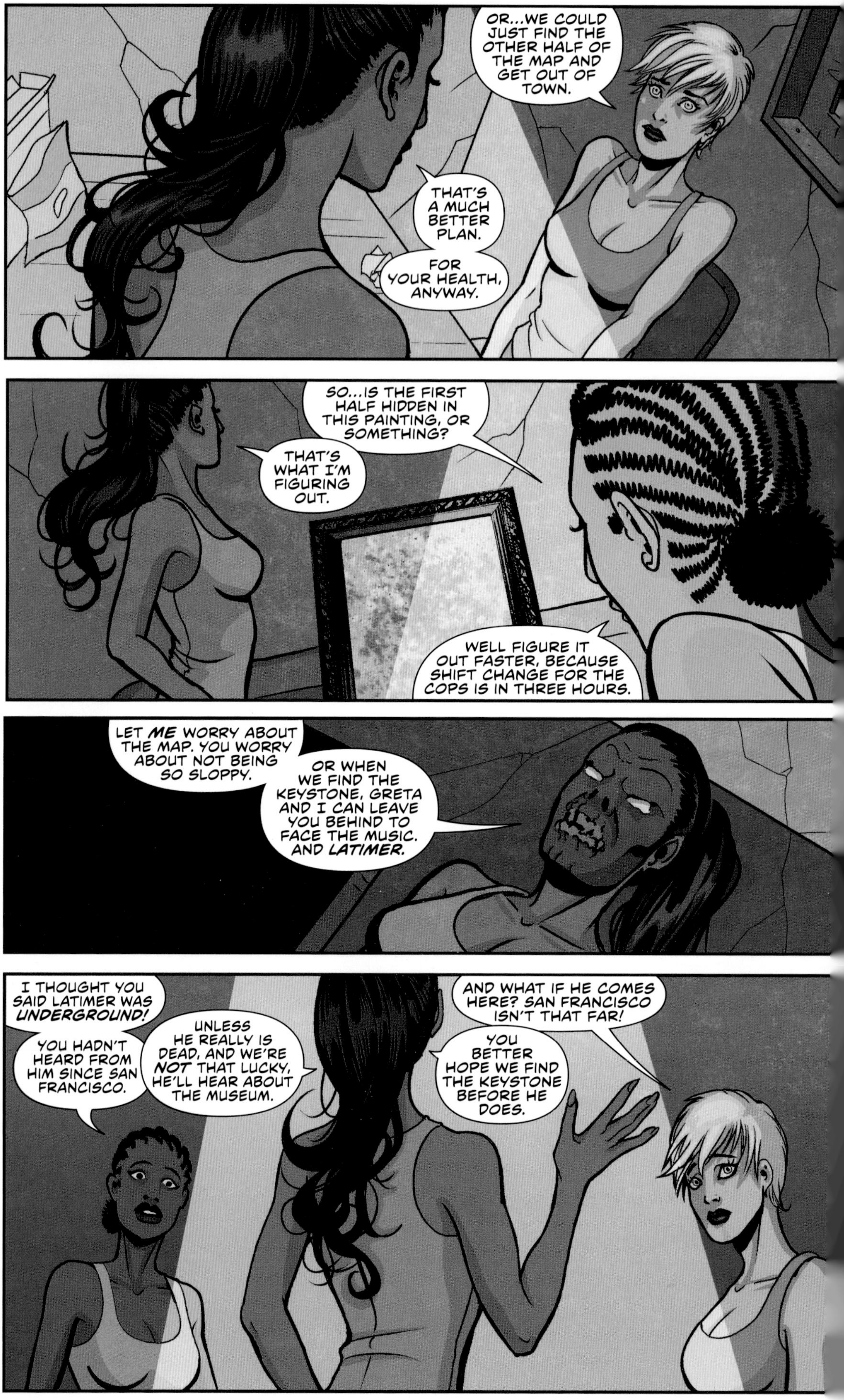
OR...WE COULD JUST FIND THE OTHER HALF OF THE MAP AND GET OUT OF TOWN.
THAT'S A MUCH BETTER PLAN.
FOR YOUR HEALTH, ANYWAY.
SO...IS THE FIRST HALF HIDDEN IN THIS PAINTING, OR SOMETHING?
THAT'S WHAT I'M FIGURING OUT.
WELL FIGURE IT OUT FASTER, BECAUSE SHIFT CHANGE FOR THE COPS IS IN THREE HOURS.
LET ME WORRY ABOUT THE MAP. YOU WORRY ABOUT NOT BEING SO SLOPPY.
OR WHEN WE FIND THE KEYSTONE, GRETA AND I CAN LEAVE YOU BEHIND TO FACE THE MUSIC. AND LATIMER.
I THOUGHT YOU SAID LATIMER WAS UNDERGROUND!
YOU HADN'T HEARD FROM HIM SINCE SAN FRANCISCO.
UNLESS HE REALLY IS DEAD, AND WE'RE NOT THAT LUCKY, HE'LL HEAR ABOUT THE MUSEUM.
AND WHAT IF HE COMES HERE? SAN FRANCISCO ISN'T THAT FAR!
YOU BETTER HOPE WE FIND THE KEYSTONE BEFORE HE DOES.

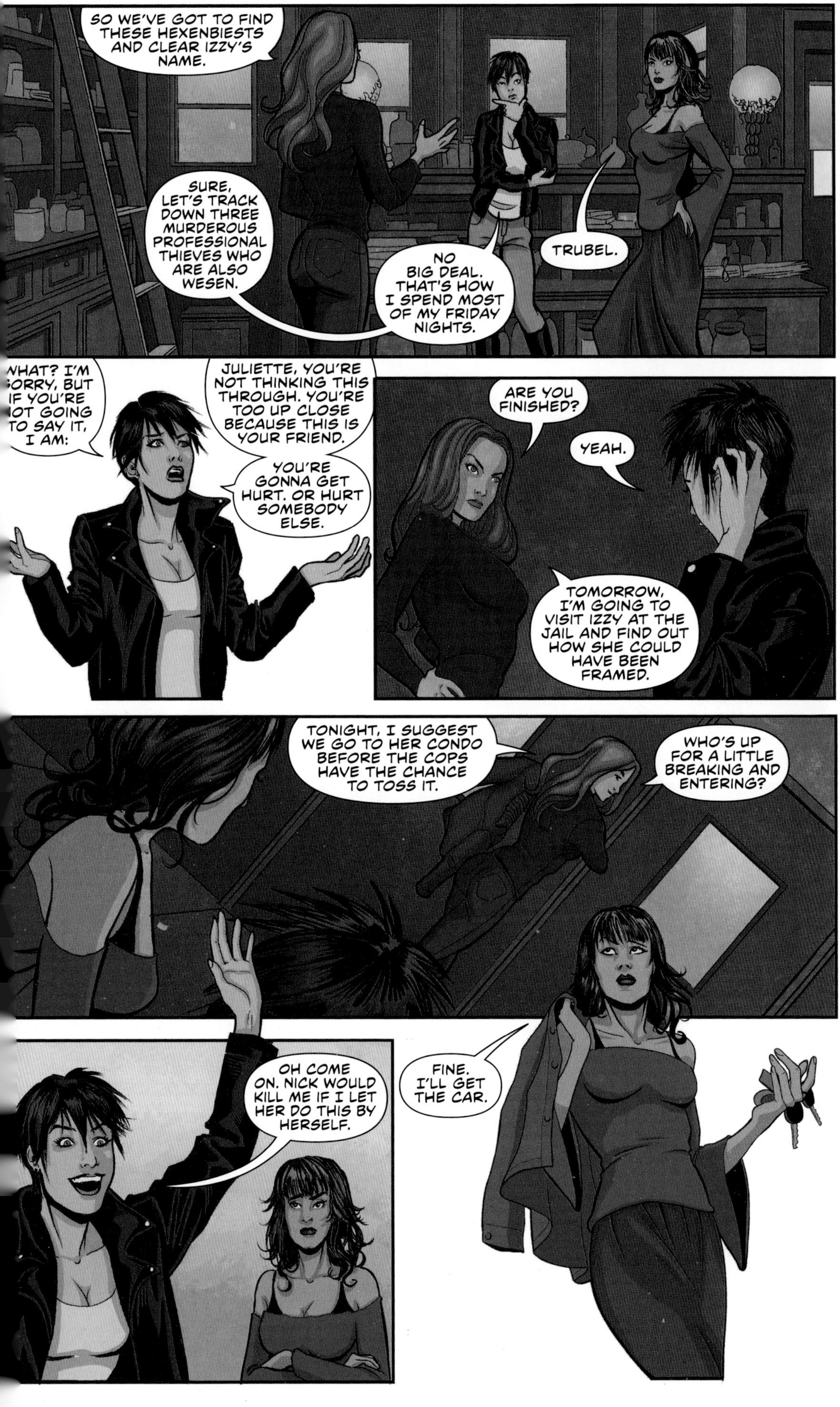
SO WE'VE GOT TO FIND THESE HEXENBIESTS AND CLEAR IZZY'S NAME.
SURE, LET'S TRACK DOWN THREE MURDEROUS PROFESSIONAL THIEVES WHO ARE ALSO WESEN.
NO BIG DEAL. THAT'S HOW I SPEND MOST OF MY FRIDAY NIGHTS.
TRUBEL.
WHAT? I'M SORRY, BUT IF YOU'RE NOT GOING TO SAY IT, I AM:
JULIETTE, YOU'RE NOT THINKING THIS THROUGH. YOU'RE TOO UP CLOSE BECAUSE THIS IS YOUR FRIEND.
YOU'RE GONNA GET HURT. OR HURT SOMEBODY ELSE.
ARE YOU FINISHED?
YEAH.
TOMORROW, I'M GOING TO VISIT IZZY AT THE JAIL AND FIND OUT HOW SHE COULD HAVE BEEN FRAMED.
TONIGHT, I SUGGEST WE GO TO HER CONDO BEFORE THE COPS HAVE THE CHANCE TO TOSS IT.
WHO'S UP FOR A LITTLE BREAKING AND ENTERING?
OH COME ON. NICK WOULD KILL ME IF I LET HER DO THIS BY HERSELF.
FINE. I'LL GET THE CAR.

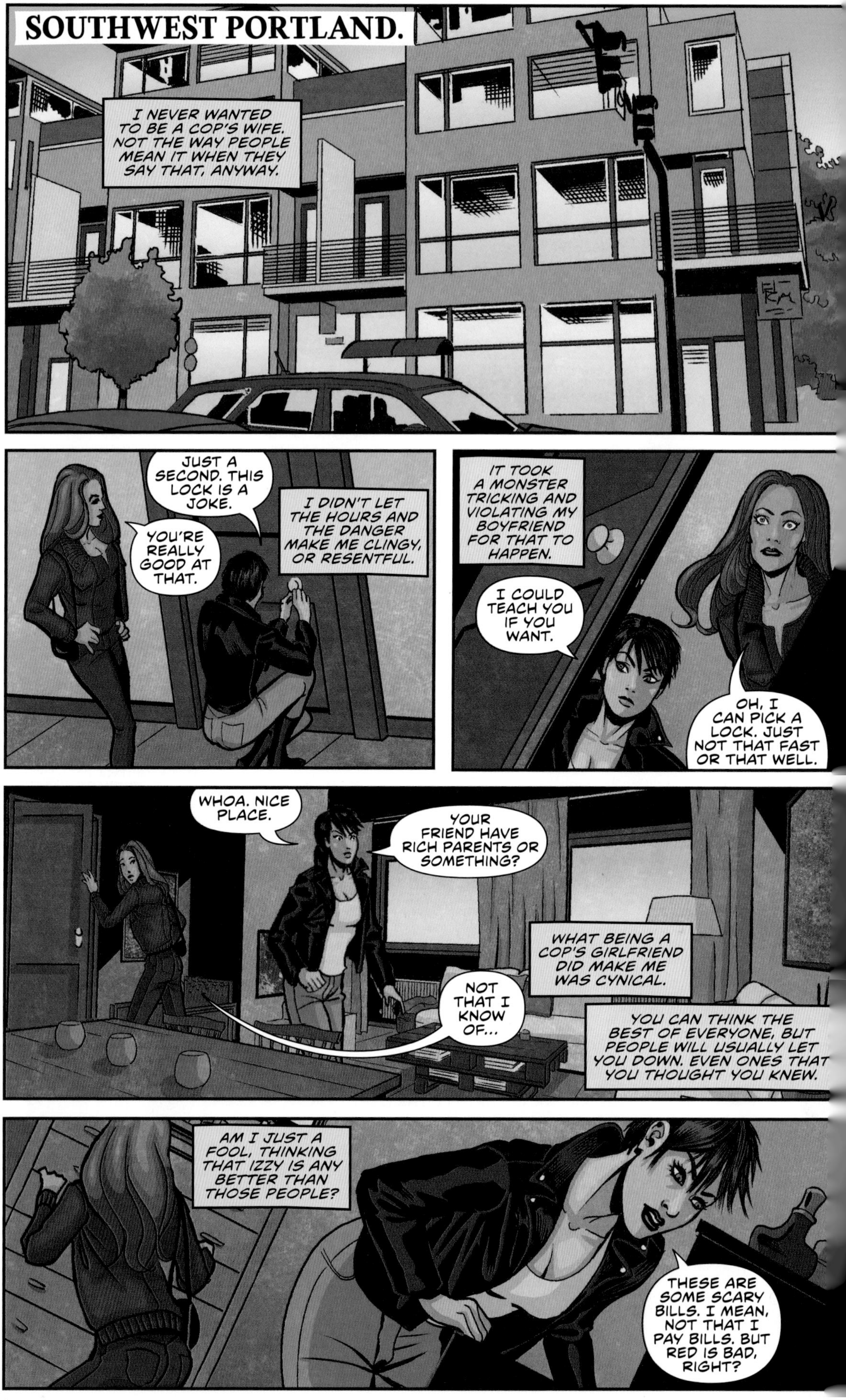
SOUTHWEST PORTLAND.
I NEVER WANTED TO BE A COP'S WIFE. NOT THE WAY PEOPLE MEAN IT WHEN THEY SAY THAT, ANYWAY.
JUST A SECOND. THIS LOCK IS A JOKE.
YOU'RE REALLY GOOD AT THAT.
I DIDN'T LET THE HOURS AND THE DANGER MAKE ME CLINGY, OR RESENTFUL.
IT TOOK A MONSTER TRICKING AND VIOLATING MY BOYFRIEND FOR THAT TO HAPPEN.
I COULD TEACH YOU IF YOU WANT.
OH, I CAN PICK A LOCK. JUST NOT THAT FAST OR THAT WELL.
WHOA. NICE PLACE.
YOUR FRIEND HAVE RICH PARENTS OR SOMETHING?
WHAT BEING A COP'S GIRLFRIEND DID MAKE ME WAS CYNICAL.
NOT THAT I KNOW OF...
YOU CAN THINK THE BEST OF EVERYONE, BUT PEOPLE WILL USUALLY LET YOU DOWN. EVEN ONES THAT YOU THOUGHT YOU KNEW.
AM I JUST A FOOL, THINKING THAT IZZY IS ANY BETTER THAN THOSE PEOPLE?
THESE ARE SOME SCARY BILLS. I MEAN, NOT THAT I PAY BILLS. BUT RED IS BAD, RIGHT?

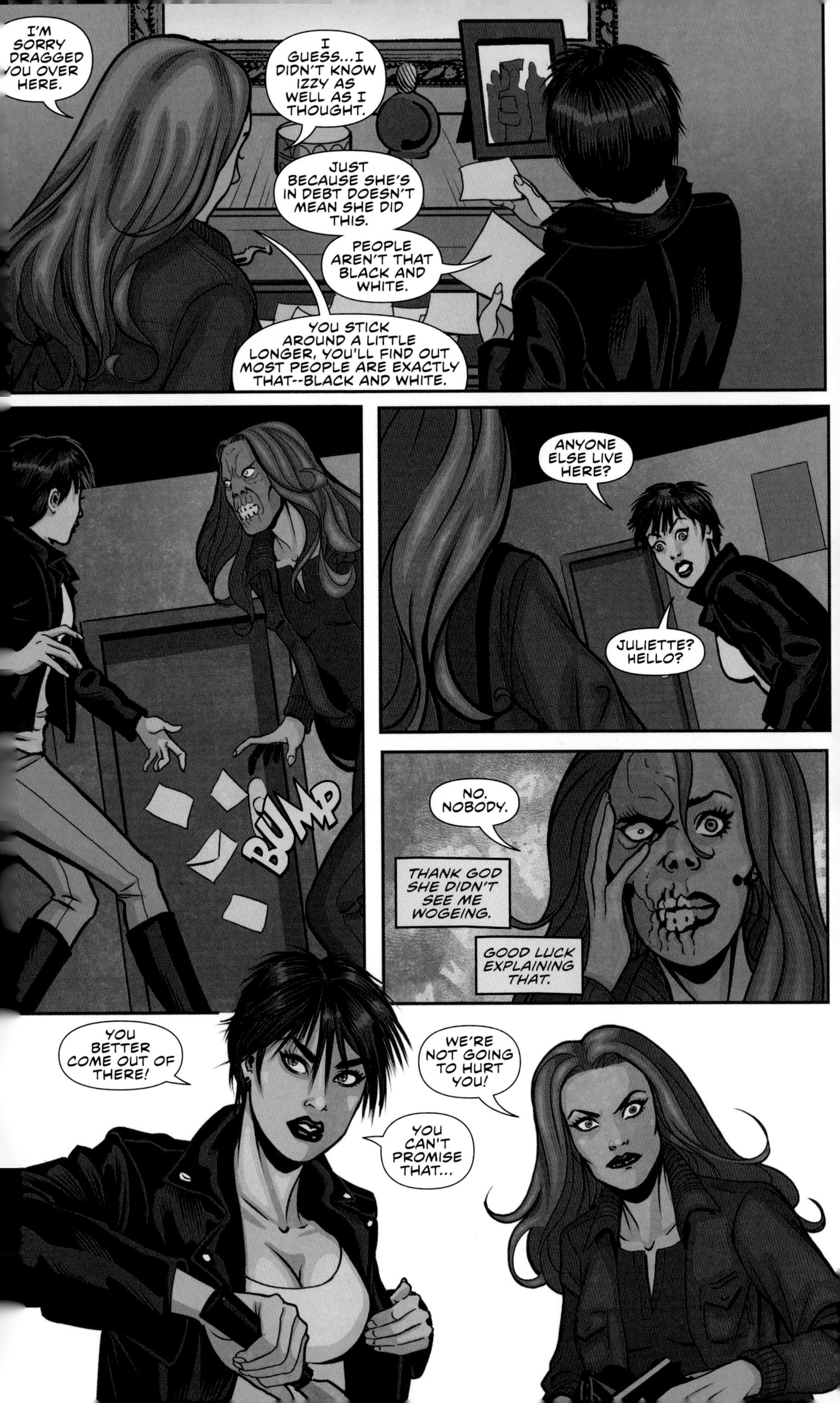
I'M SORRY DRAGGED YOU OVER HERE.
I GUESS...I DIDN'T KNOW IZZY AS WELL AS I THOUGHT.
JUST BECAUSE SHE'S IN DEBT DOESN'T MEAN SHE DID THIS.
PEOPLE AREN'T THAT BLACK AND WHITE.
YOU STICK AROUND A LITTLE LONGER, YOU'LL FIND OUT MOST PEOPLE ARE EXACTLY THAT--BLACK AND WHITE.
BUMP
ANYONE ELSE LIVE HERE?
JULIETTE? HELLO?
NO. NOBODY.
THANK GOD SHE DIDN'T SEE ME WOGEING.
GOOD LUCK EXPLAINING THAT.
YOU BETTER COME OUT OF THERE!
WE'RE NOT GOING TO HURT YOU!
YOU CAN'T PROMISE THAT...

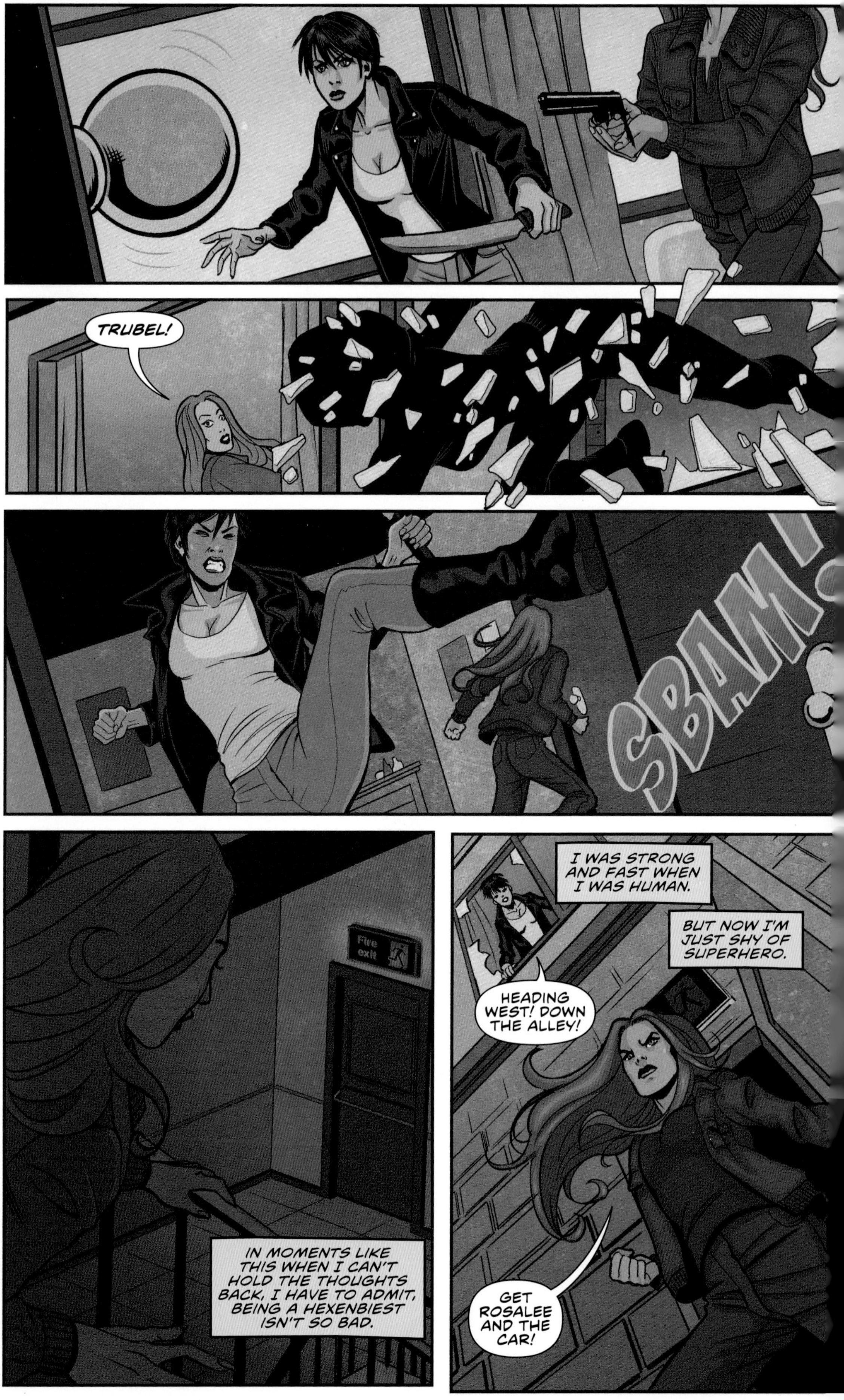
TRUBEL!
SBAM!
IN MOMENTS LIKE THIS WHEN I CAN'T HOLD THE THOUGHTS BACK, I HAVE TO ADMIT, BEING A HEXENBIEST ISN'T SO BAD.
Fire exit
I WAS STRONG AND FAST WHEN I WAS HUMAN.
BUT NOW I'M JUST SHY OF SUPERHERO.
HEADING WEST! DOWN THE ALLEY!
GET ROSALEE AND THE CAR!

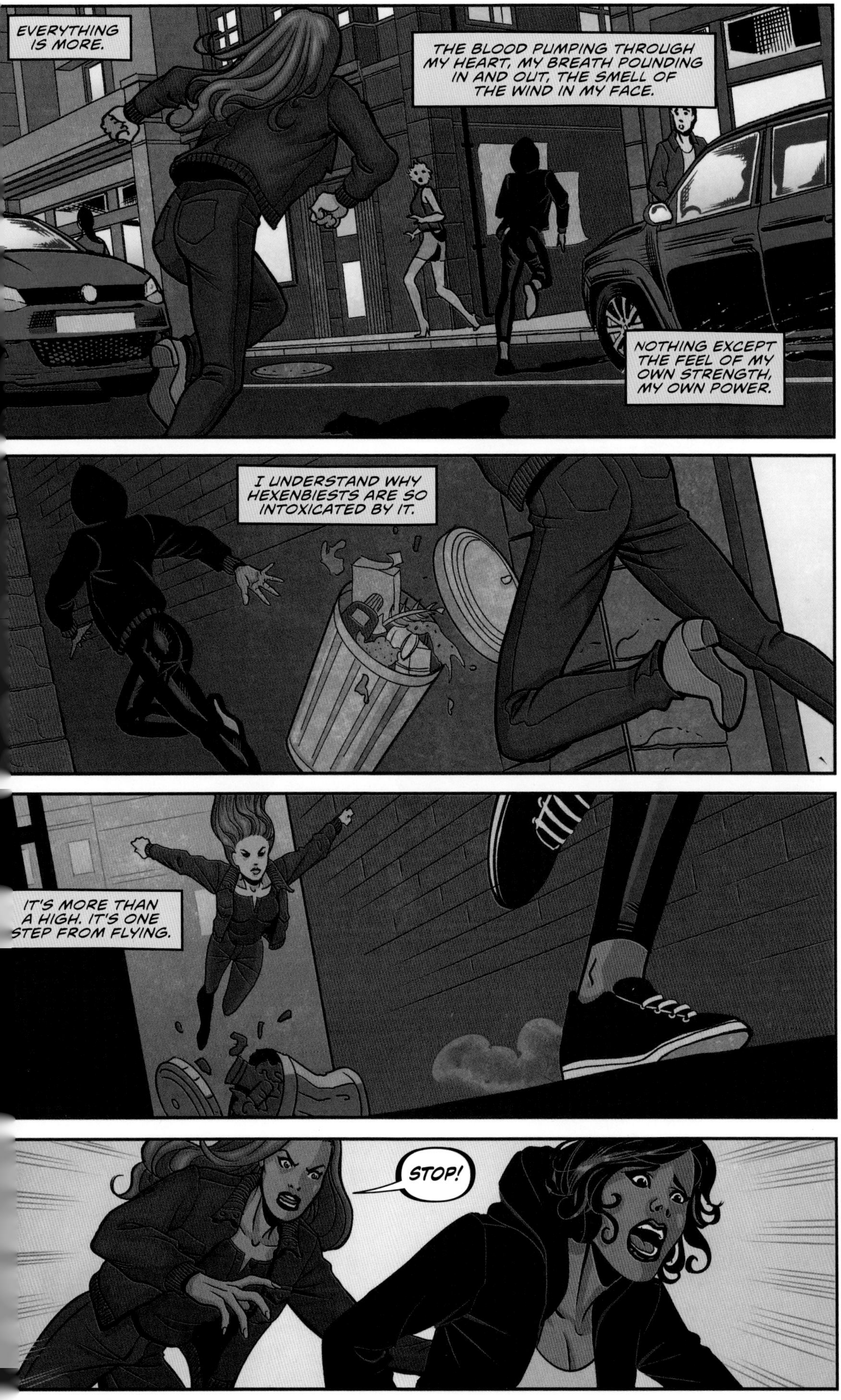
EVERYTHING IS MORE.
THE BLOOD PUMPING THROUGH MY HEART, MY BREATH POUNDING IN AND OUT, THE SMELL OF THE WIND IN MY FACE.
NOTHING EXCEPT THE FEEL OF MY OWN STRENGTH, MY OWN POWER.
I UNDERSTAND WHY HEXENBIESTS ARE SO INTOXICATED BY IT.
IT'S MORE THAN A HIGH. IT'S ONE STEP FROM FLYING.
STOP!

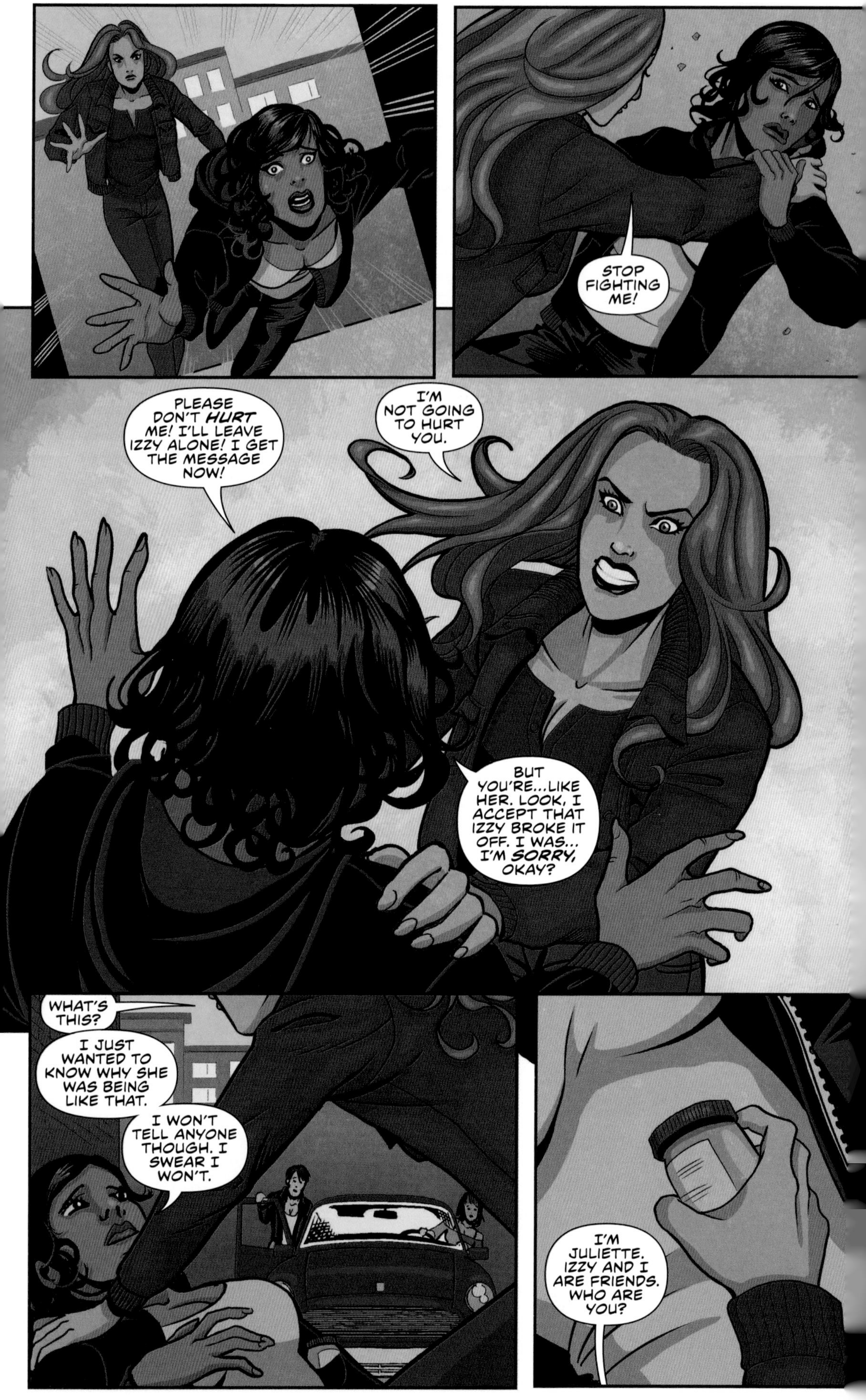
STOP FIGHTING ME!
PLEASE DON'T HURT ME! I'LL LEAVE IZZY ALONE! I GET THE MESSAGE NOW!
I'M NOT GOING TO HURT YOU.
BUT YOU'RE...LIKE HER. LOOK, I ACCEPT THAT IZZY BROKE IT OFF. I WAS... I'M SORRY, OKAY?
WHAT'S THIS?
I JUST WANTED TO KNOW WHY SHE WAS BEING LIKE THAT.
I WON'T TELL ANYONE THOUGH. I SWEAR I WON'T.
I'M JULIETTE. IZZY AND I ARE FRIENDS. WHO ARE YOU?

I'M VIOLET. VIOLET CHANG. I'M--I *WAS* IZZY'S GIRLFRIEND.

WE BROKE UP, A COUPLE OF WEEKS AGO.

AND THIS?

LOOK, IZZY MET SOMEONE ELSE, AND THAT'S FINE. BUT SHE WAS ACTING REALLY WEIRD, TAKING ALL THIS STUFF, AND I...I WAS WORRIED.

SO ONE NIGHT I FOLLOWED HER AND THIS NEW CHICK.

SHE CAUGHT ME, THIS OTHER WOMAN. SHE THREATENED ME. HER *FACE* WAS *CRAZY*, AND I THOUGHT I MUST BE HAVING A BAD REACTION OR SOMETHING.

I THOUGHT YOU WERE HER FRIENDS. SHE SAID SHE HAD FRIENDS WHO'D MESS ME UP IF I CAME AROUND AGAIN.

THIS IS A PSILOCYBIN COMPOUND.

LIKE MAGIC MUSHROOMS?

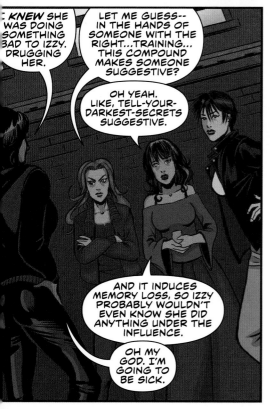

I *KNEW* SHE WAS DOING SOMETHING BAD TO IZZY. DRUGGING HER.

LET ME GUESS-- IN THE HANDS OF SOMEONE WITH THE RIGHT...TRAINING... THIS COMPOUND MAKES SOMEONE SUGGESTIVE?

OH YEAH. LIKE, TELL-YOUR-DARKEST-SECRETS SUGGESTIVE.

AND IT INDUCES MEMORY LOSS, SO IZZY PROBABLY WOULDN'T EVEN KNOW SHE DID ANYTHING UNDER THE INFLUENCE.

OH MY GOD. I'M GOING TO BE SICK.

YOU SAID YOU FOLLOWED THEM. WHERE?

TO THE MUSEUM, AFTER IT WAS CLOSED, AND THEN TO THIS SCARY DIVE BAR OVER ON WESTERN. THAT'S WHERE SHE CAUGHT ME.

YOU'D RECOGNIZE HER IF YOU SAW HER AGAIN?

I'LL NEVER FORGET THAT FACE.

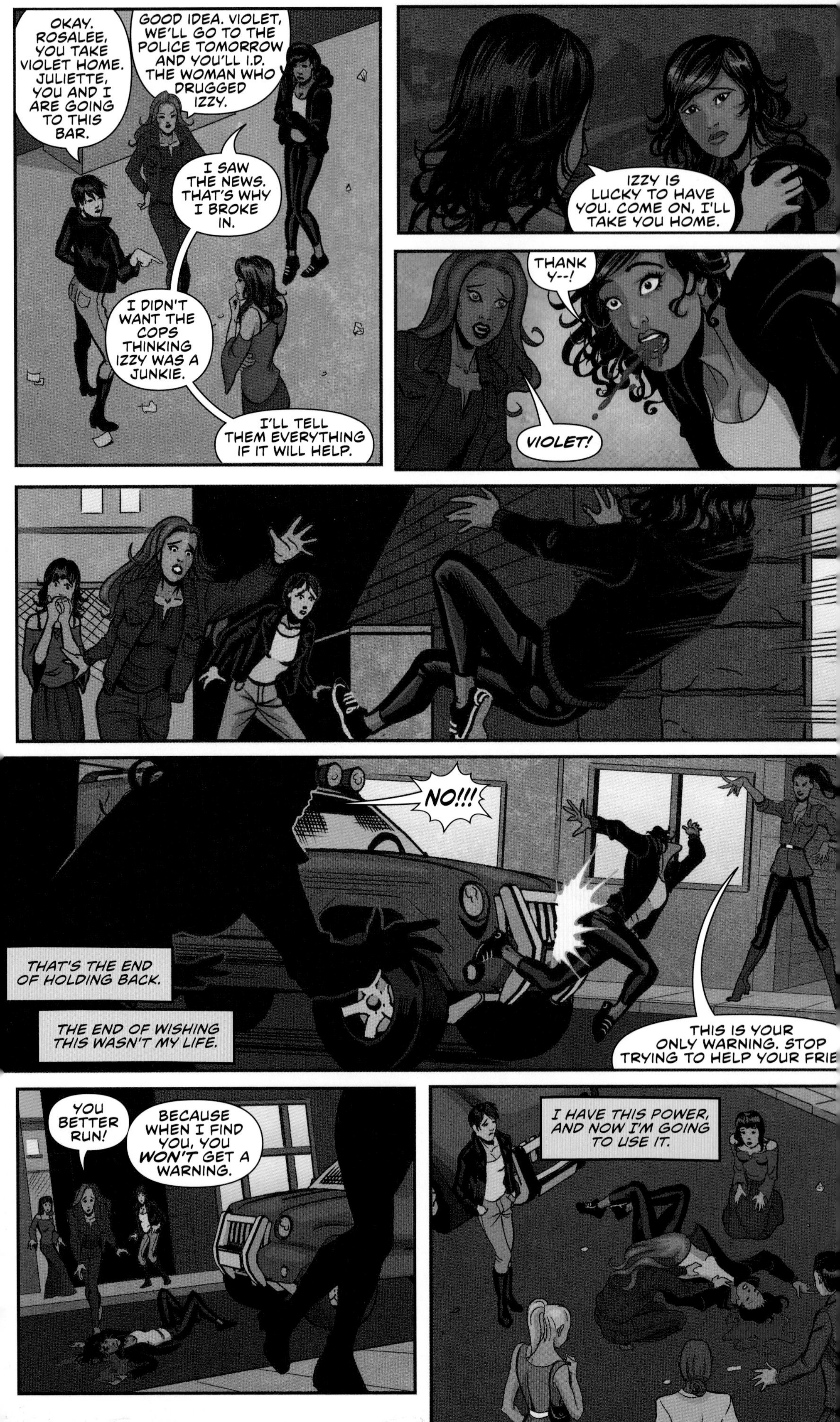
OKAY. ROSALEE, YOU TAKE VIOLET HOME. JULIETTE, YOU AND I ARE GOING TO THIS BAR.
GOOD IDEA. VIOLET, WE'LL GO TO THE POLICE TOMORROW AND YOU'LL I.D. THE WOMAN WHO DRUGGED IZZY.
I SAW THE NEWS. THAT'S WHY I BROKE IN.
I DIDN'T WANT THE COPS THINKING IZZY WAS A JUNKIE.
I'LL TELL THEM EVERYTHING IF IT WILL HELP.
IZZY IS LUCKY TO HAVE YOU. COME ON, I'LL TAKE YOU HOME.
THANK Y--!
VIOLET!
NO!!!
THAT'S THE END OF HOLDING BACK.
THE END OF WISHING THIS WASN'T MY LIFE.
THIS IS YOUR ONLY WARNING. STOP TRYING TO HELP YOUR FRIE
YOU BETTER RUN!
BECAUSE WHEN I FIND YOU, YOU *WON'T* GET A WARNING.
I HAVE THIS POWER, AND NOW I'M GOING TO USE IT.

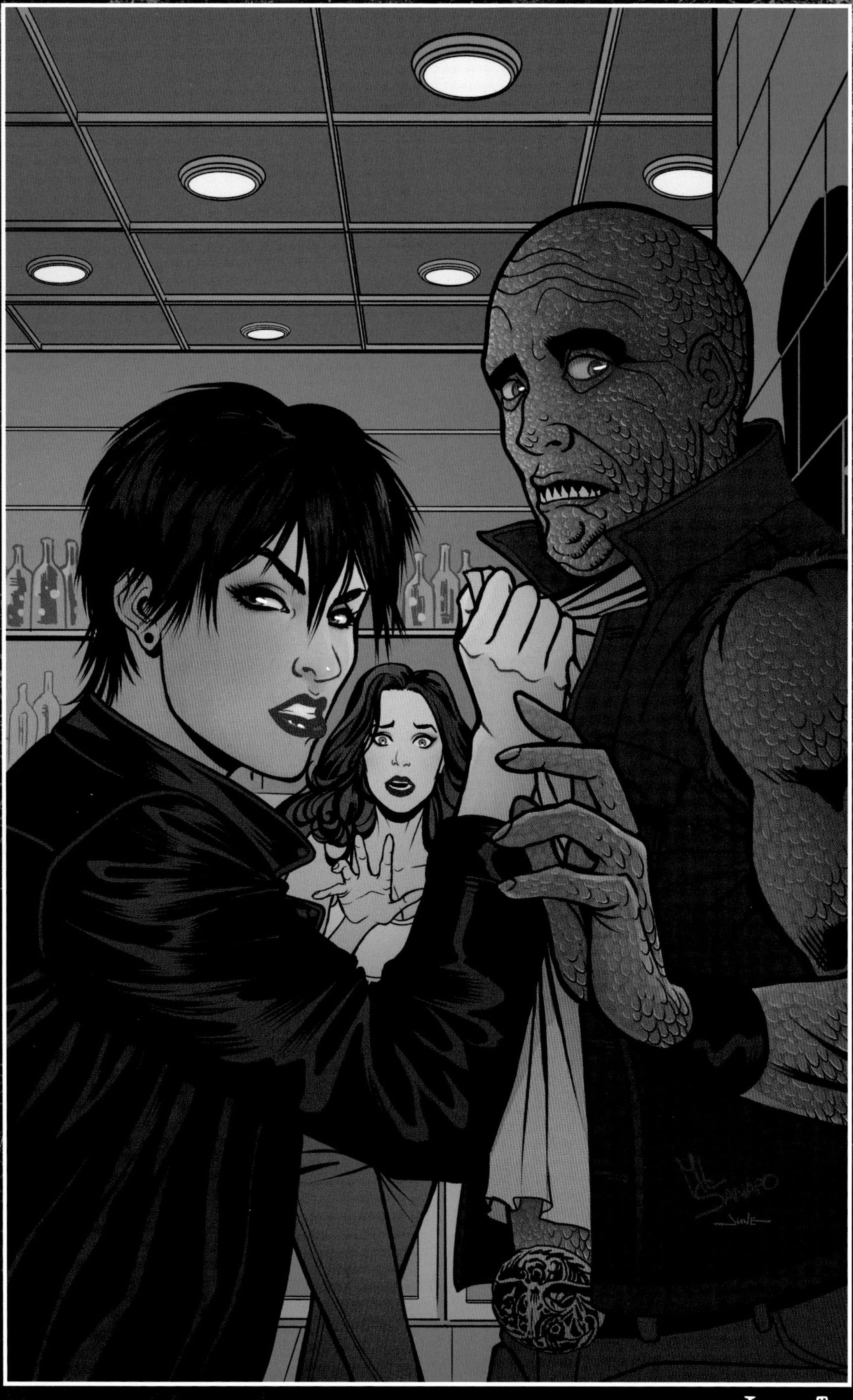

Issue Two

Art by Maria Sanapo | Colors by June Chung

Flight

Movement · Communication · Information

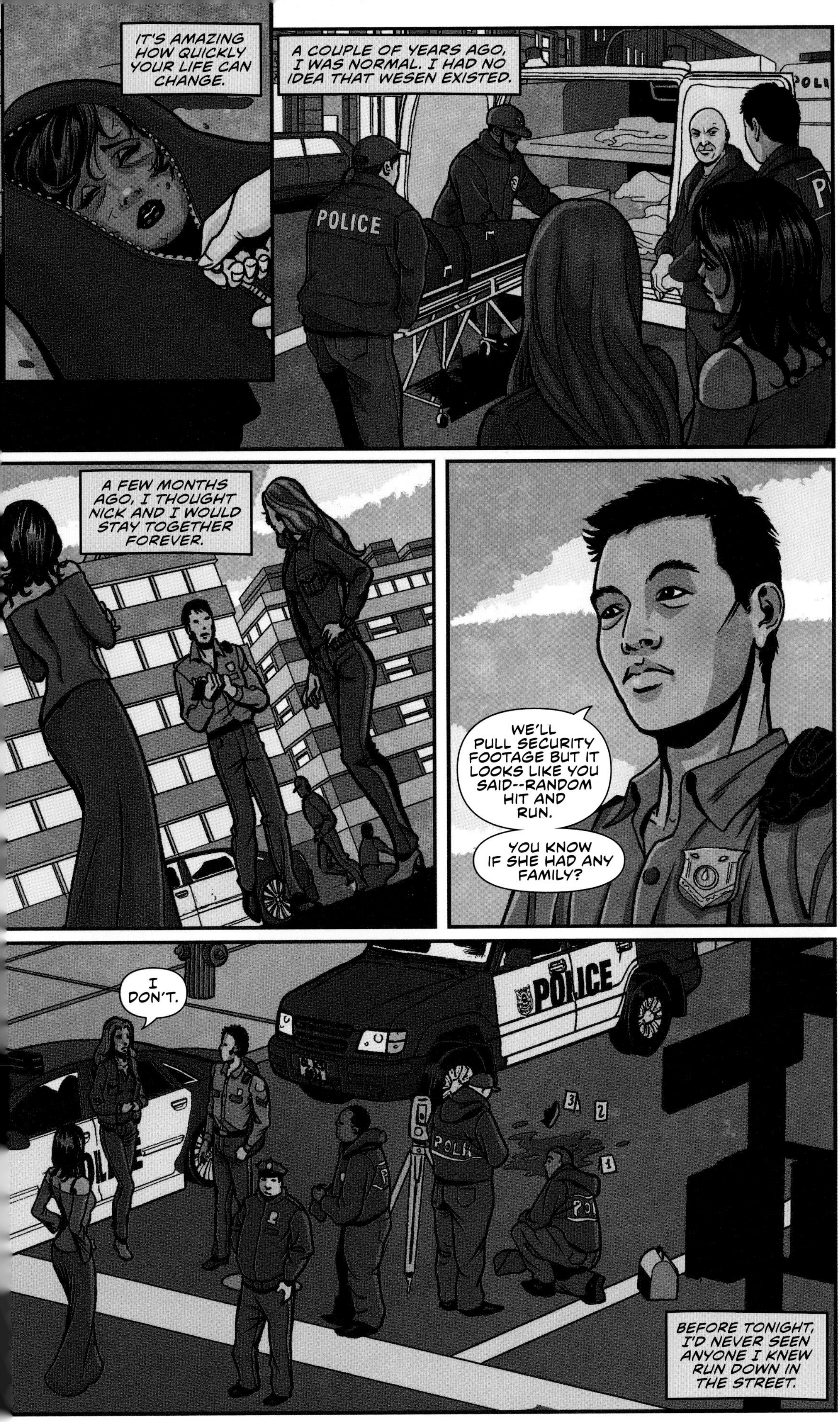
IT'S AMAZING HOW QUICKLY YOUR LIFE CAN CHANGE.
A COUPLE OF YEARS AGO, I WAS NORMAL. I HAD NO IDEA THAT WESEN EXISTED.
POLICE
A FEW MONTHS AGO, I THOUGHT NICK AND I WOULD STAY TOGETHER FOREVER.
WE'LL PULL SECURITY FOOTAGE BUT IT LOOKS LIKE YOU SAID--RANDOM HIT AND RUN.
YOU KNOW IF SHE HAD ANY FAMILY?
I DON'T.
POLICE
BEFORE TONIGHT, I'D NEVER SEEN ANYONE I KNEW RUN DOWN IN THE STREET.

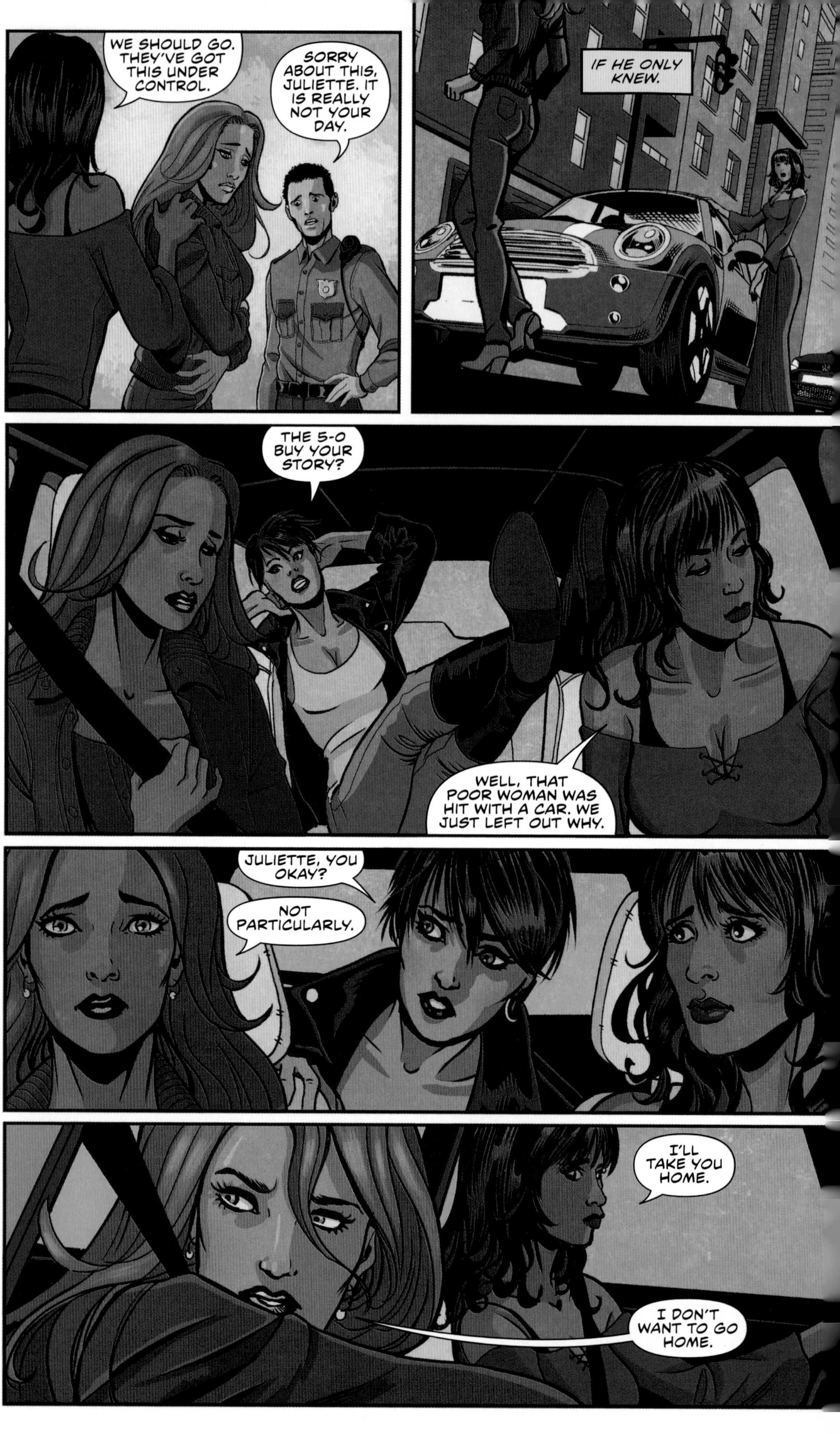
WE SHOULD GO. THEY'VE GOT THIS UNDER CONTROL.
SORRY ABOUT THIS, JULIETTE. IT IS REALLY NOT YOUR DAY.
IF HE ONLY KNEW.
THE 5-O BUY YOUR STORY?
WELL, THAT POOR WOMAN WAS HIT WITH A CAR. WE JUST LEFT OUT WHY.
JULIETTE, YOU OKAY?
NOT PARTICULARLY.
I'LL TAKE YOU HOME.
I DON'T WANT TO GO HOME.

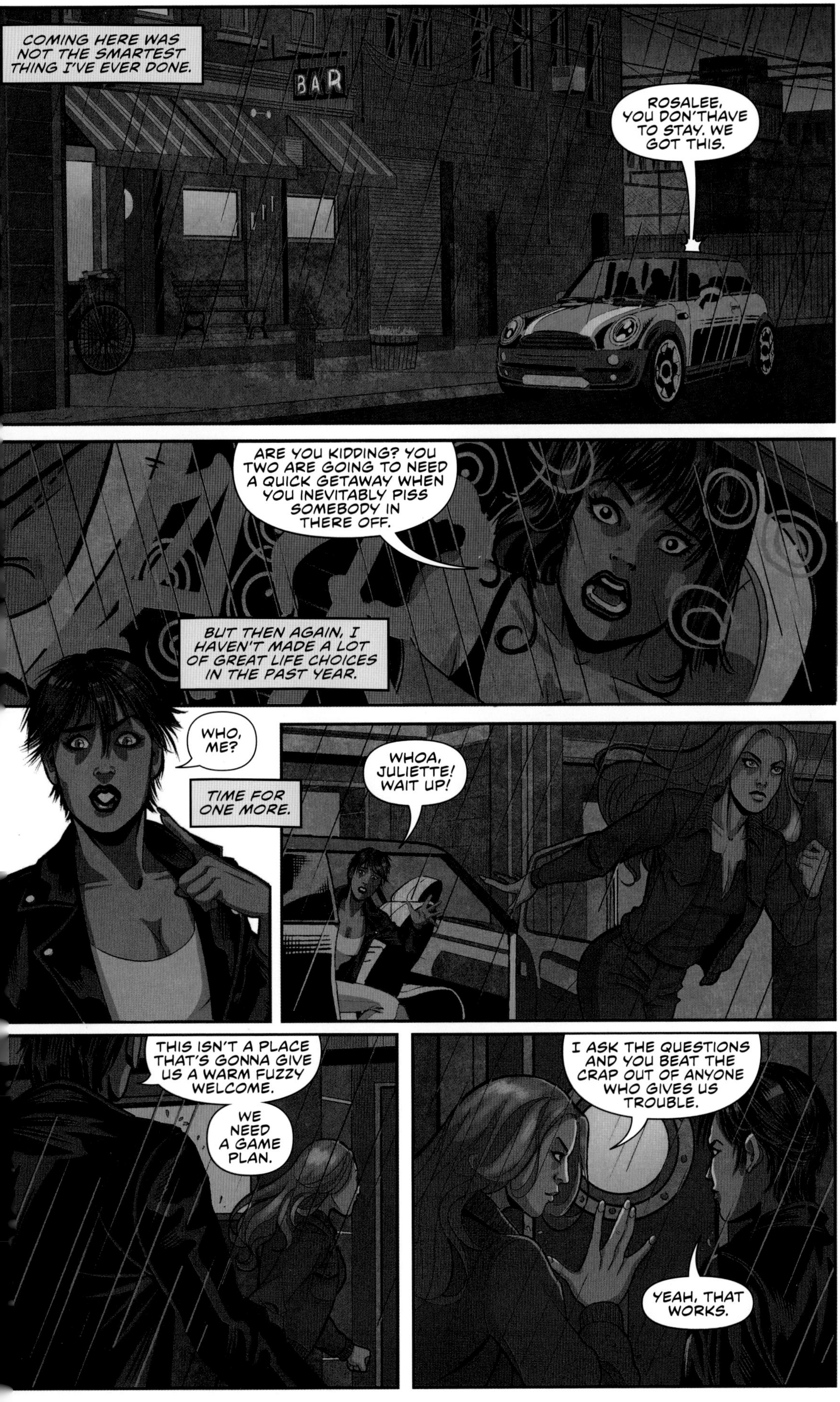
COMING HERE WAS NOT THE SMARTEST THING I'VE EVER DONE.
BAR
ROSALEE, YOU DON'THAVE TO STAY. WE GOT THIS.
ARE YOU KIDDING? YOU TWO ARE GOING TO NEED A QUICK GETAWAY WHEN YOU INEVITABLY PISS SOMEBODY IN THERE OFF.
BUT THEN AGAIN, I HAVEN'T MADE A LOT OF GREAT LIFE CHOICES IN THE PAST YEAR.
WHO, ME?
TIME FOR ONE MORE.
WHOA, JULIETTE! WAIT UP!
THIS ISN'T A PLACE THAT'S GONNA GIVE US A WARM FUZZY WELCOME.
WE NEED A GAME PLAN.
I ASK THE QUESTIONS AND YOU BEAT THE CRAP OUT OF ANYONE WHO GIVES US TROUBLE.
YEAH, THAT WORKS.

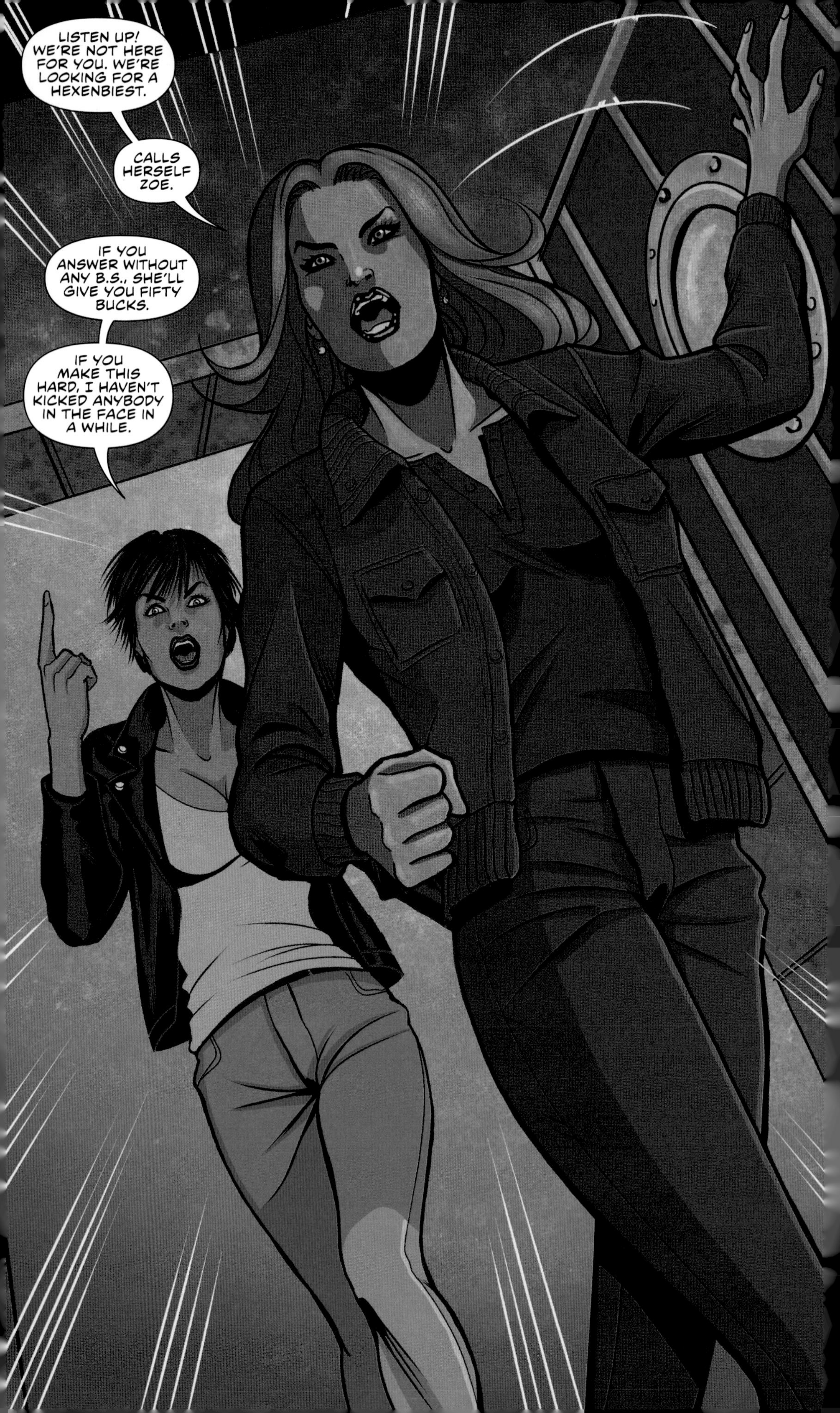
LISTEN UP! WE'RE NOT HERE FOR YOU. WE'RE LOOKING FOR A HEXENBIEST.
CALLS HERSELF ZOE.
IF YOU ANSWER WITHOUT ANY B.S., SHE'LL GIVE YOU FIFTY BUCKS.
IF YOU MAKE THIS HARD, I HAVEN'T KICKED ANYBODY IN THE FACE IN A WHILE.

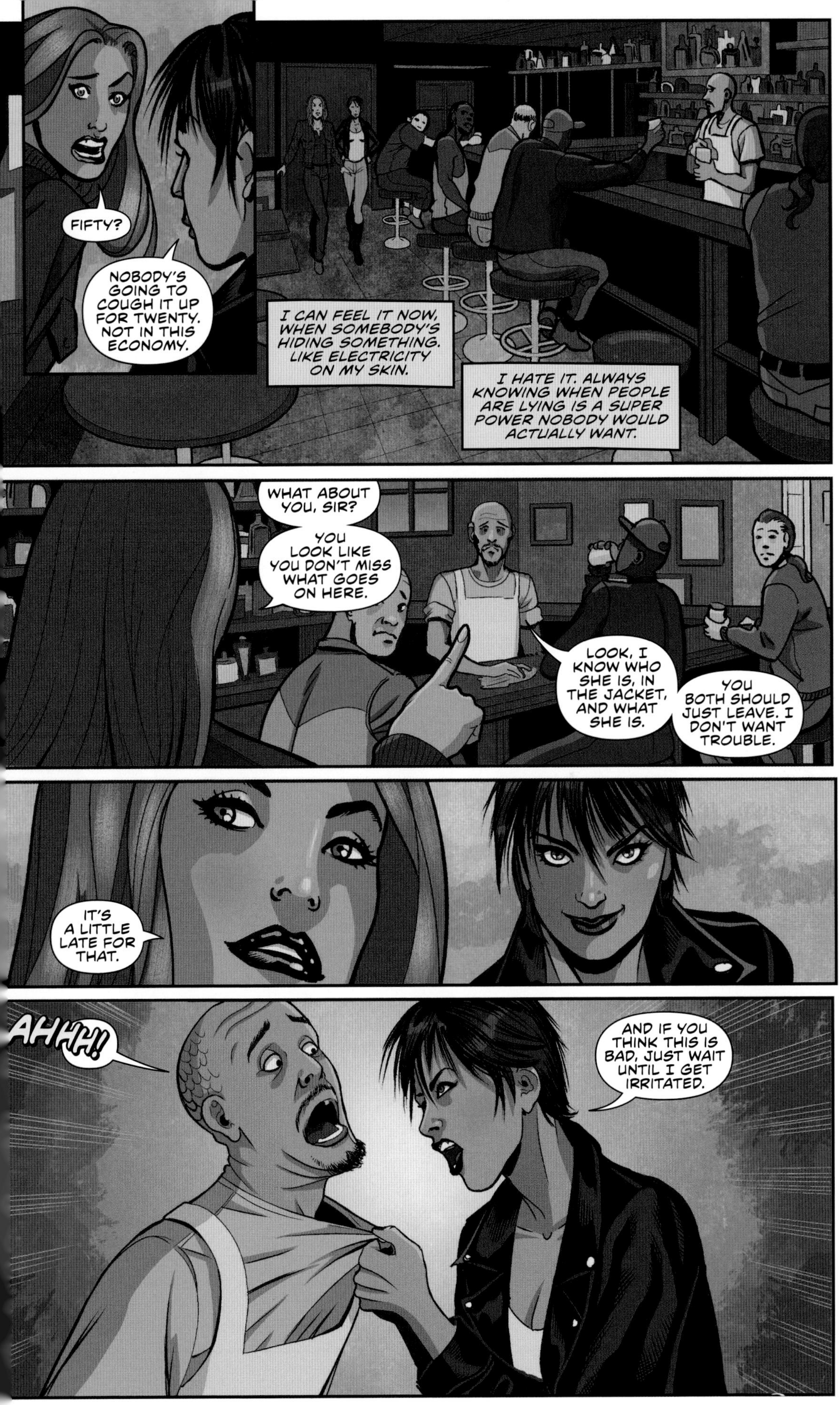
FIFTY?
NOBODY'S GOING TO COUGH IT UP FOR TWENTY. NOT IN THIS ECONOMY.
I CAN FEEL IT NOW, WHEN SOMEBODY'S HIDING SOMETHING. LIKE ELECTRICITY ON MY SKIN.
I HATE IT. ALWAYS KNOWING WHEN PEOPLE ARE LYING IS A SUPER POWER NOBODY WOULD ACTUALLY WANT.
WHAT ABOUT YOU, SIR?
YOU LOOK LIKE YOU DON'T MISS WHAT GOES ON HERE.
LOOK, I KNOW WHO SHE IS, IN THE JACKET, AND WHAT SHE IS.
YOU BOTH SHOULD JUST LEAVE. I DON'T WANT TROUBLE.
IT'S A LITTLE LATE FOR THAT.
AHHH!
AND IF YOU THINK THIS IS BAD, JUST WAIT UNTIL I GET IRRITATED.

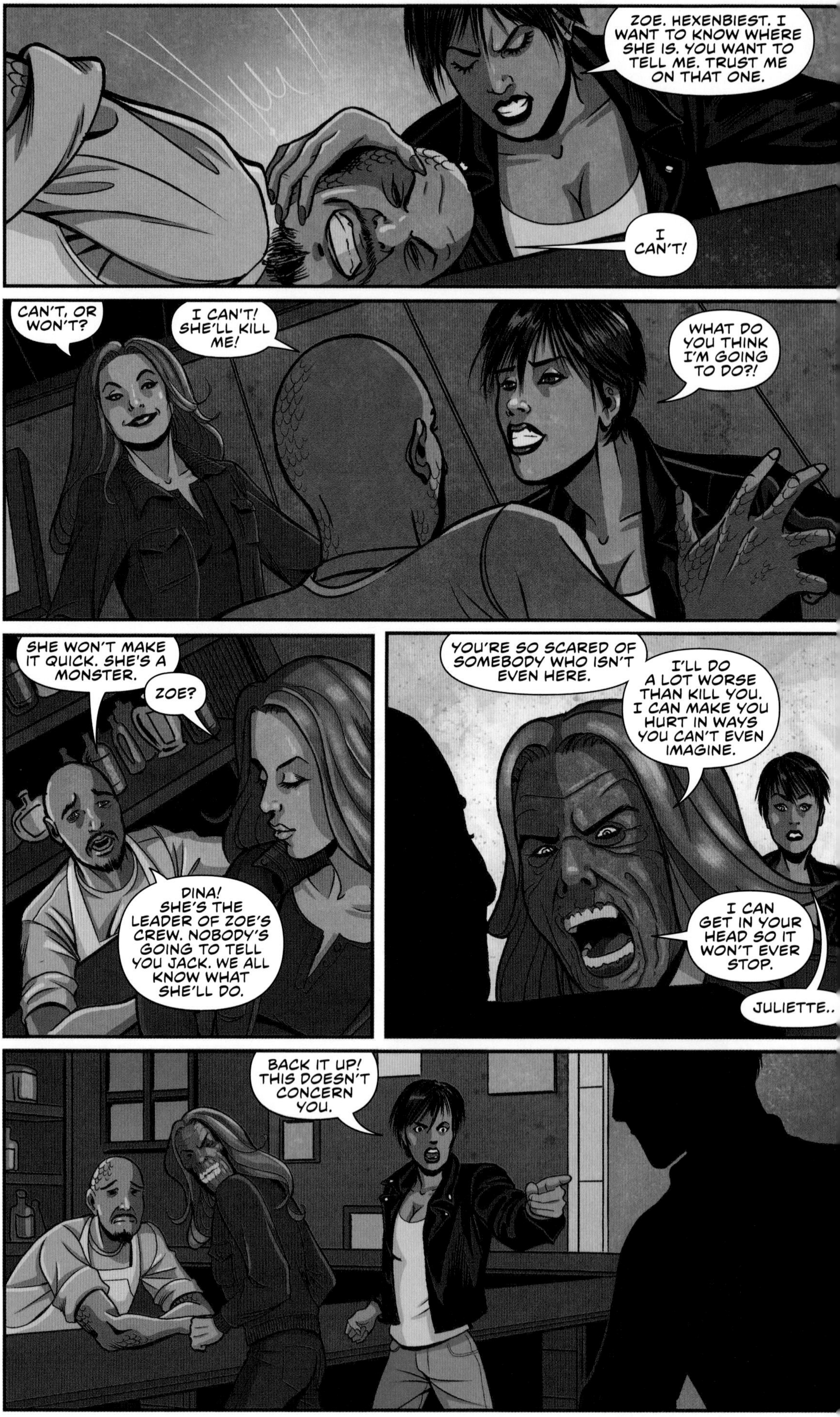
ZOE. HEXENBIEST. I WANT TO KNOW WHERE SHE IS. YOU WANT TO TELL ME. TRUST ME ON THAT ONE.
I CAN'T!
CAN'T, OR WON'T?
I CAN'T! SHE'LL KILL ME!
WHAT DO YOU THINK I'M GOING TO DO?!
SHE WON'T MAKE IT QUICK. SHE'S A MONSTER.
ZOE?
DINA! SHE'S THE LEADER OF ZOE'S CREW. NOBODY'S GOING TO TELL YOU JACK. WE ALL KNOW WHAT SHE'LL DO.
YOU'RE SO SCARED OF SOMEBODY WHO ISN'T EVEN HERE.
I'LL DO A LOT WORSE THAN KILL YOU. I CAN MAKE YOU HURT IN WAYS YOU CAN'T EVEN IMAGINE.
I CAN GET IN YOUR HEAD SO IT WON'T EVER STOP.
JULIETTE..
BACK IT UP! THIS DOESN'T CONCERN YOU.

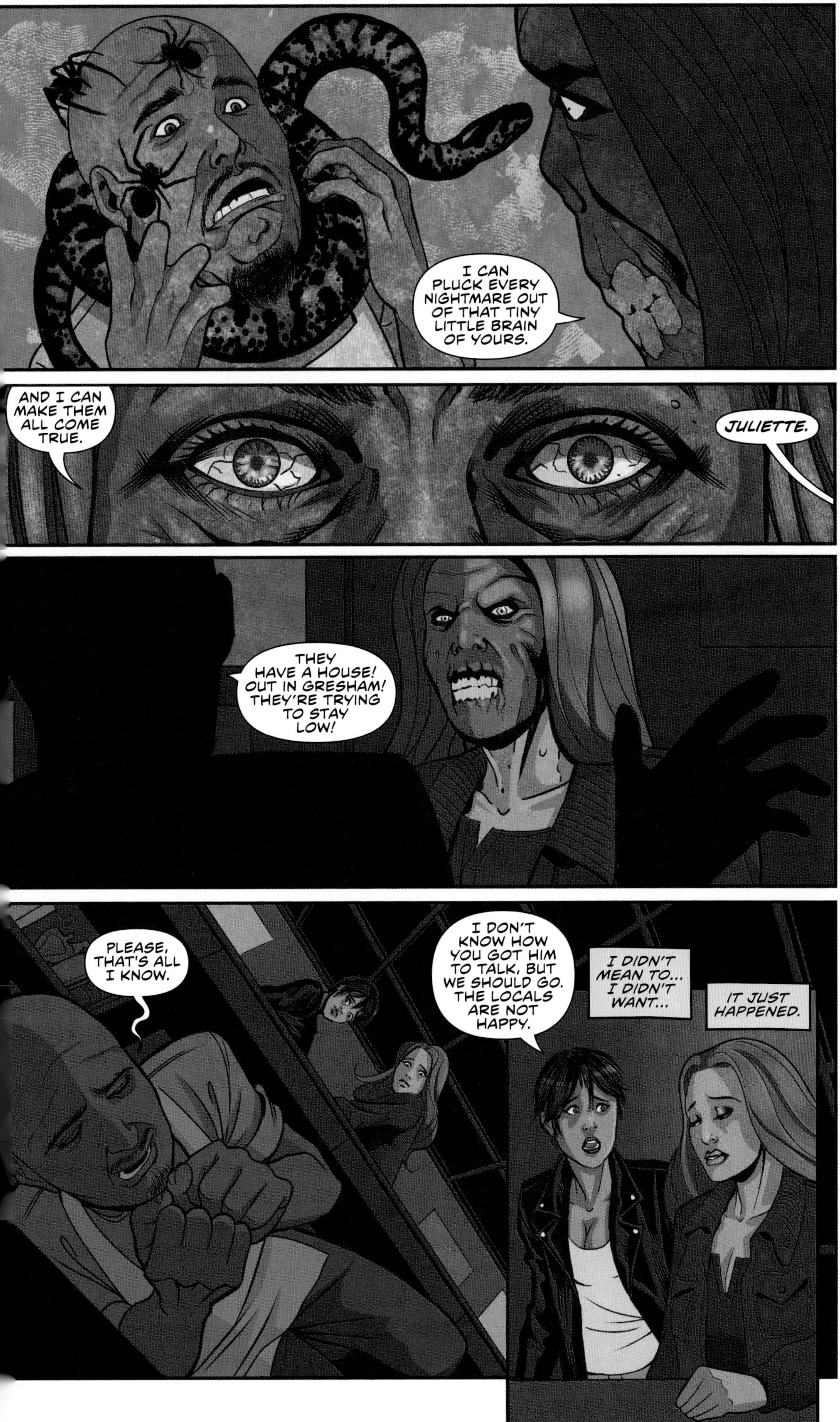
I CAN PLUCK EVERY NIGHTMARE OUT OF THAT TINY LITTLE BRAIN OF YOURS.
AND I CAN MAKE THEM ALL COME TRUE.
JULIETTE.
THEY HAVE A HOUSE! OUT IN GRESHAM! THEY'RE TRYING TO STAY LOW!
PLEASE, THAT'S ALL I KNOW.
I DON'T KNOW HOW YOU GOT HIM TO TALK, BUT WE SHOULD GO. THE LOCALS ARE NOT HAPPY.
I DIDN'T MEAN TO... I DIDN'T WANT...
IT JUST HAPPENED.

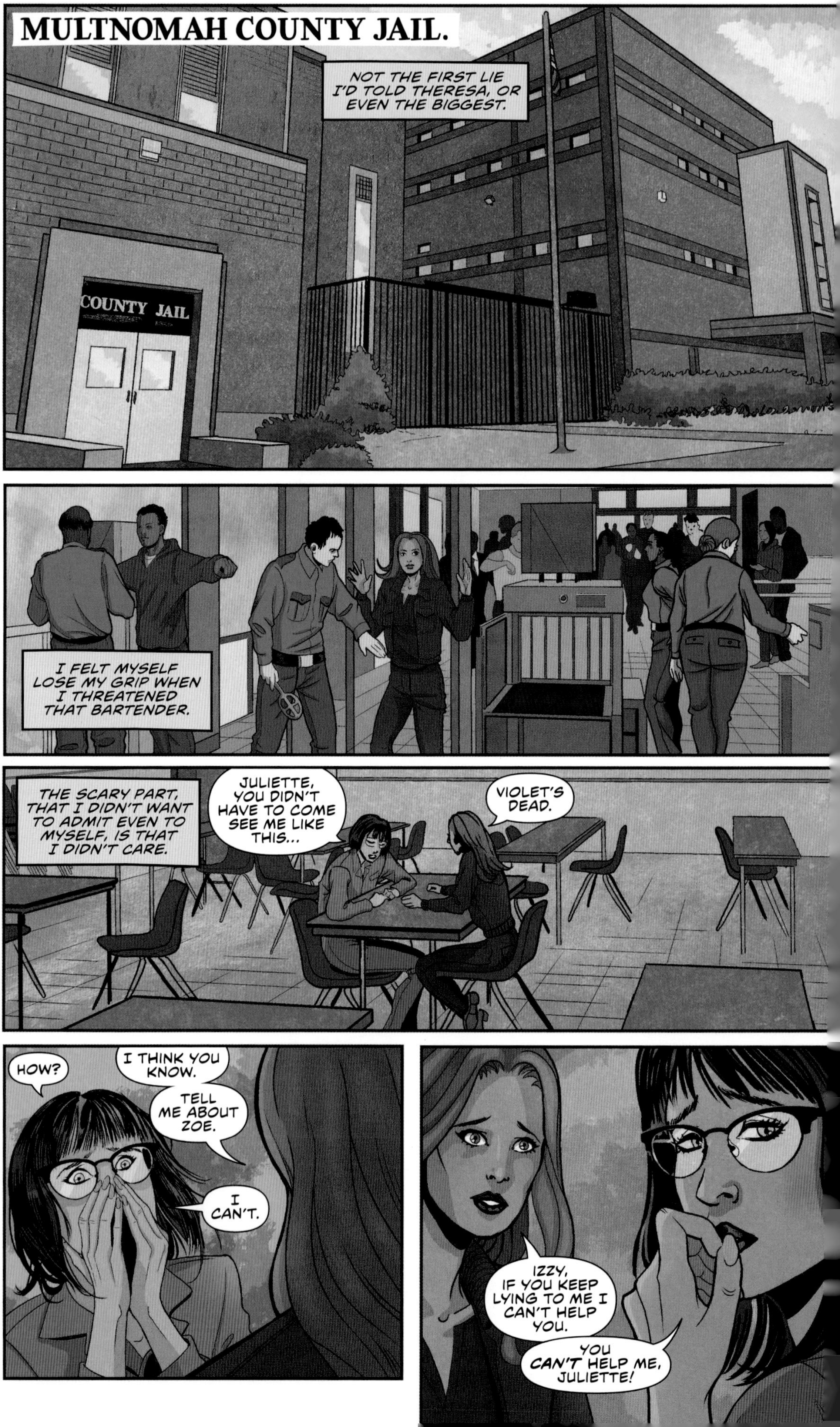
MULTNOMAH COUNTY JAIL.
NOT THE FIRST LIE I'D TOLD THERESA, OR EVEN THE BIGGEST.
COUNTY JAIL
I FELT MYSELF LOSE MY GRIP WHEN I THREATENED THAT BARTENDER.
THE SCARY PART, THAT I DIDN'T WANT TO ADMIT EVEN TO MYSELF, IS THAT I DIDN'T CARE.
JULIETTE, YOU DIDN'T HAVE TO COME SEE ME LIKE THIS...
VIOLET'S DEAD.
HOW?
I THINK YOU KNOW.
TELL ME ABOUT ZOE.
I CAN'T.
IZZY, IF YOU KEEP LYING TO ME I CAN'T HELP YOU.
YOU *CAN'T* HELP ME, JULIETTE!

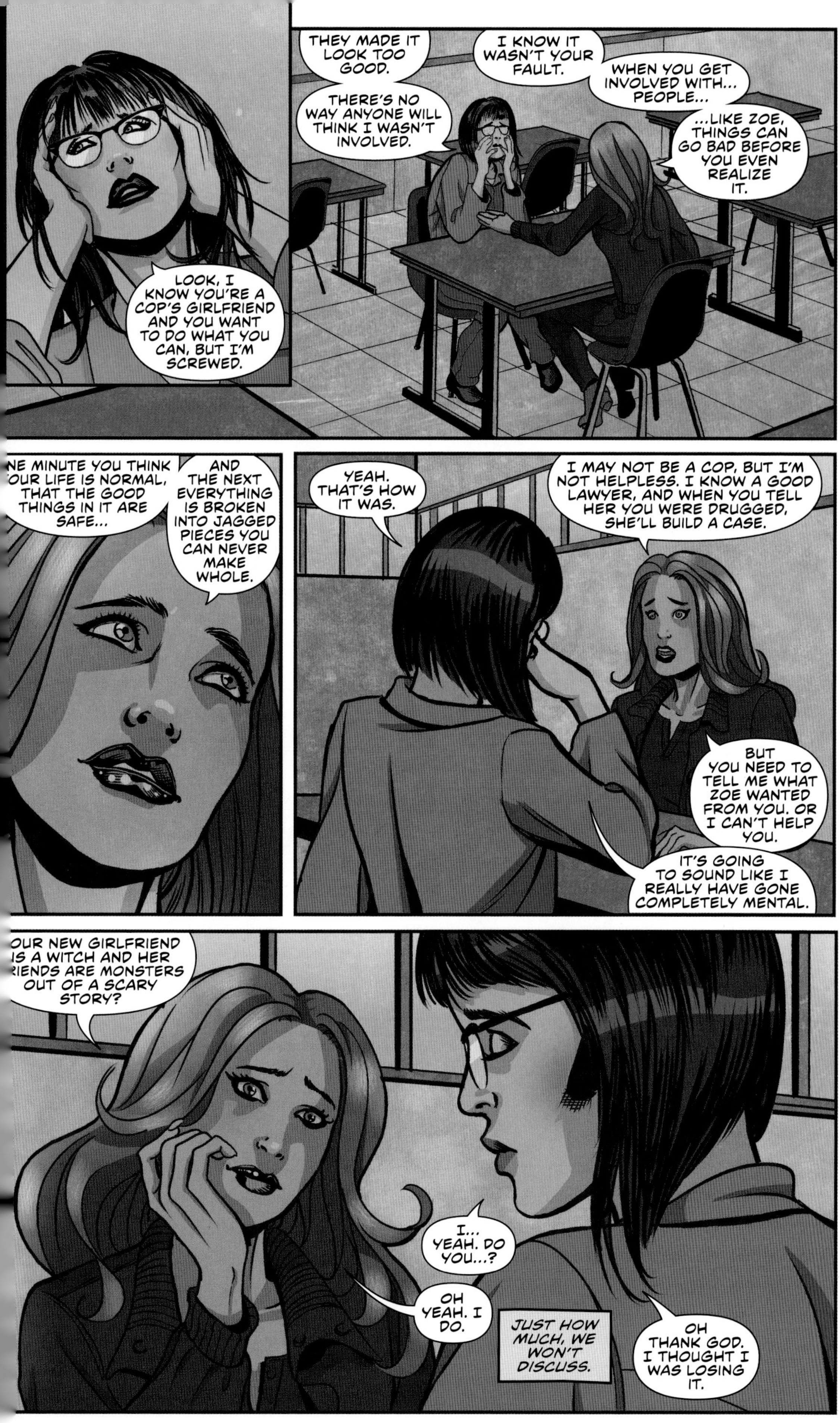
THEY MADE IT LOOK TOO GOOD.
THERE'S NO WAY ANYONE WILL THINK I WASN'T INVOLVED.
I KNOW IT WASN'T YOUR FAULT.
WHEN YOU GET INVOLVED WITH... PEOPLE...
...LIKE ZOE, THINGS CAN GO BAD BEFORE YOU EVEN REALIZE IT.
LOOK, I KNOW YOU'RE A COP'S GIRLFRIEND AND YOU WANT TO DO WHAT YOU CAN, BUT I'M SCREWED.
NE MINUTE YOU THINK OUR LIFE IS NORMAL, THAT THE GOOD THINGS IN IT ARE SAFE...
AND THE NEXT EVERYTHING IS BROKEN INTO JAGGED PIECES YOU CAN NEVER MAKE WHOLE.
YEAH. THAT'S HOW IT WAS.
I MAY NOT BE A COP, BUT I'M NOT HELPLESS. I KNOW A GOOD LAWYER, AND WHEN YOU TELL HER YOU WERE DRUGGED, SHE'LL BUILD A CASE.
BUT YOU NEED TO TELL ME WHAT ZOE WANTED FROM YOU. OR I CAN'T HELP YOU.
IT'S GOING TO SOUND LIKE I REALLY HAVE GONE COMPLETELY MENTAL.
OUR NEW GIRLFRIEND IS A WITCH AND HER RIENDS ARE MONSTERS OUT OF A SCARY STORY?
I... YEAH. DO YOU...?
OH YEAH. I DO.
JUST HOW MUCH, WE WON'T DISCUSS.
OH THANK GOD. I THOUGHT I WAS LOSING IT.

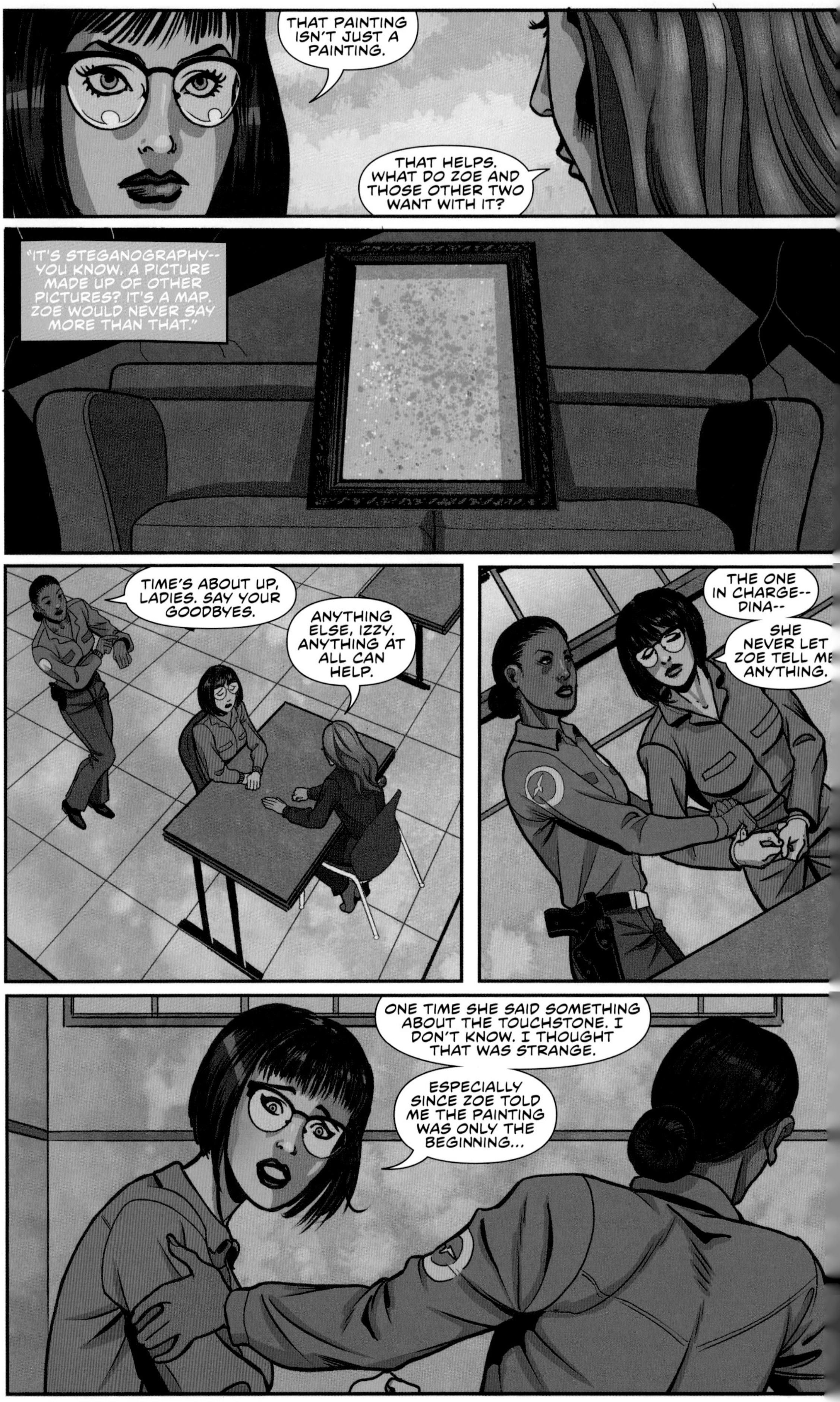
THAT PAINTING ISN'T JUST A PAINTING.
THAT HELPS. WHAT DO ZOE AND THOSE OTHER TWO WANT WITH IT?
"IT'S STEGANOGRAPHY-- YOU KNOW, A PICTURE MADE UP OF OTHER PICTURES? IT'S A MAP. ZOE WOULD NEVER SAY MORE THAN THAT."
TIME'S ABOUT UP, LADIES. SAY YOUR GOODBYES.
ANYTHING ELSE, IZZY. ANYTHING AT ALL CAN HELP.
THE ONE IN CHARGE-- DINA--
SHE NEVER LET ZOE TELL ME ANYTHING.
ONE TIME SHE SAID SOMETHING ABOUT THE TOUCHSTONE. I DON'T KNOW. I THOUGHT THAT WAS STRANGE.
ESPECIALLY SINCE ZOE TOLD ME THE PAINTING WAS ONLY THE BEGINNING...

THINGS LOOK DIFFERENT IN DAYLIGHT. ESPECIALLY WHEN YOU REGRET THE NIGHT BEFORE.

POOR IZZY. THIS MUST BE THE WORST DAY OF HER LIFE.

SECOND WORST, MAYBE. THE ONE WHERE YOU FIND OUT ABOUT WESEN IS ALWAYS NUMBER ONE.

AND HOW ARE YOU HOLDING UP?

DID TRUBEL RAT ME OUT?

SHE MIGHT HAVE MENTIONED YOU PHYSICALLY ASSAULTING A CERTAIN BARTENDER, YES.

THOSE WEREN'T THREATS. THAT'S THE THING. I REALLY WOULD HAVE RIPPED THAT MAN'S MIND APART.

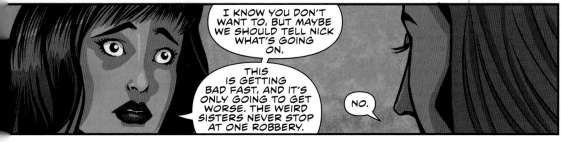

I KNOW YOU DON'T WANT TO, BUT MAYBE WE SHOULD TELL NICK WHAT'S GOING ON.

THIS IS GETTING BAD FAST, AND IT'S ONLY GOING TO GET WORSE. THE WEIRD SISTERS NEVER STOP AT ONE ROBBERY.

NO.

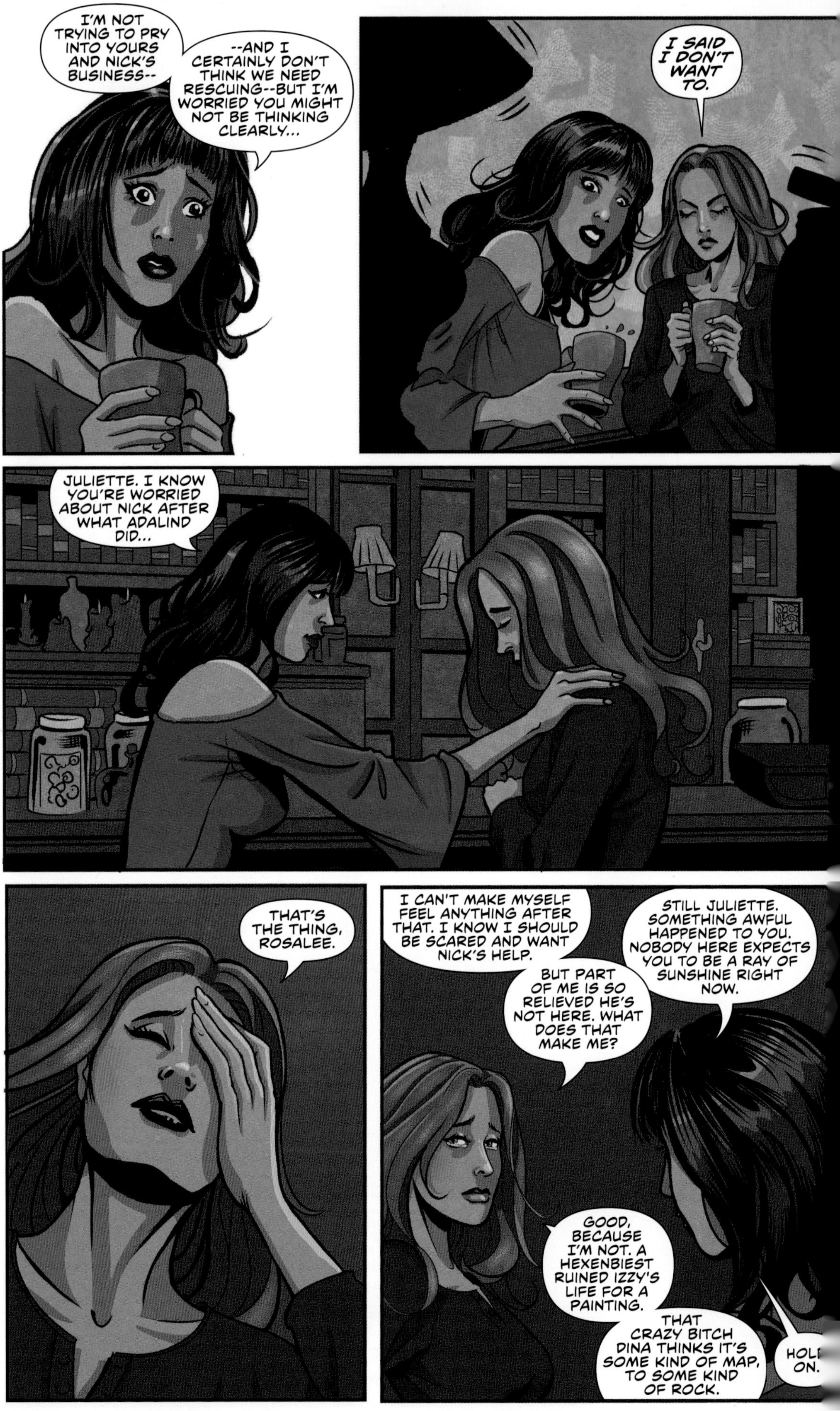
I'M NOT TRYING TO PRY INTO YOURS AND NICK'S BUSINESS--
--AND I CERTAINLY DON'T THINK WE NEED RESCUING--BUT I'M WORRIED YOU MIGHT NOT BE THINKING CLEARLY...
I SAID I DON'T WANT TO.
JULIETTE. I KNOW YOU'RE WORRIED ABOUT NICK AFTER WHAT ADALIND DID...
THAT'S THE THING, ROSALEE.
I CAN'T MAKE MYSELF FEEL ANYTHING AFTER THAT. I KNOW I SHOULD BE SCARED AND WANT NICK'S HELP.
BUT PART OF ME IS SO RELIEVED HE'S NOT HERE. WHAT DOES THAT MAKE ME?
STILL JULIETTE. SOMETHING AWFUL HAPPENED TO YOU. NOBODY HERE EXPECTS YOU TO BE A RAY OF SUNSHINE RIGHT NOW.
GOOD, BECAUSE I'M NOT. A HEXENBIEST RUINED IZZY'S LIFE FOR A PAINTING.
THAT CRAZY BITCH DINA THINKS IT'S SOME KIND OF MAP, TO SOME KIND OF ROCK.
HOL ON.

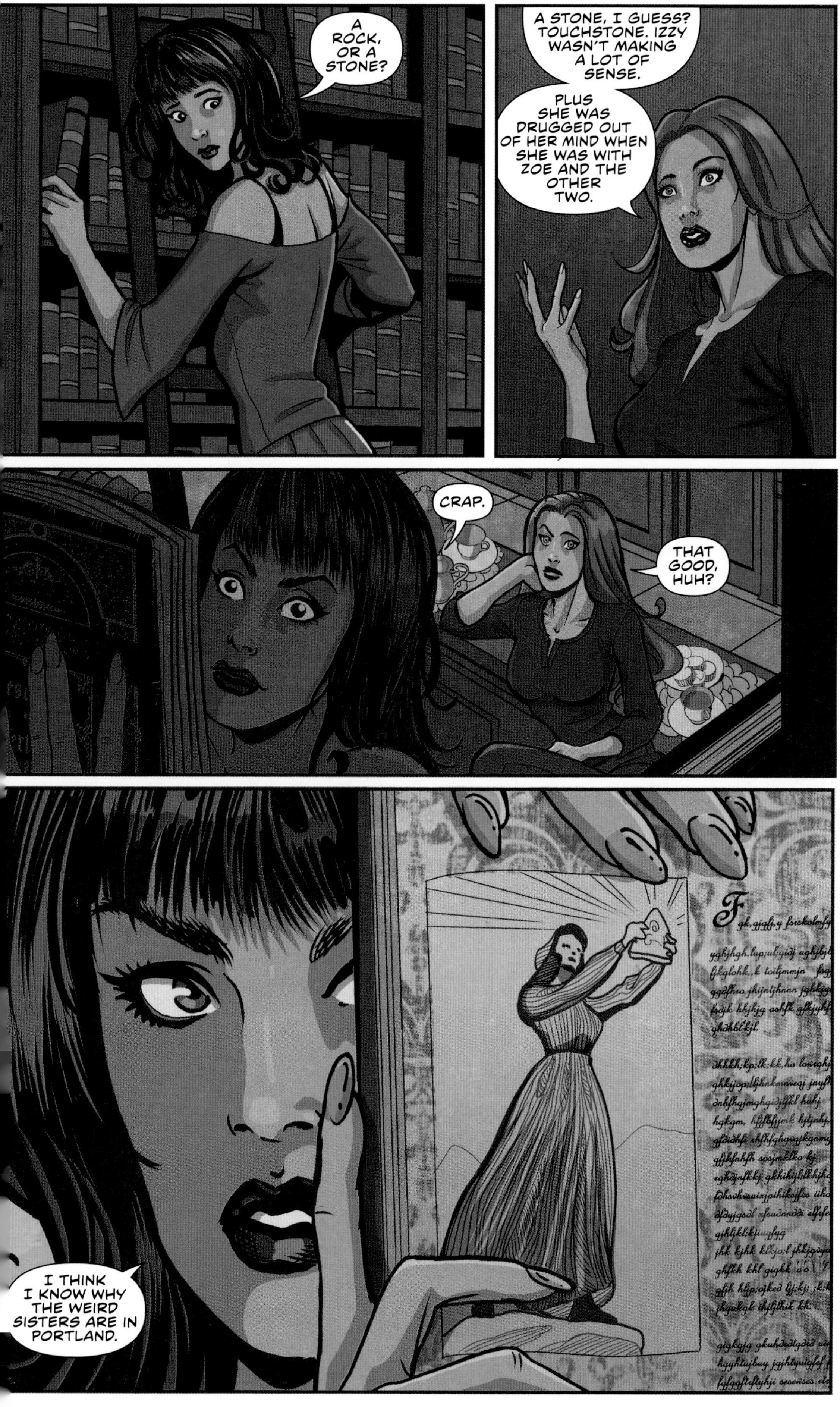
A ROCK, OR A STONE?
A STONE, I GUESS? TOUCHSTONE. IZZY WASN'T MAKING A LOT OF SENSE.
PLUS SHE WAS DRUGGED OUT OF HER MIND WHEN SHE WAS WITH ZOE AND THE OTHER TWO.
CRAP.
THAT GOOD, HUH?
I THINK I KNOW WHY THE WEIRD SISTERS ARE IN PORTLAND.

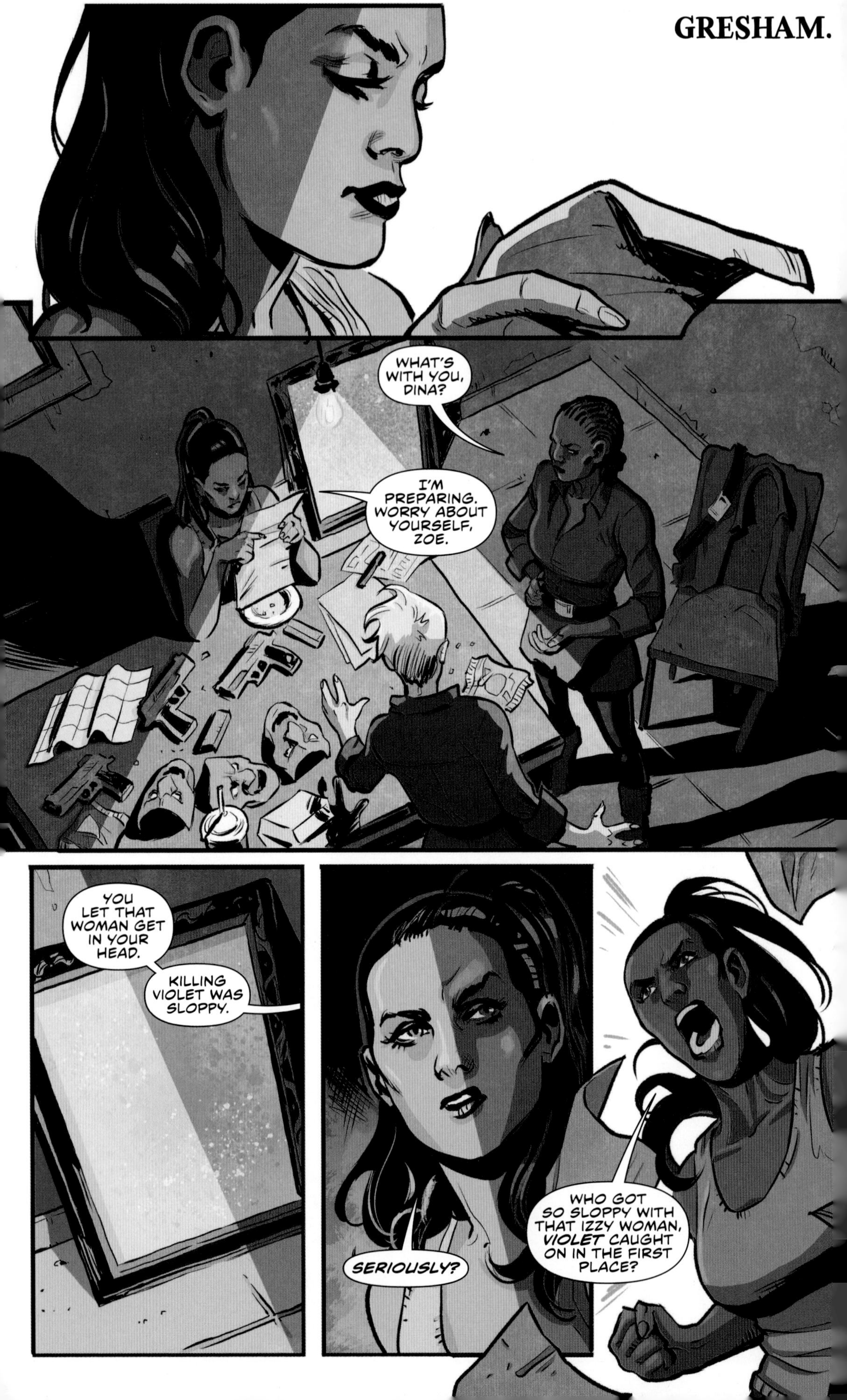
GRESHAM.
WHAT'S WITH YOU, DINA?
I'M PREPARING. WORRY ABOUT YOURSELF, ZOE.
YOU LET THAT WOMAN GET IN YOUR HEAD.
KILLING VIOLET WAS SLOPPY.
SERIOUSLY?
WHO GOT SO SLOPPY WITH THAT IZZY WOMAN, VIOLET CAUGHT ON IN THE FIRST PLACE?

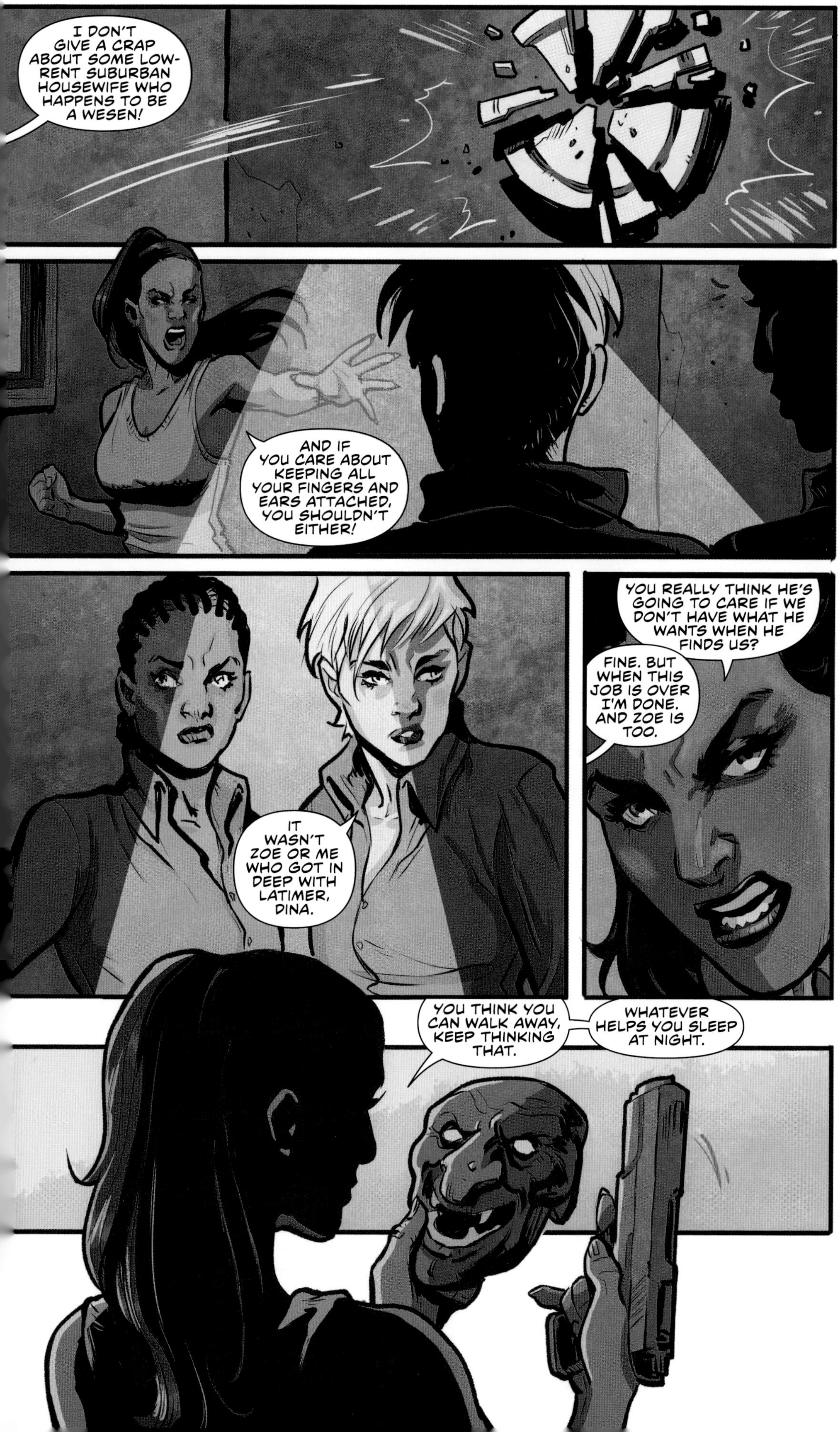
I DON'T GIVE A CRAP ABOUT SOME LOW-RENT SUBURBAN HOUSEWIFE WHO HAPPENS TO BE A WESEN!
AND IF YOU CARE ABOUT KEEPING ALL YOUR FINGERS AND EARS ATTACHED, YOU SHOULDN'T EITHER!
IT WASN'T ZOE OR ME WHO GOT IN DEEP WITH LATIMER, DINA.
YOU REALLY THINK HE'S GOING TO CARE IF WE DON'T HAVE WHAT HE WANTS WHEN HE FINDS US?
FINE. BUT WHEN THIS JOB IS OVER I'M DONE. AND ZOE IS TOO.
YOU THINK YOU CAN WALK AWAY, KEEP THINKING THAT.
WHATEVER HELPS YOU SLEEP AT NIGHT.

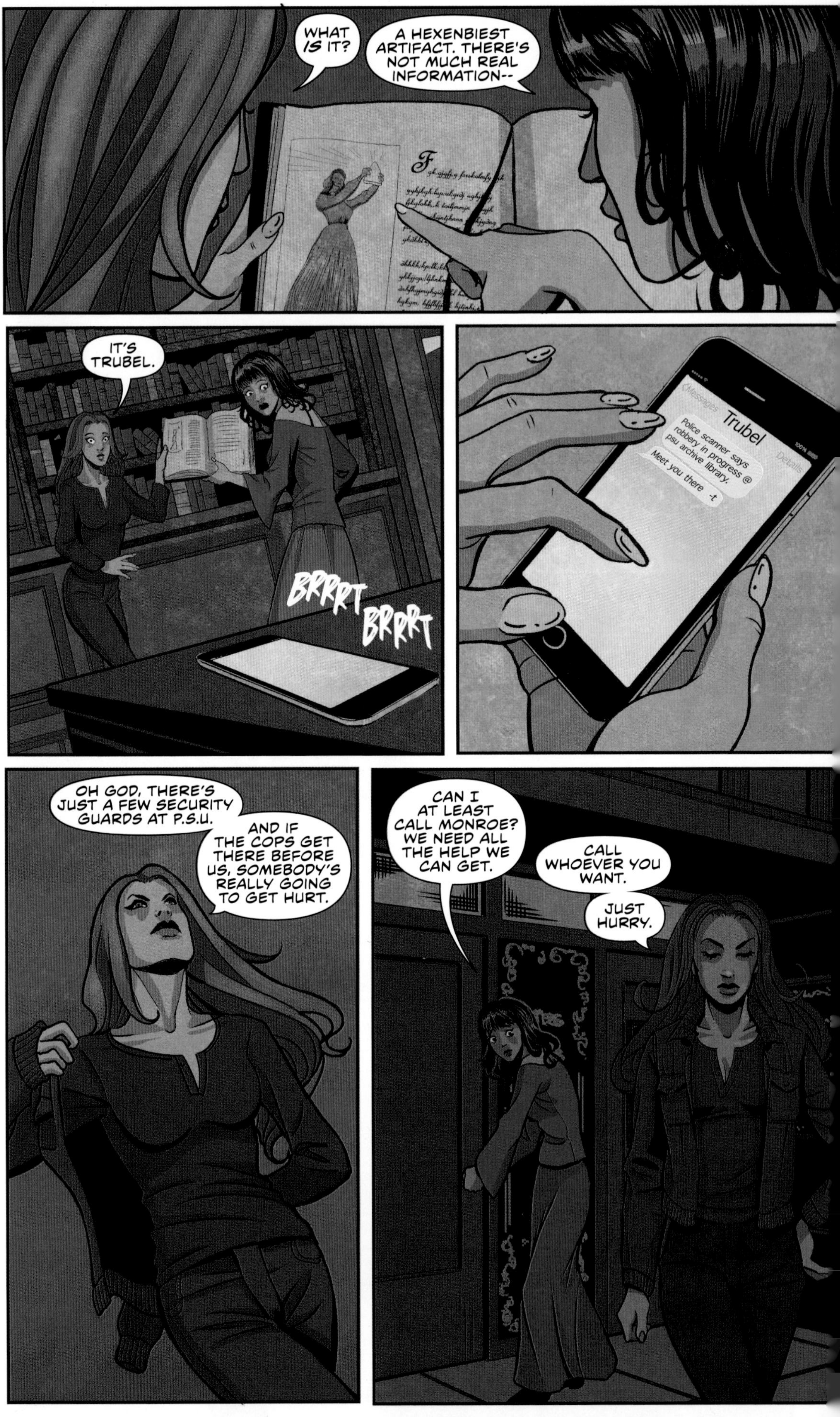
WHAT *IS* IT?
A HEXENBIEST ARTIFACT. THERE'S NOT MUCH REAL INFORMATION--
IT'S TRUBEL.
BRRRT BRRRT
Trubel
Police scanner says robbery in progress @ psu archive library.
Meet you there -t
OH GOD, THERE'S JUST A FEW SECURITY GUARDS AT P.S.U.
AND IF THE COPS GET THERE BEFORE US, SOMEBODY'S REALLY GOING TO GET HURT.
CAN I AT LEAST CALL MONROE? WE NEED ALL THE HELP WE CAN GET.
CALL WHOEVER YOU WANT.
JUST HURRY.

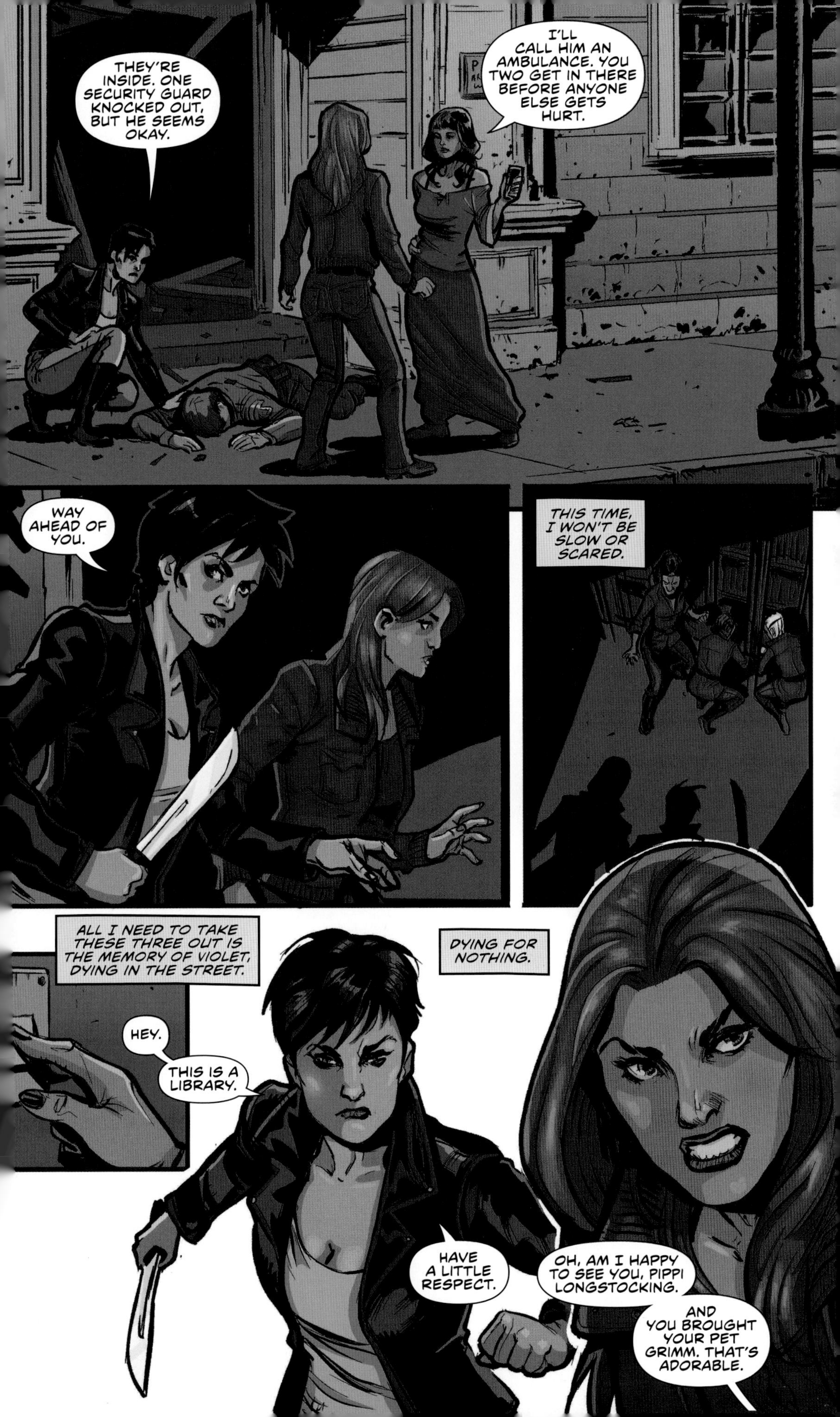
THEY'RE INSIDE. ONE SECURITY GUARD KNOCKED OUT, BUT HE SEEMS OKAY.
I'LL CALL HIM AN AMBULANCE. YOU TWO GET IN THERE BEFORE ANYONE ELSE GETS HURT.
WAY AHEAD OF YOU.
THIS TIME, I WON'T BE SLOW OR SCARED.
ALL I NEED TO TAKE THESE THREE OUT IS THE MEMORY OF VIOLET, DYING IN THE STREET.
DYING FOR NOTHING.
HEY.
THIS IS A LIBRARY.
HAVE A LITTLE RESPECT.
OH, AM I HAPPY TO SEE YOU, PIPPI LONGSTOCKING.
AND YOU BROUGHT YOUR PET GRIMM. THAT'S ADORABLE.

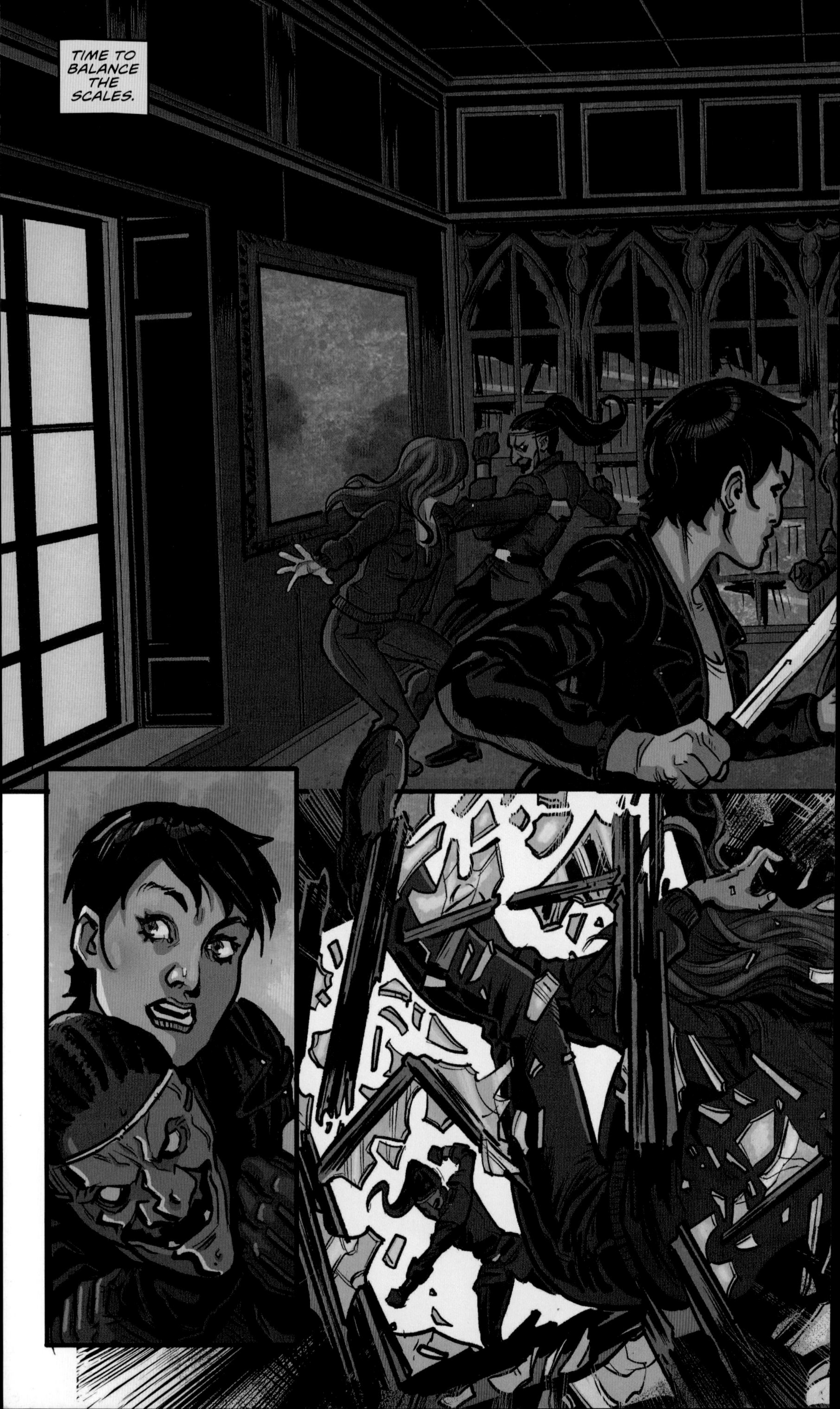
TIME TO BALANCE THE SCALES.

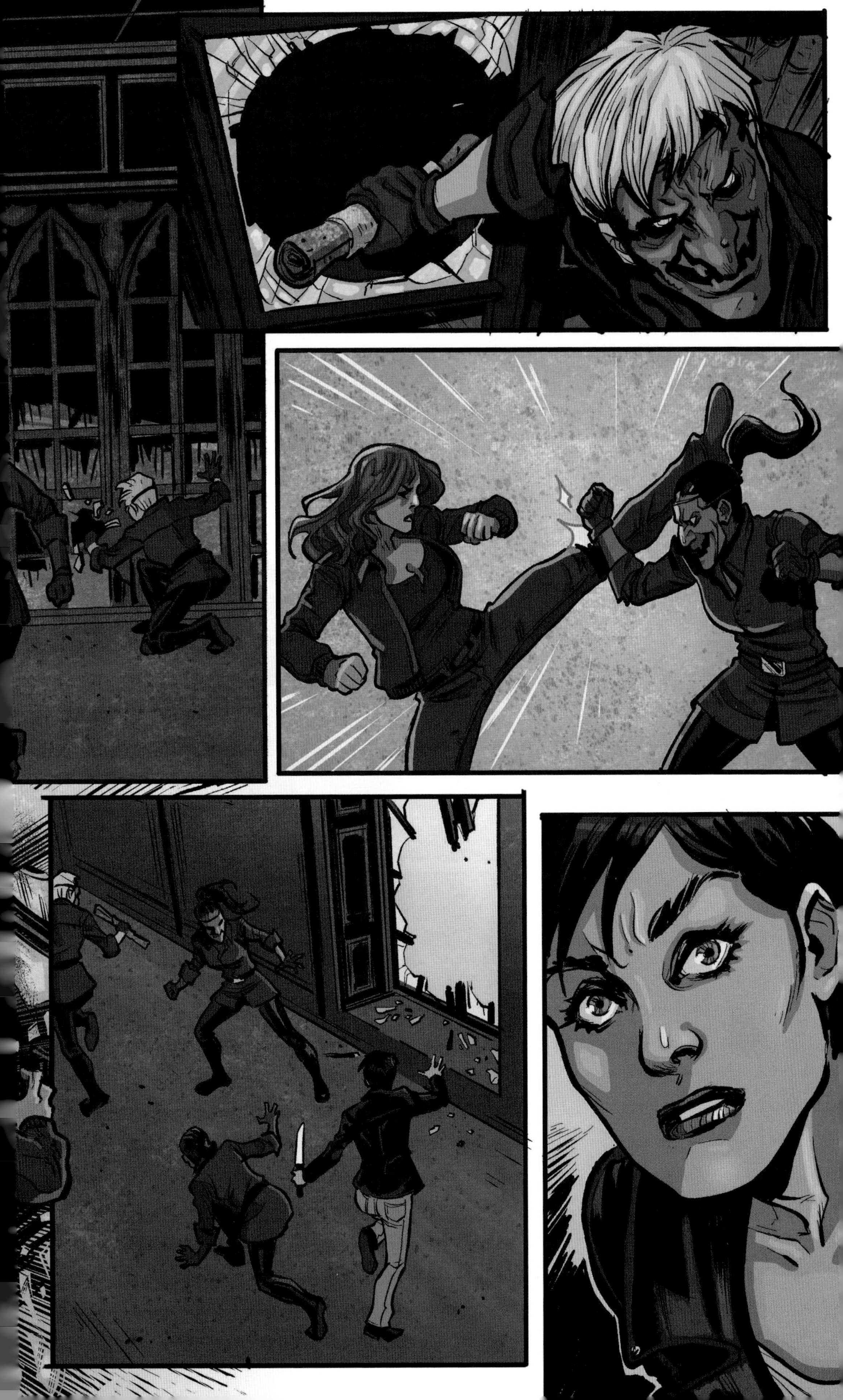

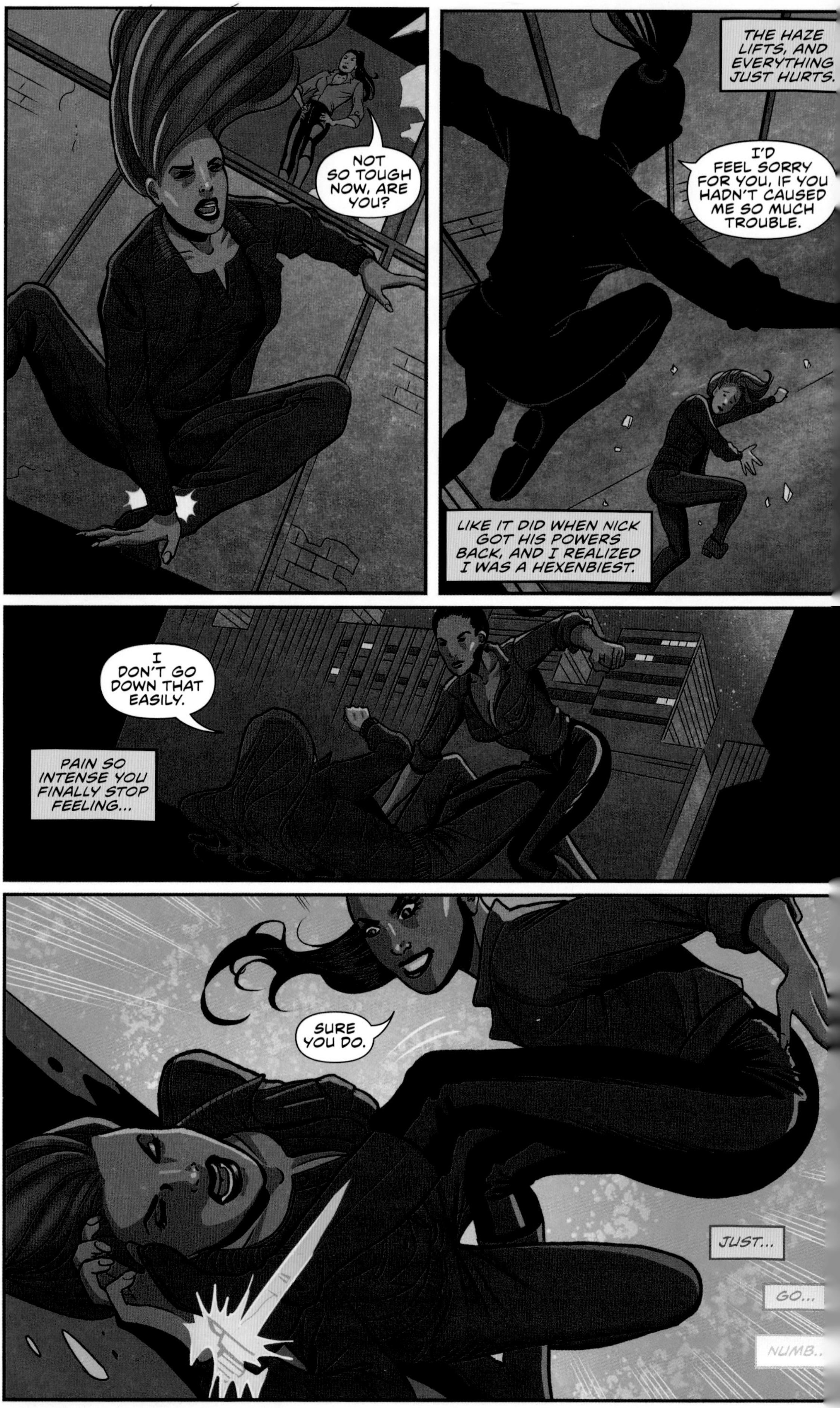
NOT SO TOUGH NOW, ARE YOU?
THE HAZE LIFTS, AND EVERYTHING JUST HURTS.
I'D FEEL SORRY FOR YOU, IF YOU HADN'T CAUSED ME SO MUCH TROUBLE.
LIKE IT DID WHEN NICK GOT HIS POWERS BACK, AND I REALIZED I WAS A HEXENBIEST.
I DON'T GO DOWN THAT EASILY.
PAIN SO INTENSE YOU FINALLY STOP FEELING...
SURE YOU DO.
JUST...
GO...
NUMB..

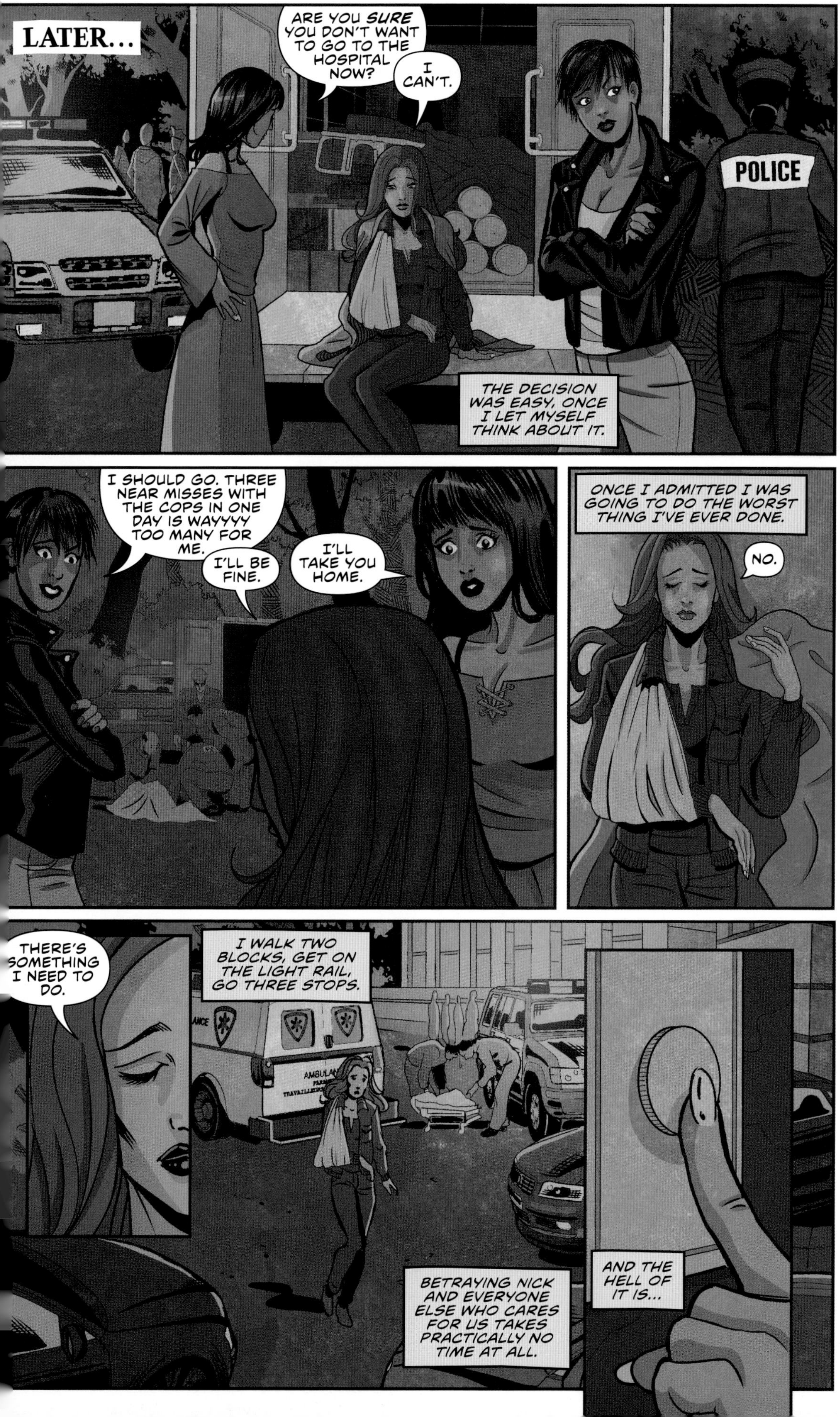
LATER...
ARE YOU SURE YOU DON'T WANT TO GO TO THE HOSPITAL NOW?
I CAN'T.
POLICE
THE DECISION WAS EASY, ONCE I LET MYSELF THINK ABOUT IT.
I SHOULD GO. THREE NEAR MISSES WITH THE COPS IN ONE DAY IS WAYYYY TOO MANY FOR ME.
I'LL BE FINE.
I'LL TAKE YOU HOME.
ONCE I ADMITTED I WAS GOING TO DO THE WORST THING I'VE EVER DONE.
NO.
THERE'S SOMETHING I NEED TO DO.
I WALK TWO BLOCKS, GET ON THE LIGHT RAIL, GO THREE STOPS.
BETRAYING NICK AND EVERYONE ELSE WHO CARES FOR US TAKES PRACTICALLY NO TIME AT ALL.
AND THE HELL OF IT IS...

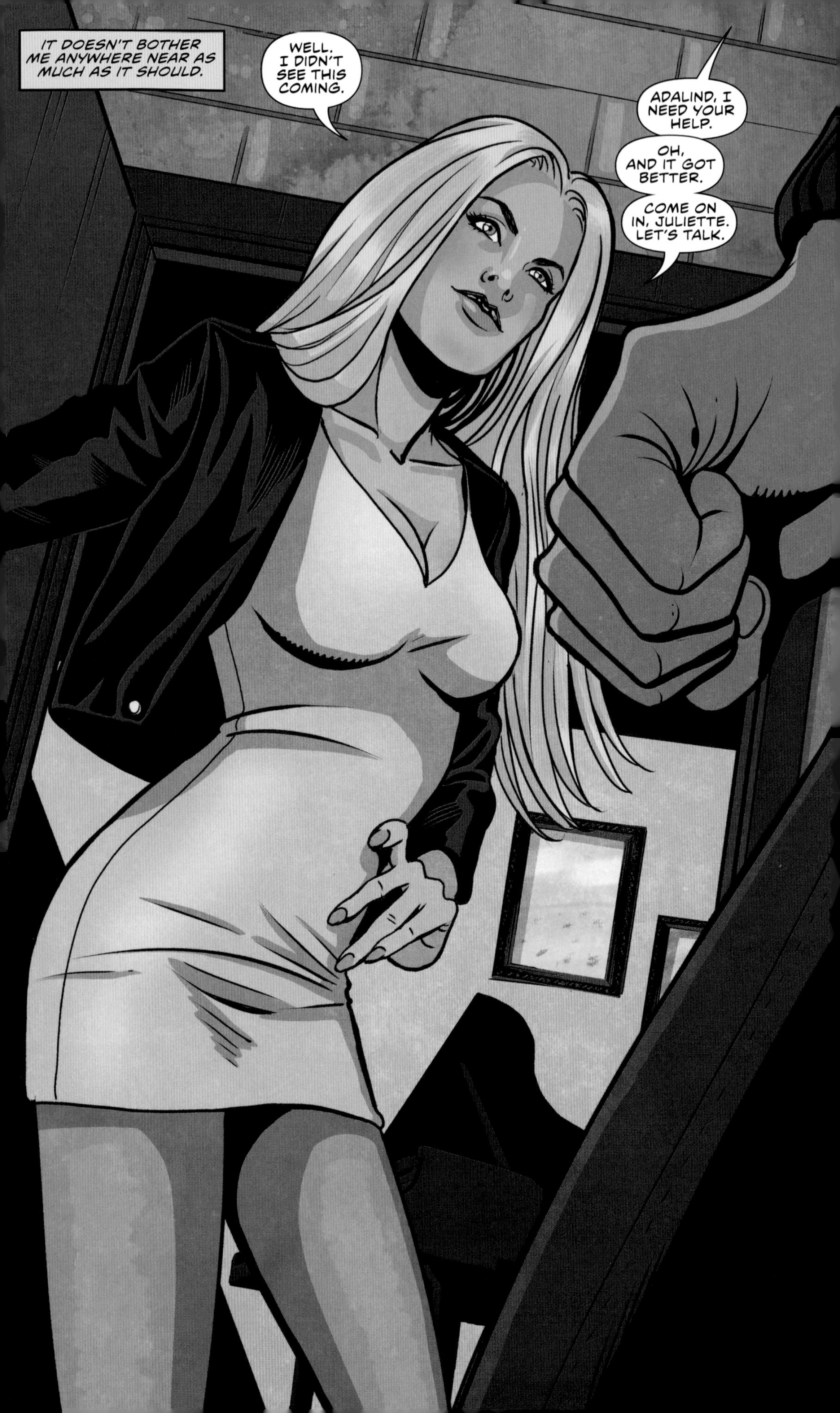

IT DOESN'T BOTHER ME ANYWHERE NEAR AS MUCH AS IT SHOULD.
WELL. I DIDN'T SEE THIS COMING.
ADALIND, I NEED YOUR HELP.
OH, AND IT GOT BETTER.
COME ON IN, JULIETTE. LET'S TALK.

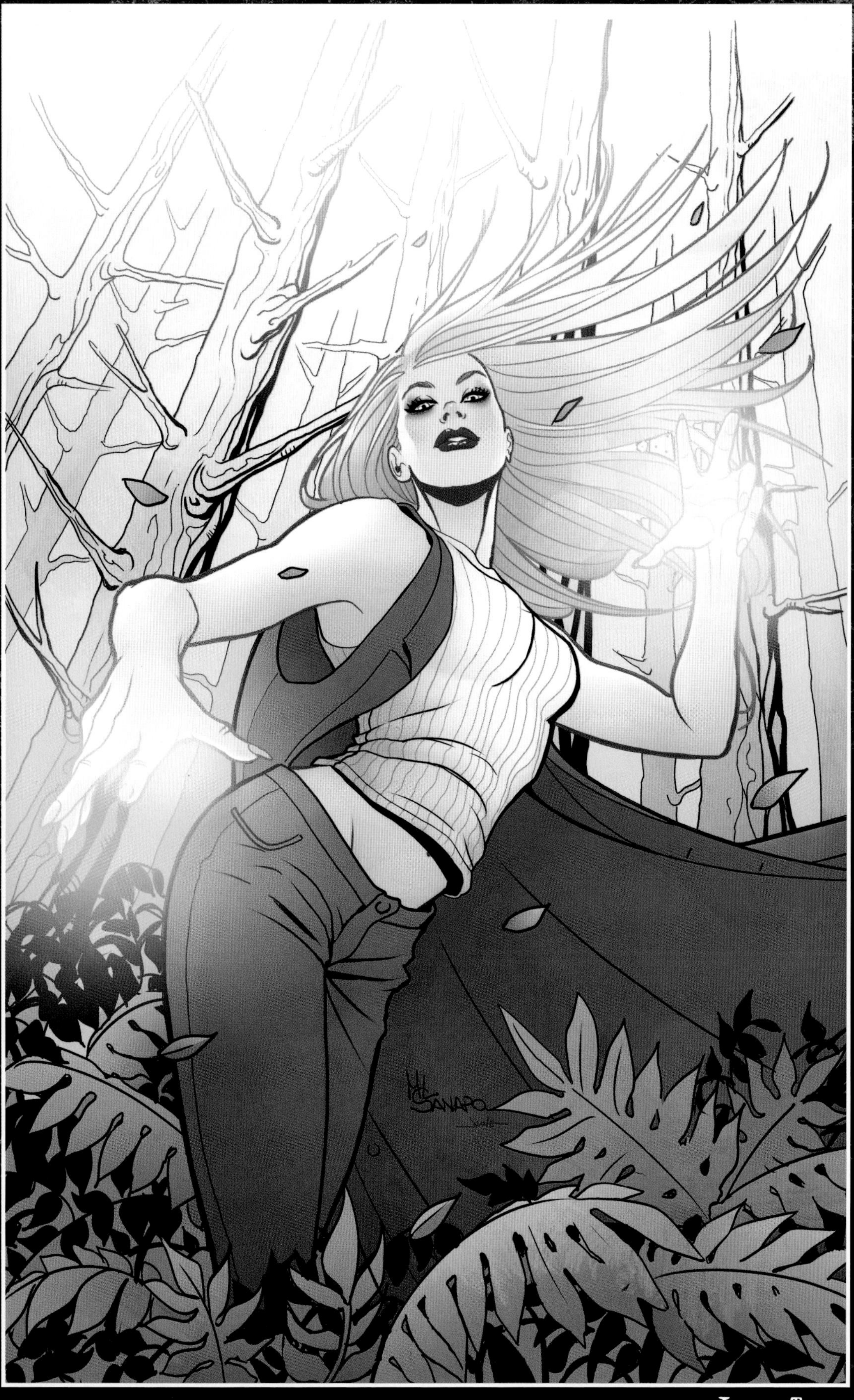

Issue Three

Art by Maria Sanapo | Colors by June Chung

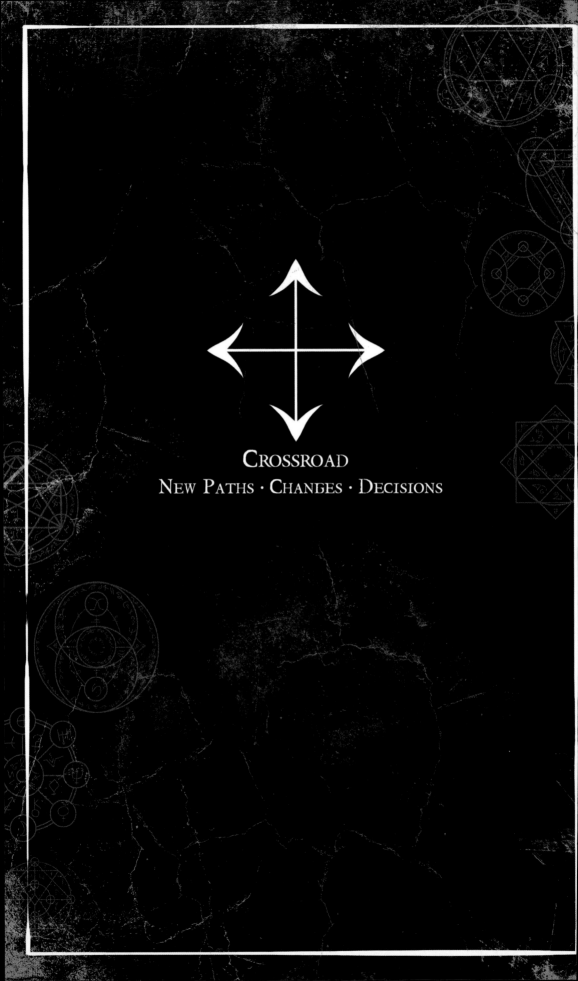

CROSSROAD
NEW PATHS · CHANGES · DECISIONS

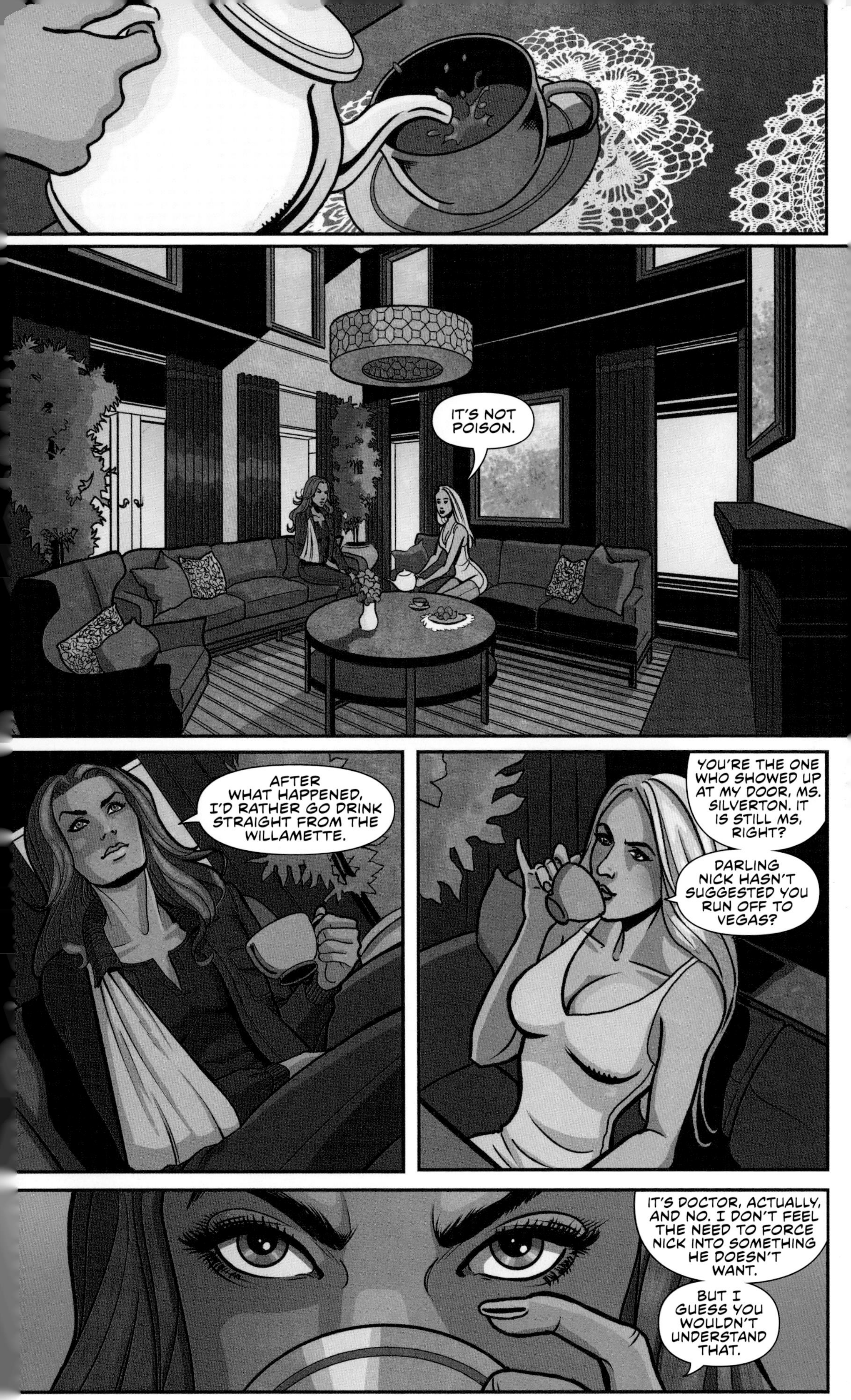
IT'S NOT POISON.
AFTER WHAT HAPPENED, I'D RATHER GO DRINK STRAIGHT FROM THE WILLAMETTE.
YOU'RE THE ONE WHO SHOWED UP AT MY DOOR, MS. SILVERTON. IT IS STILL MS, RIGHT?
DARLING NICK HASN'T SUGGESTED YOU RUN OFF TO VEGAS?
IT'S DOCTOR, ACTUALLY, AND NO. I DON'T FEEL THE NEED TO FORCE NICK INTO SOMETHING HE DOESN'T WANT.
BUT I GUESS YOU WOULDN'T UNDERSTAND THAT.

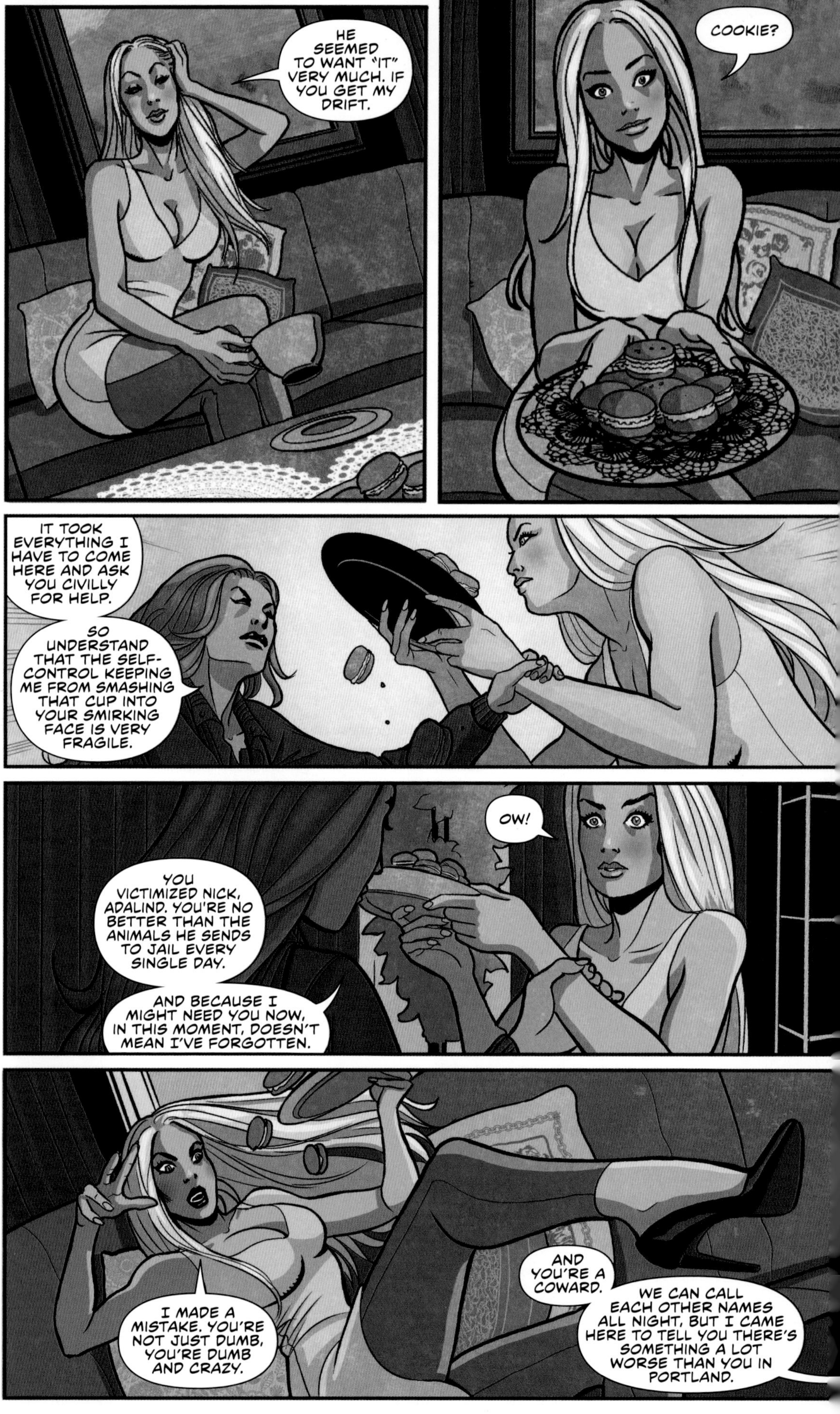
HE SEEMED TO WANT "IT" VERY MUCH. IF YOU GET MY DRIFT.
COOKIE?
IT TOOK EVERYTHING I HAVE TO COME HERE AND ASK YOU CIVILLY FOR HELP.
SO UNDERSTAND THAT THE SELF-CONTROL KEEPING ME FROM SMASHING THAT CUP INTO YOUR SMIRKING FACE IS VERY FRAGILE.
OW!
YOU VICTIMIZED NICK, ADALIND. YOU'RE NO BETTER THAN THE ANIMALS HE SENDS TO JAIL EVERY SINGLE DAY.
AND BECAUSE I MIGHT NEED YOU NOW, IN THIS MOMENT, DOESN'T MEAN I'VE FORGOTTEN.
I MADE A MISTAKE. YOU'RE NOT JUST DUMB, YOU'RE DUMB AND CRAZY.
AND YOU'RE A COWARD.
WE CAN CALL EACH OTHER NAMES ALL NIGHT, BUT I CAME HERE TO TELL YOU THERE'S SOMETHING A LOT WORSE THAN YOU IN PORTLAND.

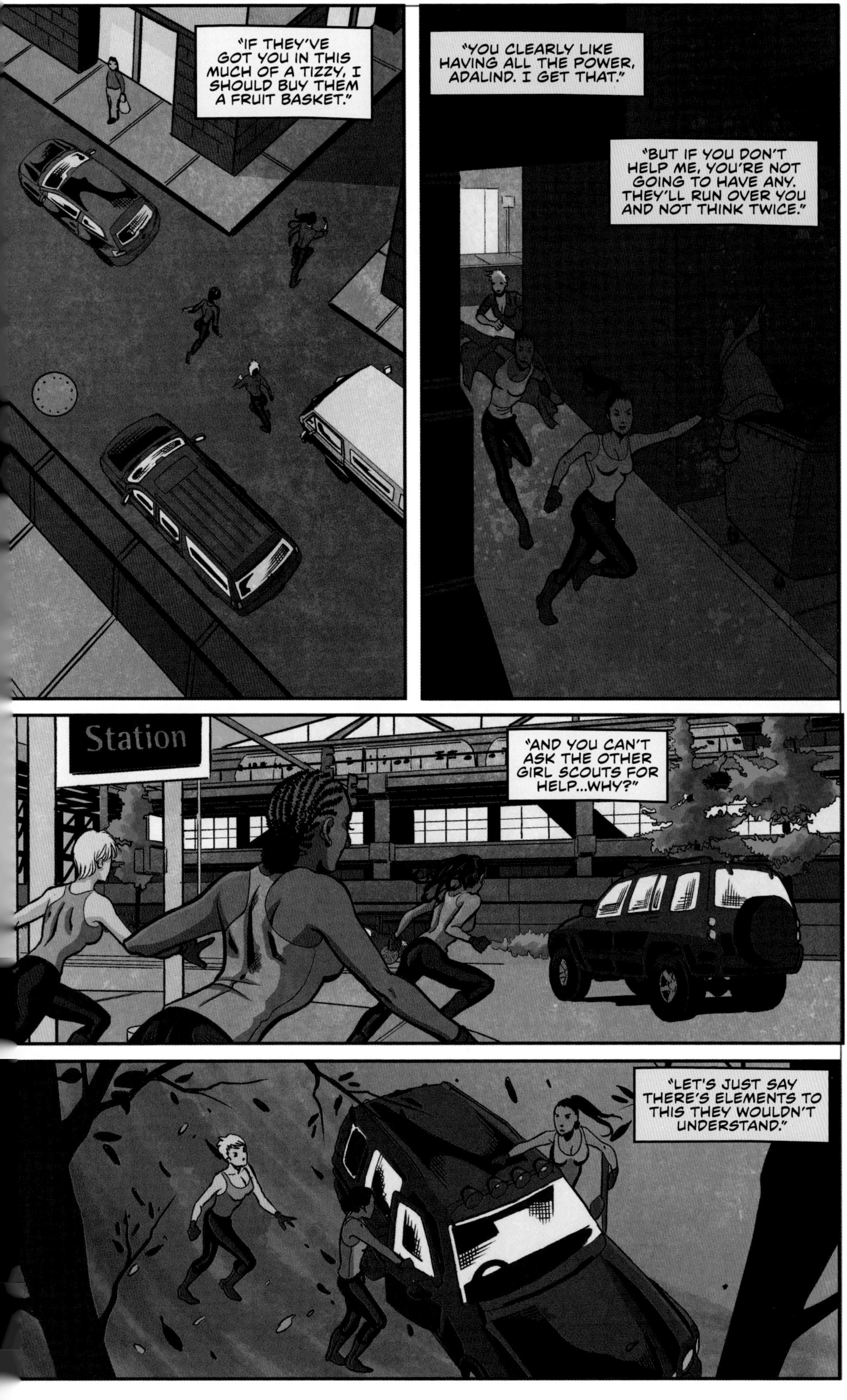
"IF THEY'VE GOT YOU IN THIS MUCH OF A TIZZY, I SHOULD BUY THEM A FRUIT BASKET."
"YOU CLEARLY LIKE HAVING ALL THE POWER, ADALIND. I GET THAT."
"BUT IF YOU DON'T HELP ME, YOU'RE NOT GOING TO HAVE ANY. THEY'LL RUN OVER YOU AND NOT THINK TWICE."
Station
"AND YOU CAN'T ASK THE OTHER GIRL SCOUTS FOR HELP...WHY?"
"LET'S JUST SAY THERE'S ELEMENTS TO THIS THEY WOULDN'T UNDERSTAND."

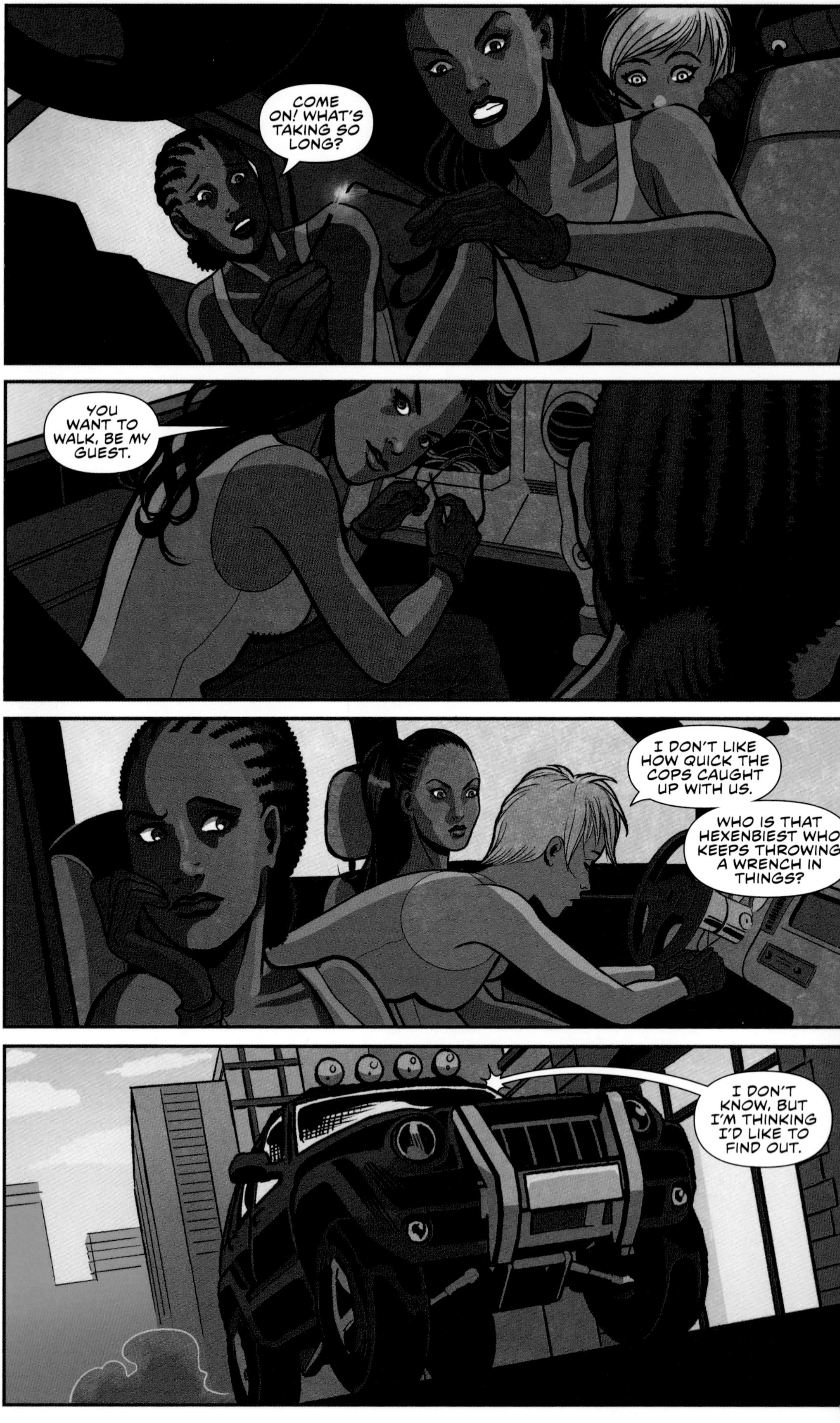
COME ON! WHAT'S TAKING SO LONG?
YOU WANT TO WALK, BE MY GUEST.
I DON'T LIKE HOW QUICK THE COPS CAUGHT UP WITH US.
WHO IS THAT HEXENBIEST WHO KEEPS THROWING A WRENCH IN THINGS?
I DON'T KNOW, BUT I'M THINKING I'D LIKE TO FIND OUT.

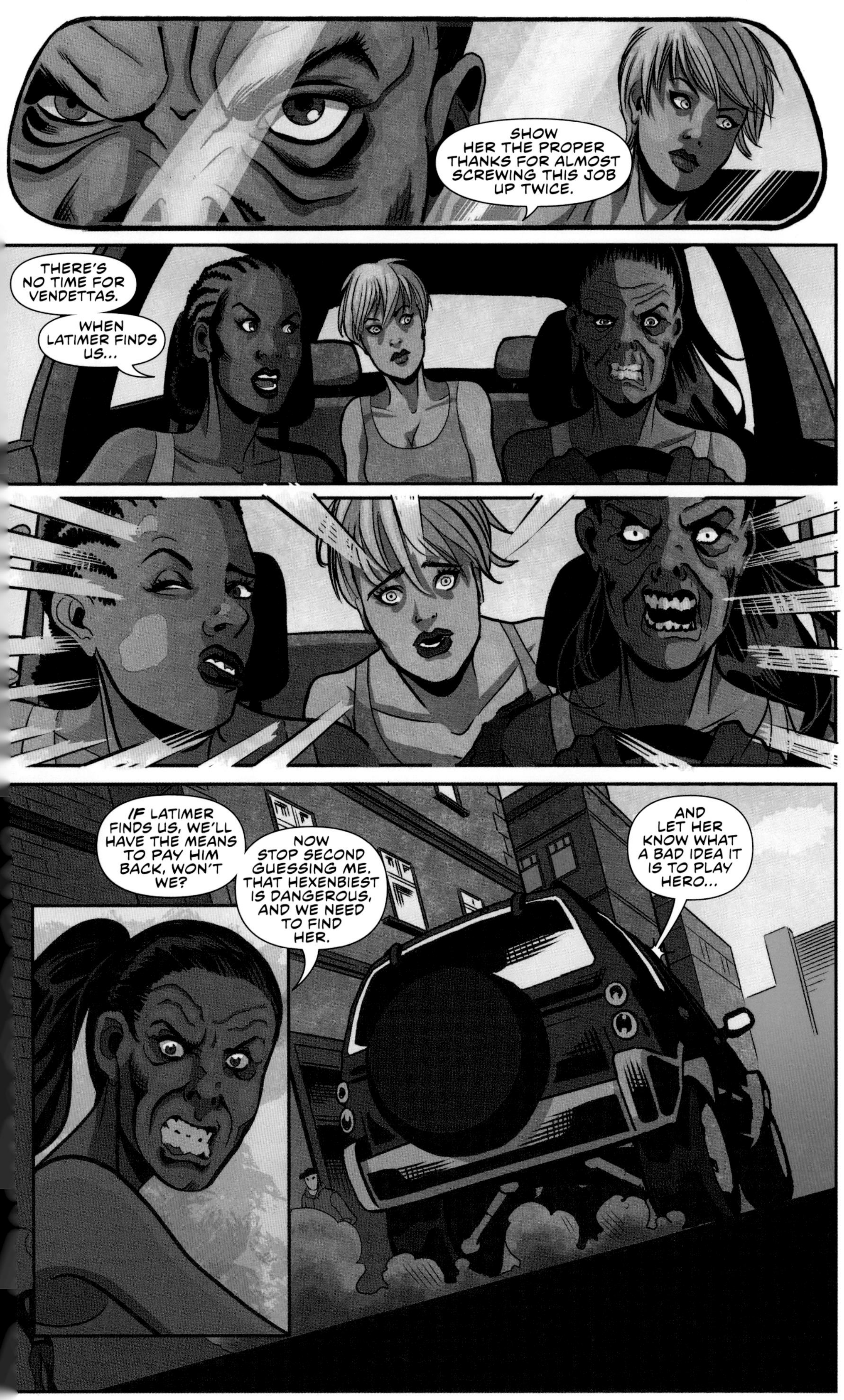
SHOW HER THE PROPER THANKS FOR ALMOST SCREWING THIS JOB UP TWICE.
THERE'S NO TIME FOR VENDETTAS.
WHEN LATIMER FINDS US...
IF LATIMER FINDS US, WE'LL HAVE THE MEANS TO PAY HIM BACK, WON'T WE?
NOW STOP SECOND GUESSING ME. THAT HEXENBIEST IS DANGEROUS, AND WE NEED TO FIND HER.
AND LET HER KNOW WHAT A BAD IDEA IT IS TO PLAY HERO...

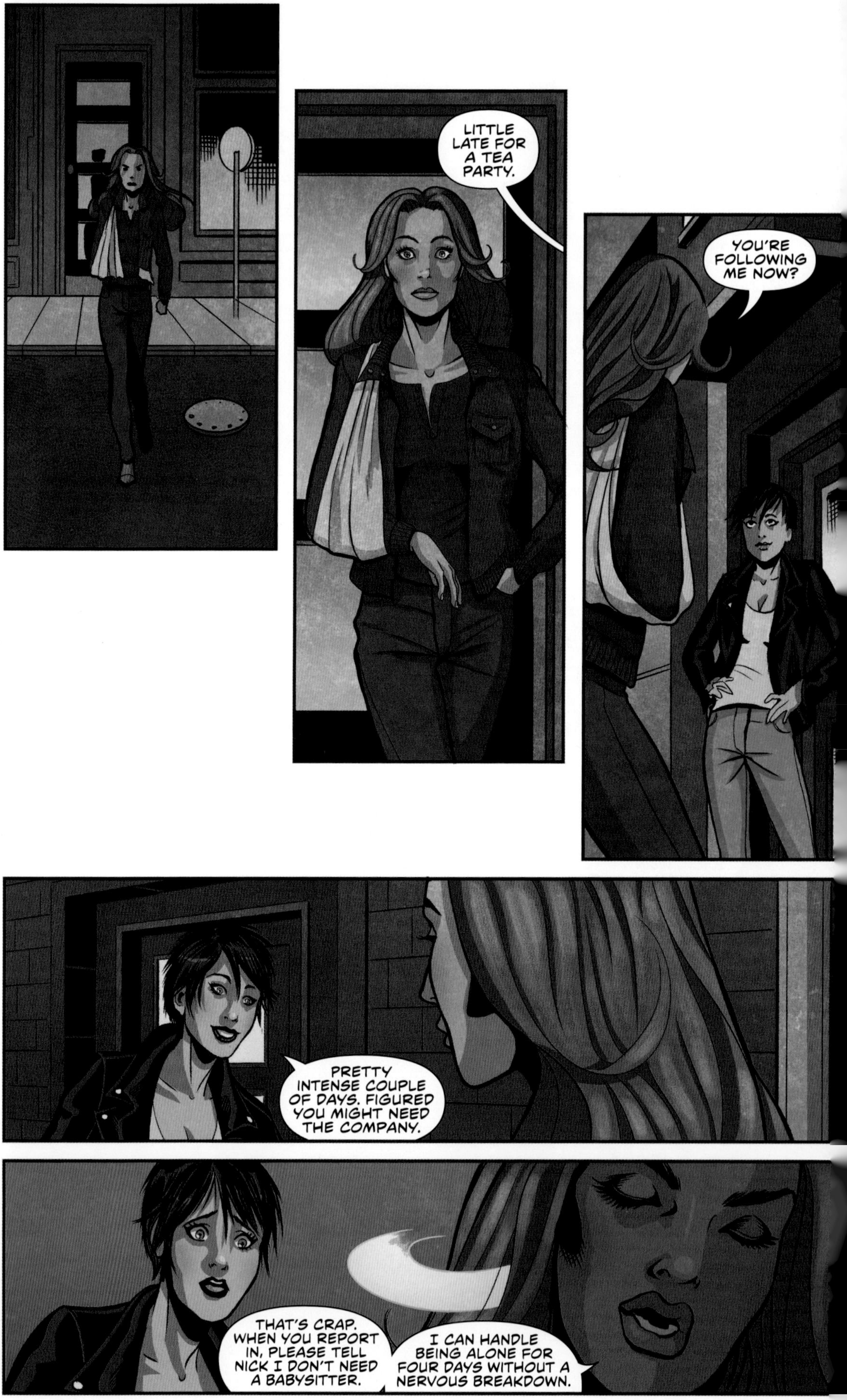
LITTLE LATE FOR A TEA PARTY.
YOU'RE FOLLOWING ME NOW?
PRETTY INTENSE COUPLE OF DAYS. FIGURED YOU MIGHT NEED THE COMPANY.
THAT'S CRAP. WHEN YOU REPORT IN, PLEASE TELL NICK I DON'T NEED A BABYSITTER.
I CAN HANDLE BEING ALONE FOR FOUR DAYS WITHOUT A NERVOUS BREAKDOWN.

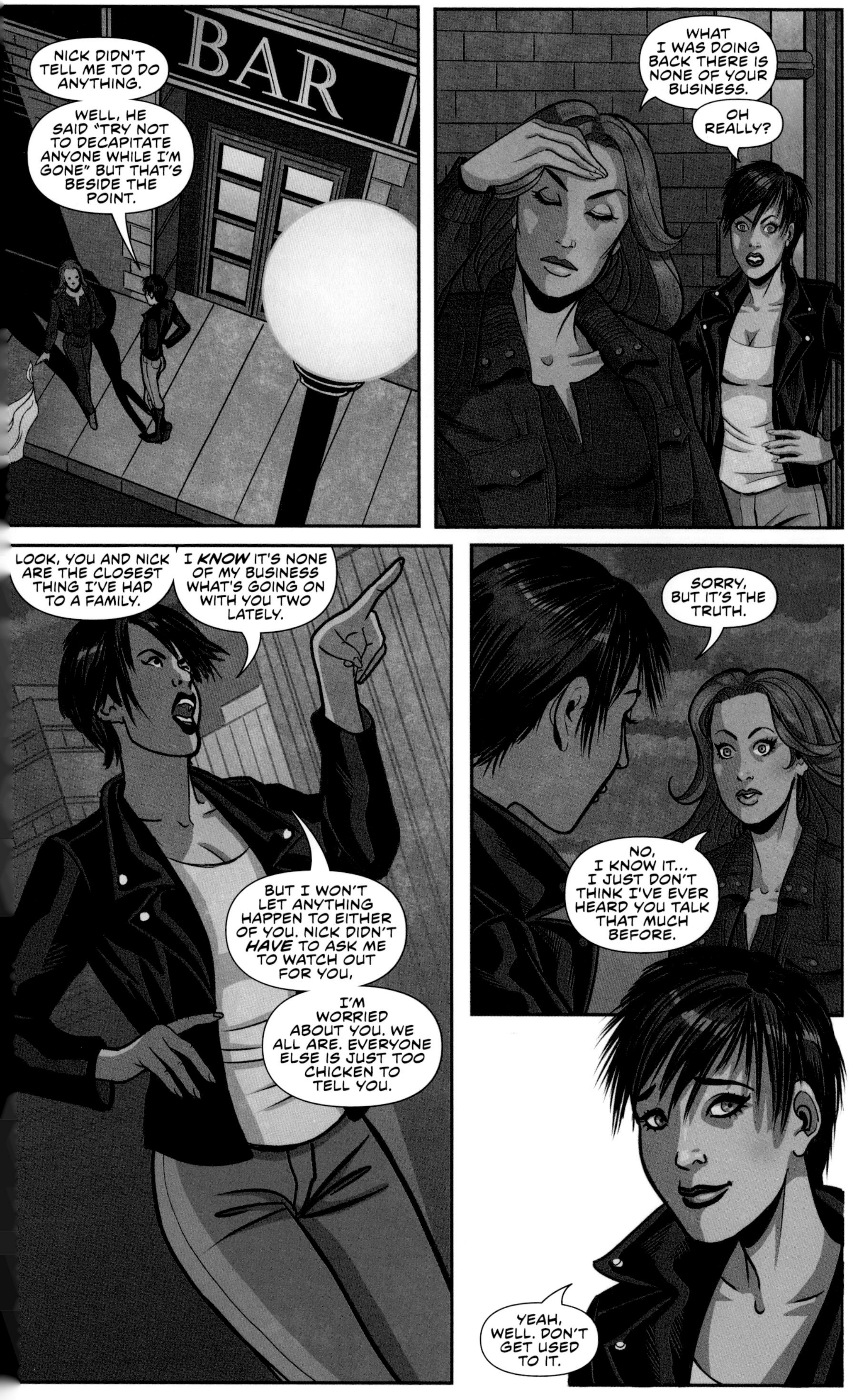
BAR
NICK DIDN'T TELL ME TO DO ANYTHING.
WELL, HE SAID "TRY NOT TO DECAPITATE ANYONE WHILE I'M GONE" BUT THAT'S BESIDE THE POINT.
WHAT I WAS DOING BACK THERE IS NONE OF YOUR BUSINESS.
OH REALLY?
LOOK, YOU AND NICK ARE THE CLOSEST THING I'VE HAD TO A FAMILY.
I **KNOW** IT'S NONE OF MY BUSINESS WHAT'S GOING ON WITH YOU TWO LATELY.
BUT I WON'T LET ANYTHING HAPPEN TO EITHER OF YOU. NICK DIDN'T **HAVE** TO ASK ME TO WATCH OUT FOR YOU,
I'M WORRIED ABOUT YOU. WE ALL ARE. EVERYONE ELSE IS JUST TOO CHICKEN TO TELL YOU.
SORRY, BUT IT'S THE TRUTH.
NO, I KNOW IT... I JUST DON'T THINK I'VE EVER HEARD YOU TALK THAT MUCH BEFORE.
YEAH, WELL. DON'T GET USED TO IT.

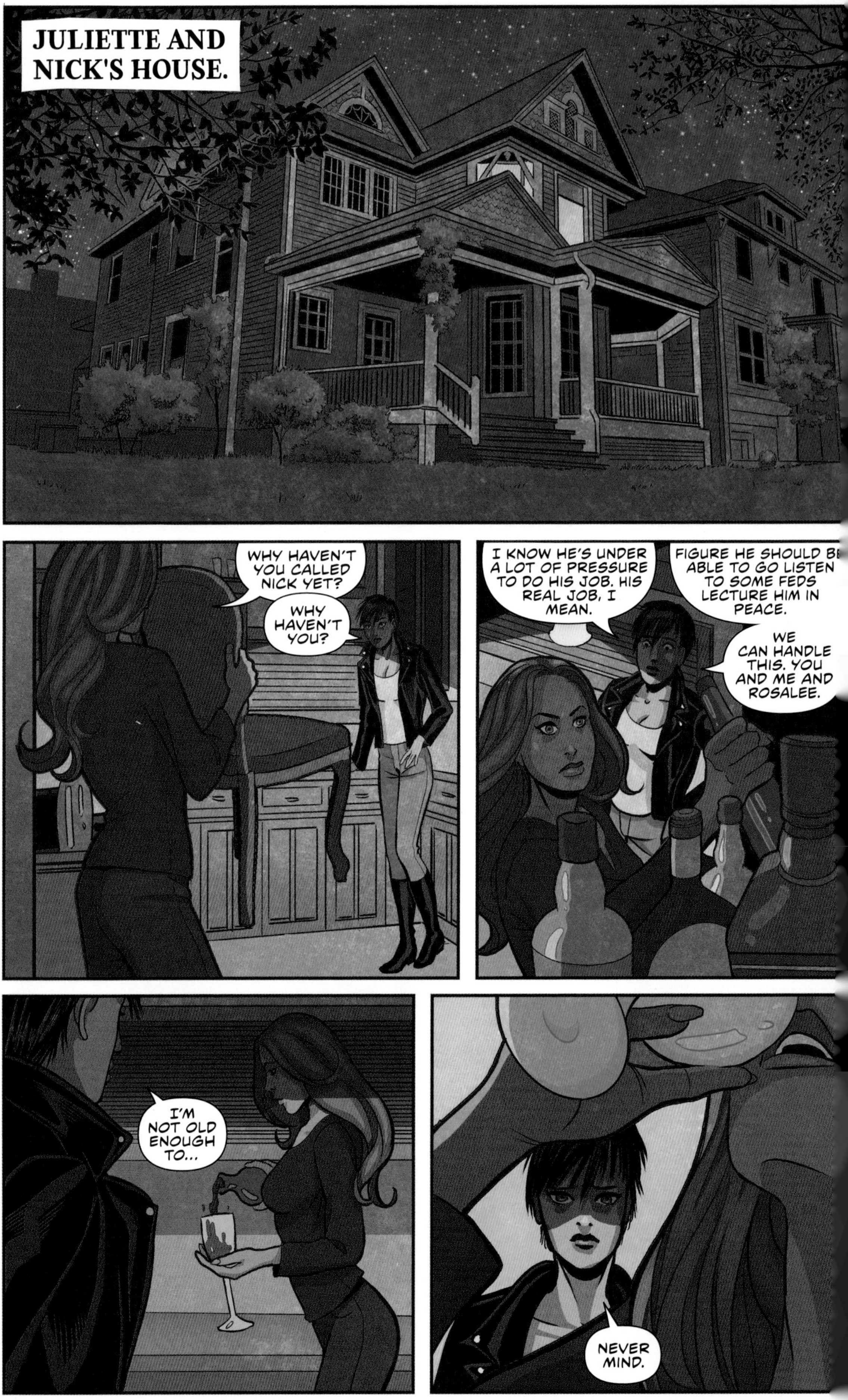
JULIETTE AND NICK'S HOUSE.
WHY HAVEN'T YOU CALLED NICK YET?
WHY HAVEN'T YOU?
I KNOW HE'S UNDER A LOT OF PRESSURE TO DO HIS JOB. HIS REAL JOB, I MEAN.
FIGURE HE SHOULD BE ABLE TO GO LISTEN TO SOME FEDS LECTURE HIM IN PEACE.
WE CAN HANDLE THIS. YOU AND ME AND ROSALEE.
I'M NOT OLD ENOUGH TO...
NEVER MIND.

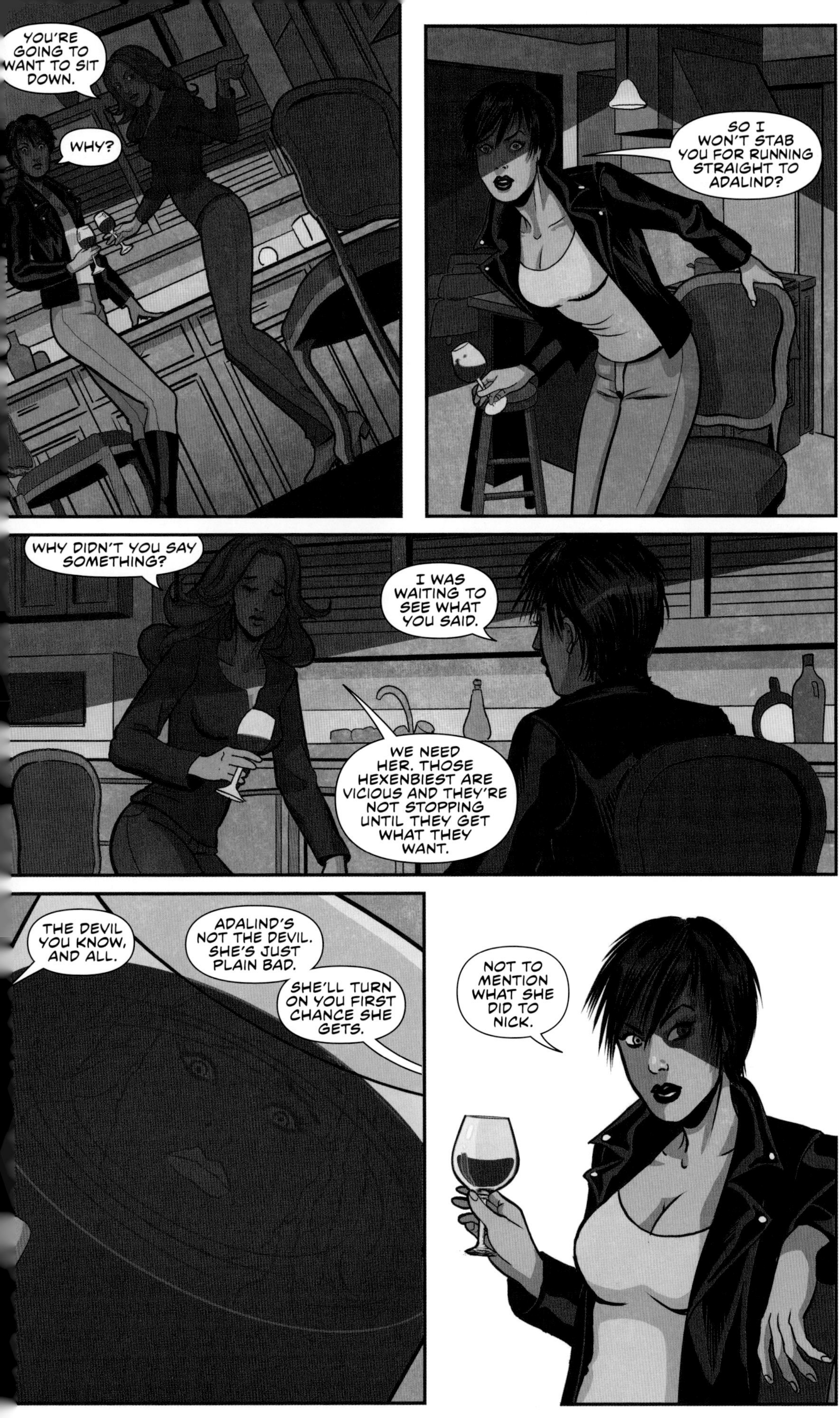
YOU'RE GOING TO WANT TO SIT DOWN.
WHY?
SO I WON'T STAB YOU FOR RUNNING STRAIGHT TO ADALIND?
WHY DIDN'T YOU SAY SOMETHING?
I WAS WAITING TO SEE WHAT YOU SAID.
WE NEED HER. THOSE HEXENBIEST ARE VICIOUS AND THEY'RE NOT STOPPING UNTIL THEY GET WHAT THEY WANT.
THE DEVIL YOU KNOW, AND ALL.
ADALIND'S NOT THE DEVIL. SHE'S JUST PLAIN BAD.
SHE'LL TURN ON YOU FIRST CHANCE SHE GETS.
NOT TO MENTION WHAT SHE DID TO NICK.

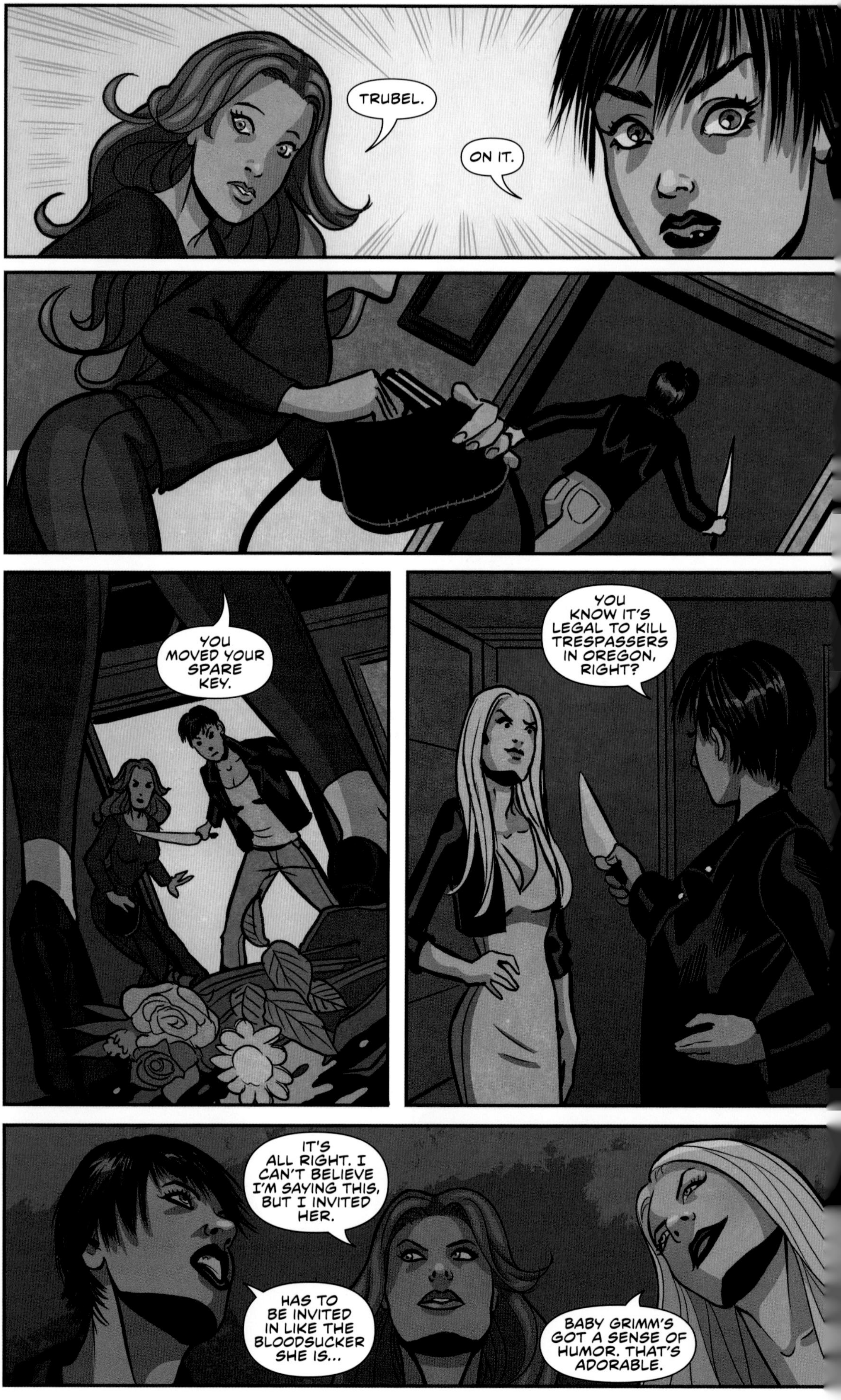
TRUBEL.
ON IT.
YOU MOVED YOUR SPARE KEY.
YOU KNOW IT'S LEGAL TO KILL TRESPASSERS IN OREGON, RIGHT?
IT'S ALL RIGHT. I CAN'T BELIEVE I'M SAYING THIS, BUT I INVITED HER.
HAS TO BE INVITED IN LIKE THE BLOODSUCKER SHE IS...
BABY GRIMM'S GOT A SENSE OF HUMOR. THAT'S ADORABLE.

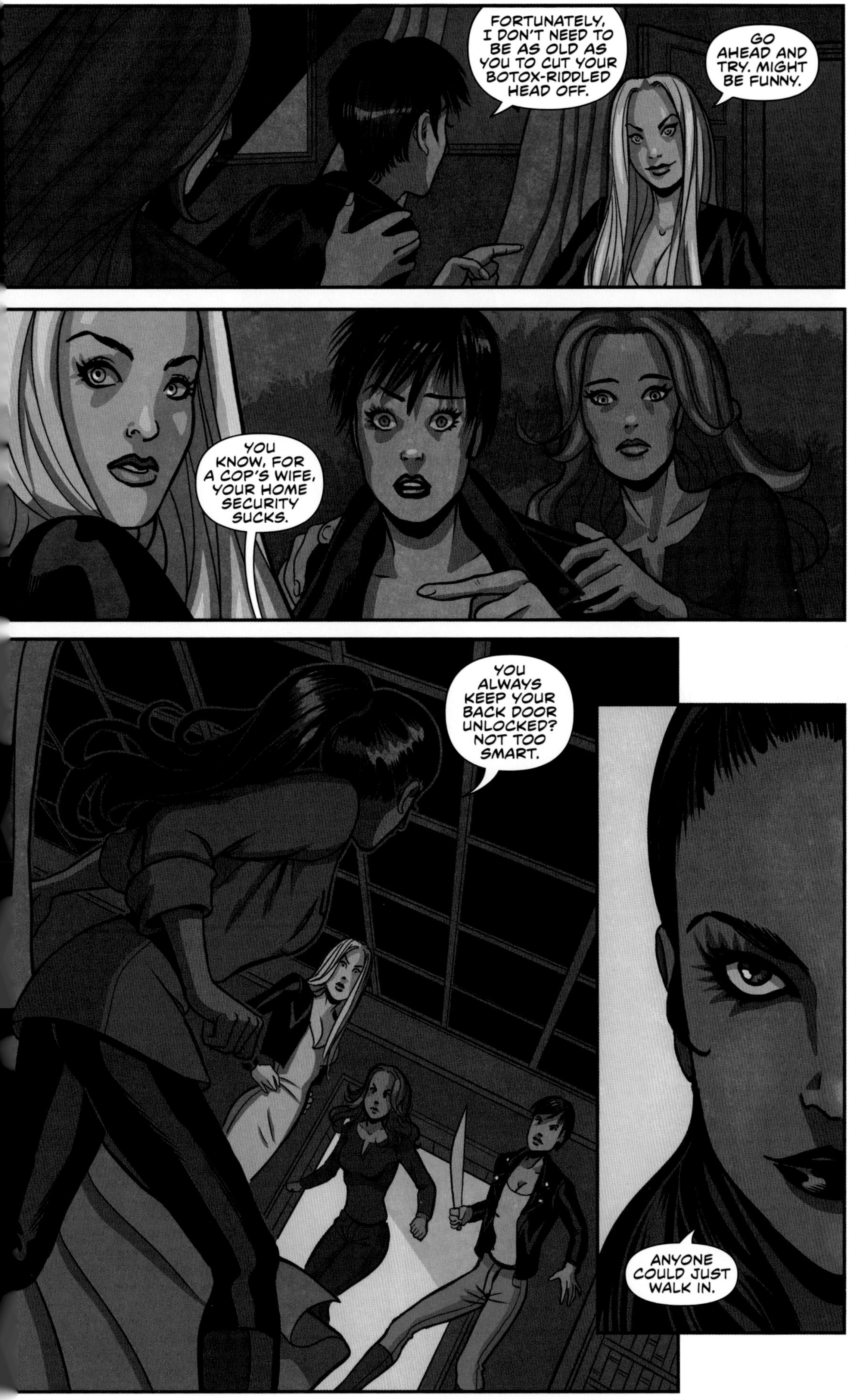
FORTUNATELY, I DON'T NEED TO BE AS OLD AS YOU TO CUT YOUR BOTOX-RIDDLED HEAD OFF.
GO AHEAD AND TRY. MIGHT BE FUNNY.
YOU KNOW, FOR A COP'S WIFE, YOUR HOME SECURITY SUCKS.
YOU ALWAYS KEEP YOUR BACK DOOR UNLOCKED? NOT TOO SMART.
ANYONE COULD JUST WALK IN.

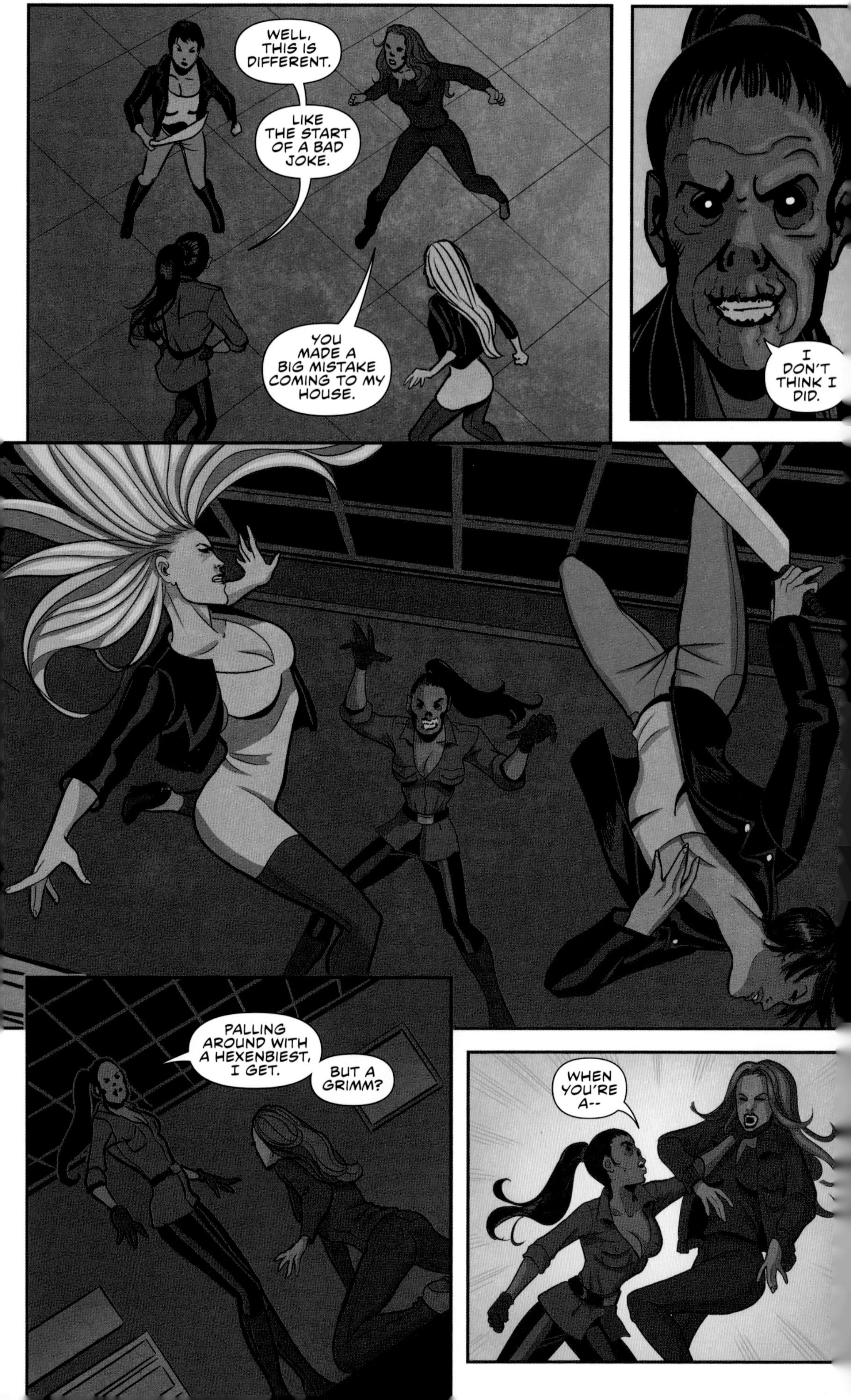
WELL, THIS IS DIFFERENT.
LIKE THE START OF A BAD JOKE.
YOU MADE A BIG MISTAKE COMING TO MY HOUSE.
I DON'T THINK I DID.
PALLING AROUND WITH A HEXENBIEST, I GET.
BUT A GRIMM?
WHEN YOU'RE A--

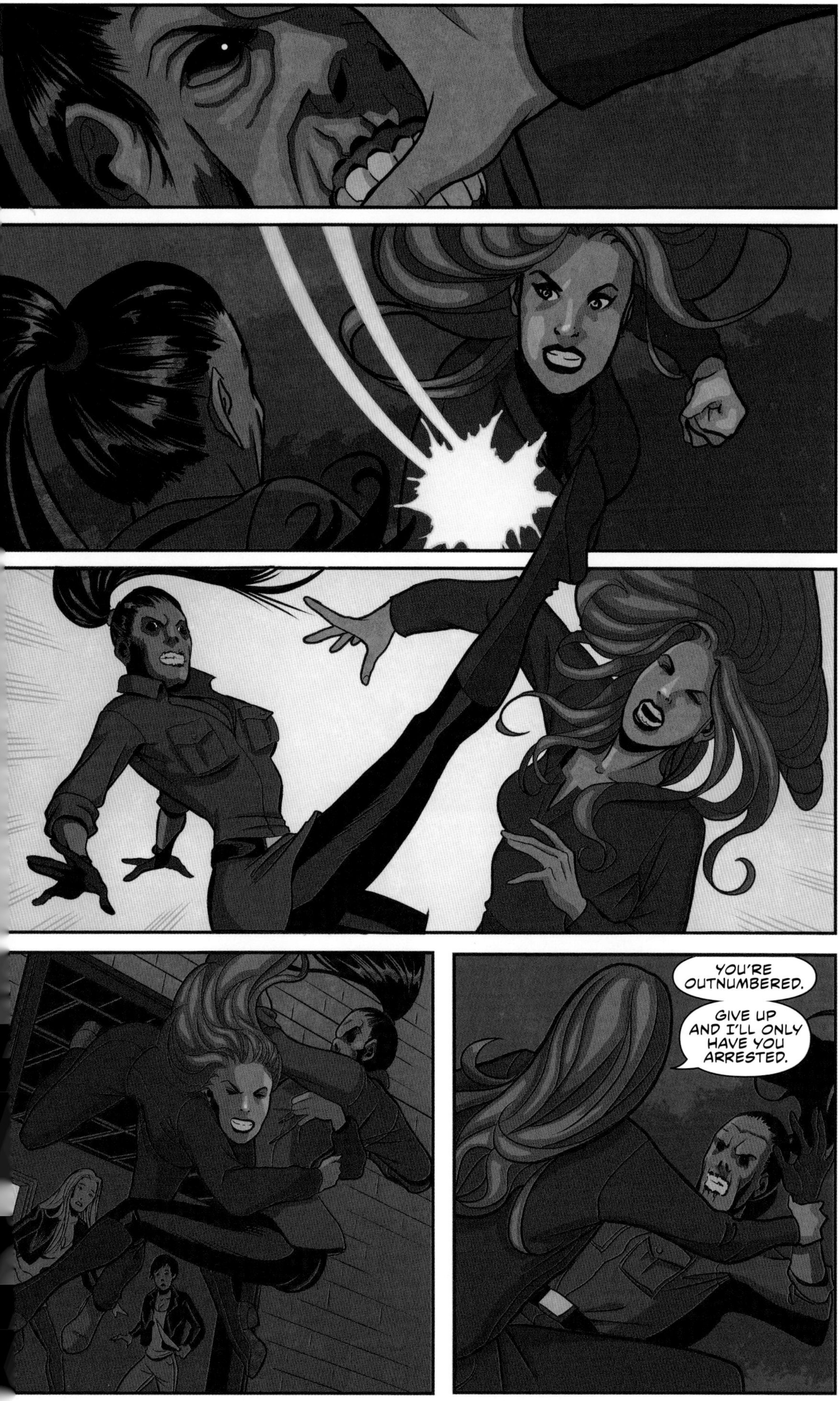
YOU'RE OUTNUMBERED.
GIVE UP AND I'LL ONLY HAVE YOU ARRESTED.

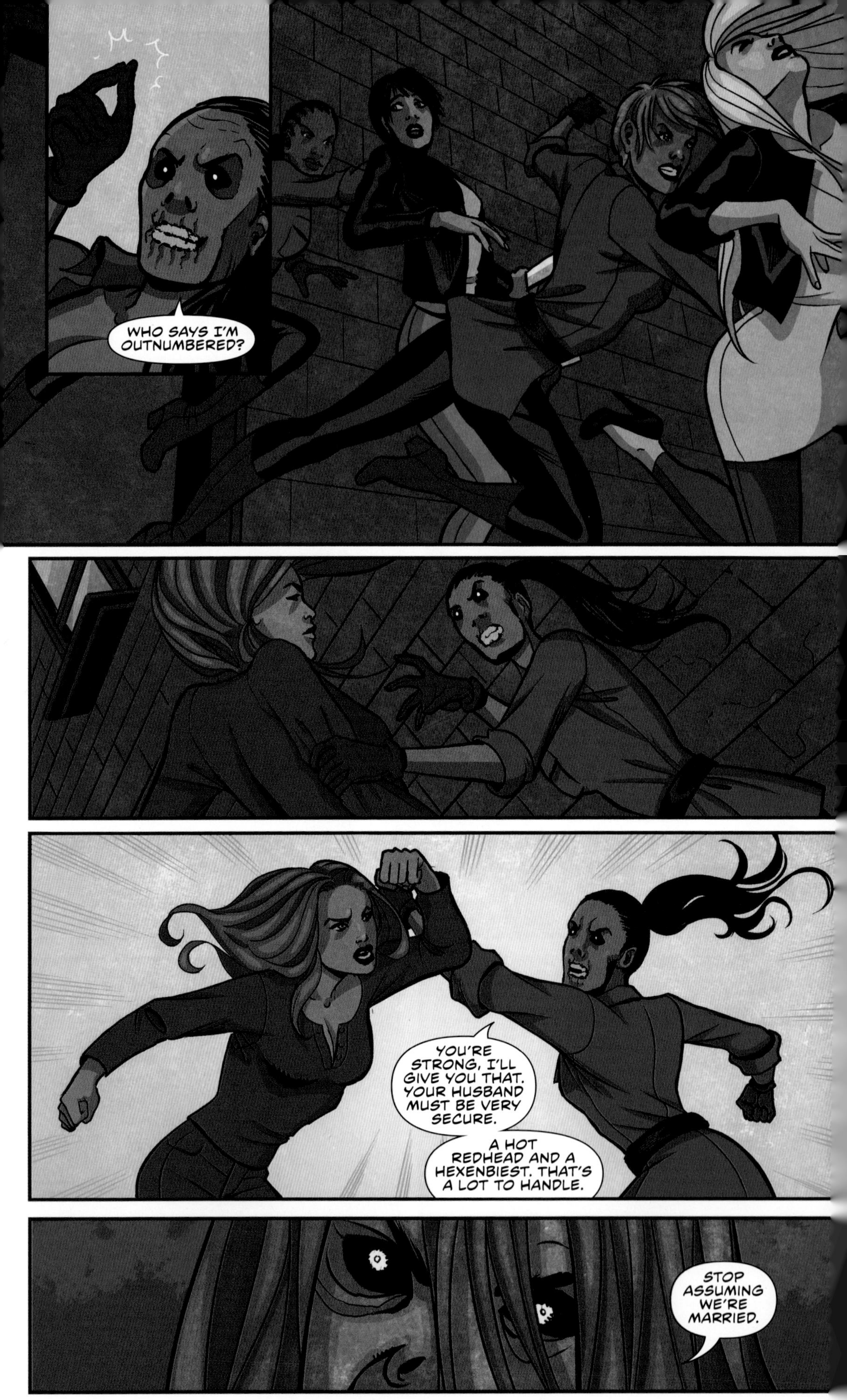
WHO SAYS I'M OUTNUMBERED?
YOU'RE STRONG, I'LL GIVE YOU THAT. YOUR HUSBAND MUST BE VERY SECURE.
A HOT REDHEAD AND A HEXENBIEST. THAT'S A LOT TO HANDLE.
STOP ASSUMING WE'RE MARRIED.

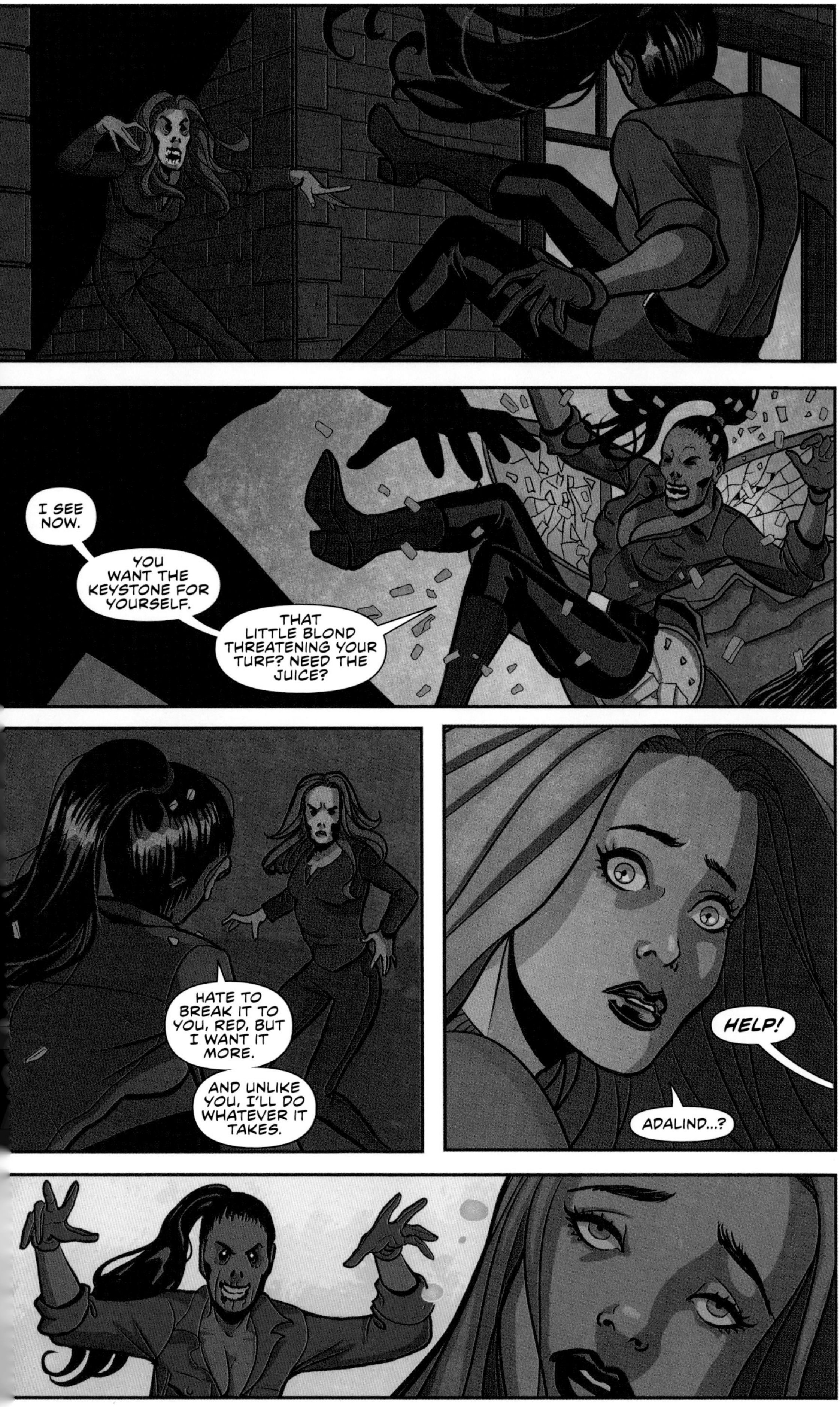
I SEE NOW.
YOU WANT THE KEYSTONE FOR YOURSELF.
THAT LITTLE BLOND THREATENING YOUR TURF? NEED THE JUICE?
HATE TO BREAK IT TO YOU, RED, BUT I WANT IT MORE.
AND UNLIKE YOU, I'LL DO WHATEVER IT TAKES.
HELP!
ADALIND...?

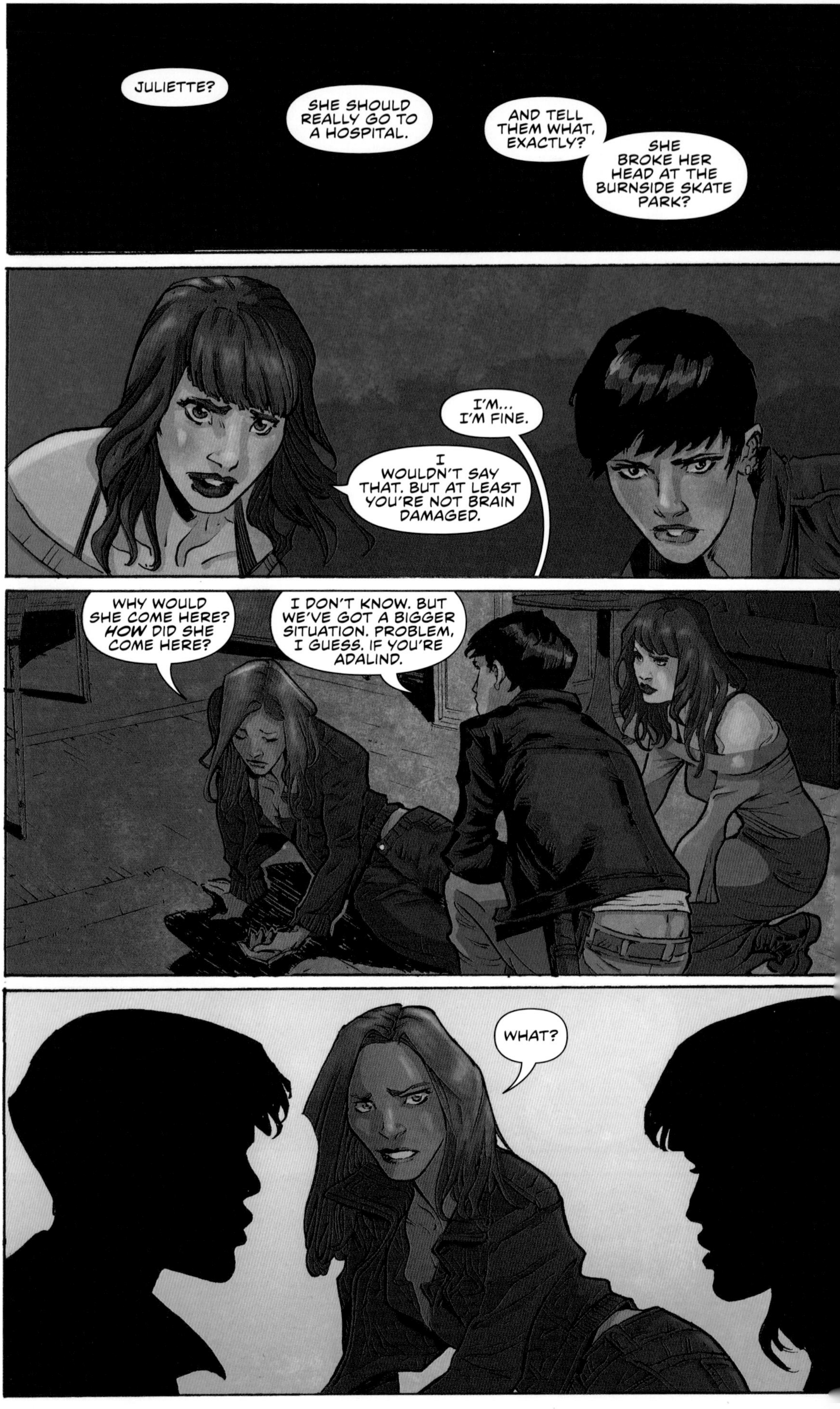
JULIETTE?
SHE SHOULD REALLY GO TO A HOSPITAL.
AND TELL THEM WHAT, EXACTLY?
SHE BROKE HER HEAD AT THE BURNSIDE SKATE PARK?
I'M... I'M FINE.
I WOULDN'T SAY THAT. BUT AT LEAST YOU'RE NOT BRAIN DAMAGED.
WHY WOULD SHE COME HERE? HOW DID SHE COME HERE?
I DON'T KNOW. BUT WE'VE GOT A BIGGER SITUATION. PROBLEM, I GUESS. IF YOU'RE ADALIND.
WHAT?

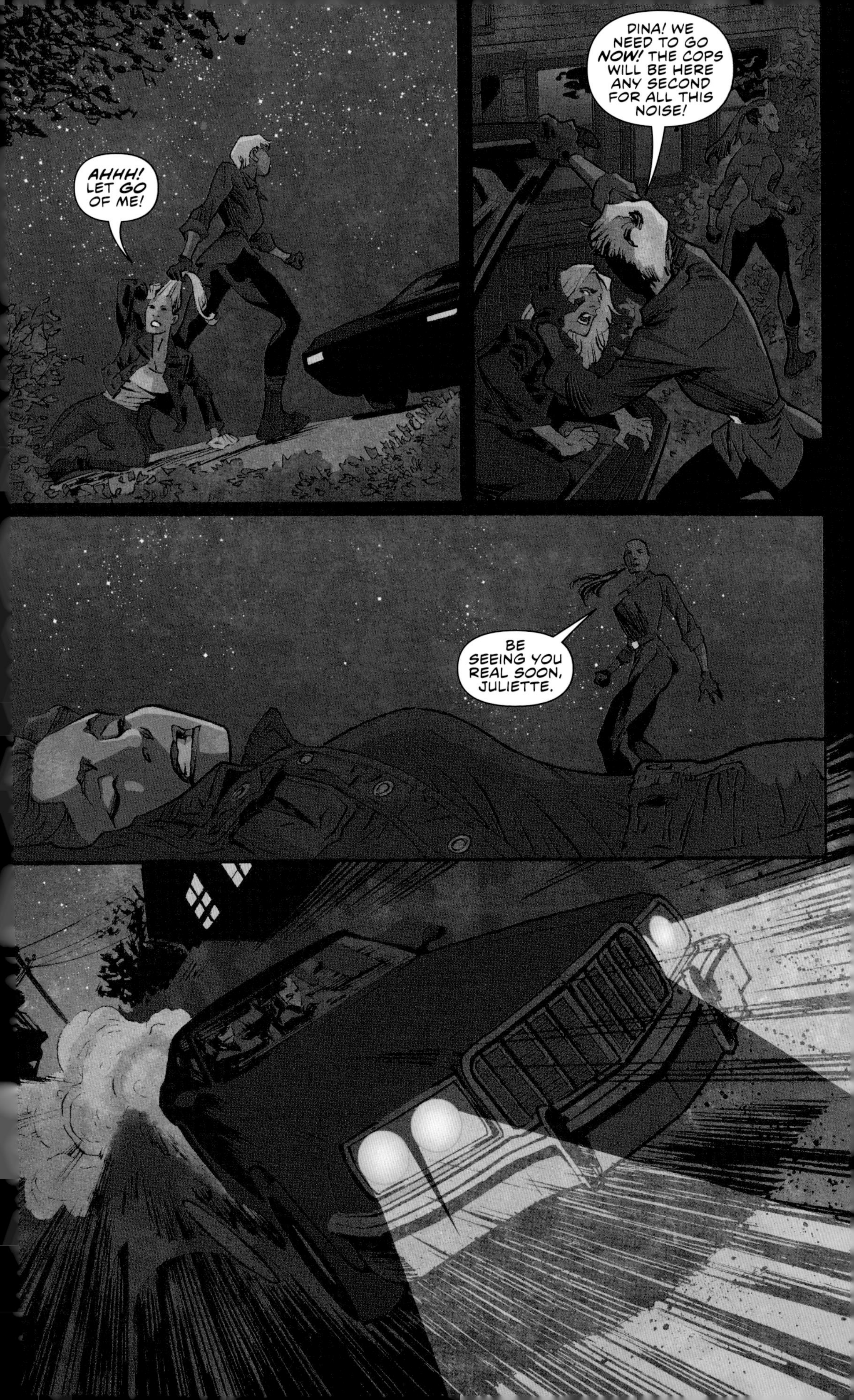
AHHH! LET GO OF ME!
DINA! WE NEED TO GO NOW! THE COPS WILL BE HERE ANY SECOND FOR ALL THIS NOISE!
BE SEEING YOU REAL SOON, JULIETTE.

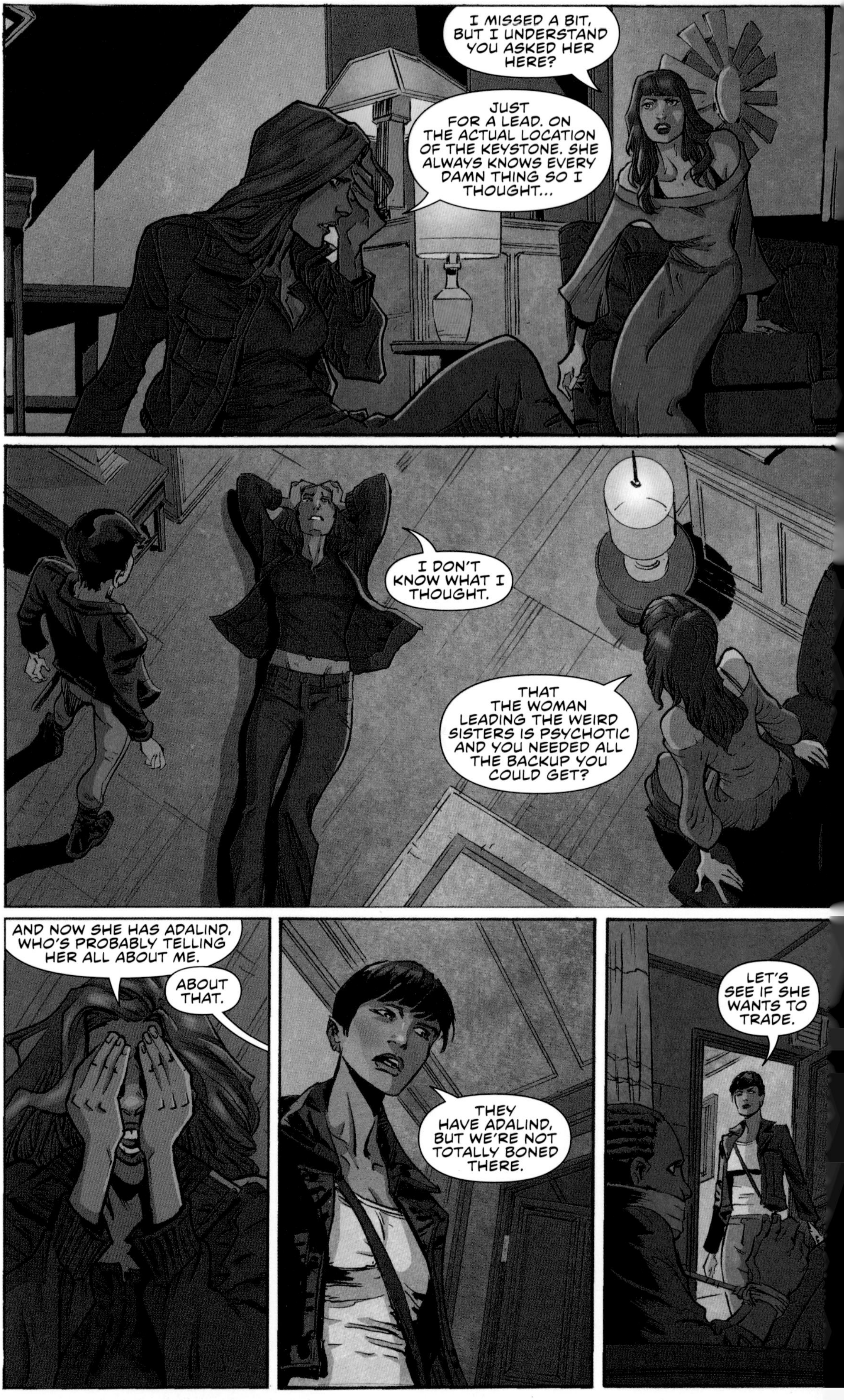

I MISSED A BIT, BUT I UNDERSTAND YOU ASKED HER HERE?
JUST FOR A LEAD. ON THE ACTUAL LOCATION OF THE KEYSTONE. SHE ALWAYS KNOWS EVERY DAMN THING SO I THOUGHT...
I DON'T KNOW WHAT I THOUGHT.
THAT THE WOMAN LEADING THE WEIRD SISTERS IS PSYCHOTIC AND YOU NEEDED ALL THE BACKUP YOU COULD GET?
AND NOW SHE HAS ADALIND, WHO'S PROBABLY TELLING HER ALL ABOUT ME.
ABOUT THAT.
THEY HAVE ADALIND, BUT WE'RE NOT TOTALLY BONED THERE.
LET'S SEE IF SHE WANTS TO TRADE.

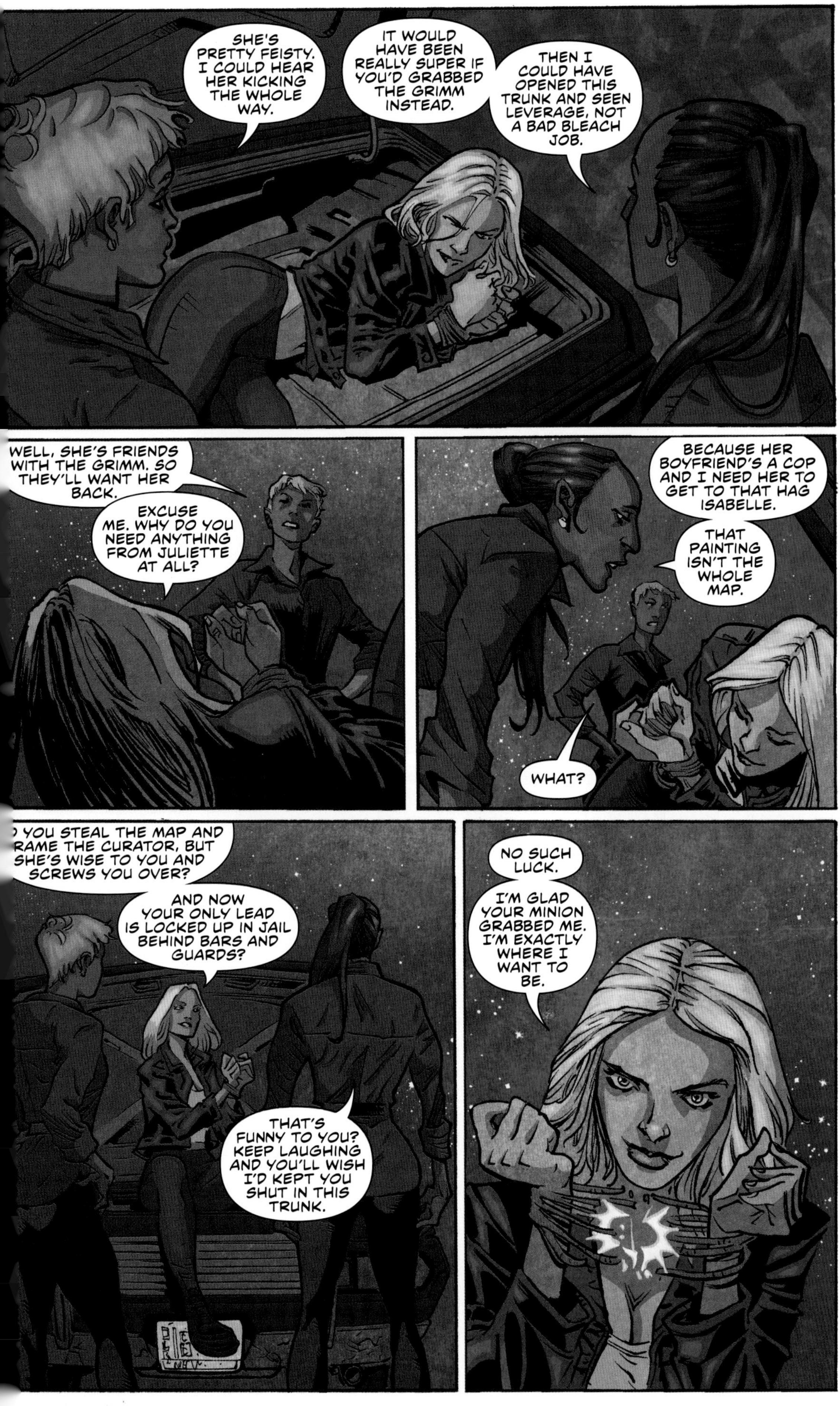
SHE'S PRETTY FEISTY. I COULD HEAR HER KICKING THE WHOLE WAY.
IT WOULD HAVE BEEN REALLY SUPER IF YOU'D GRABBED THE GRIMM INSTEAD.
THEN I COULD HAVE OPENED THIS TRUNK AND SEEN LEVERAGE, NOT A BAD BLEACH JOB.
WELL, SHE'S FRIENDS WITH THE GRIMM. SO THEY'LL WANT HER BACK.
EXCUSE ME. WHY DO YOU NEED ANYTHING FROM JULIETTE AT ALL?
BECAUSE HER BOYFRIEND'S A COP AND I NEED HER TO GET TO THAT HAG ISABELLE.
THAT PAINTING ISN'T THE WHOLE MAP.
WHAT?
YOU STEAL THE MAP AND RAME THE CURATOR, BUT SHE'S WISE TO YOU AND SCREWS YOU OVER?
AND NOW YOUR ONLY LEAD IS LOCKED UP IN JAIL BEHIND BARS AND GUARDS?
THAT'S FUNNY TO YOU? KEEP LAUGHING AND YOU'LL WISH I'D KEPT YOU SHUT IN THIS TRUNK.
NO SUCH LUCK.
I'M GLAD YOUR MINION GRABBED ME. I'M EXACTLY WHERE I WANT TO BE.

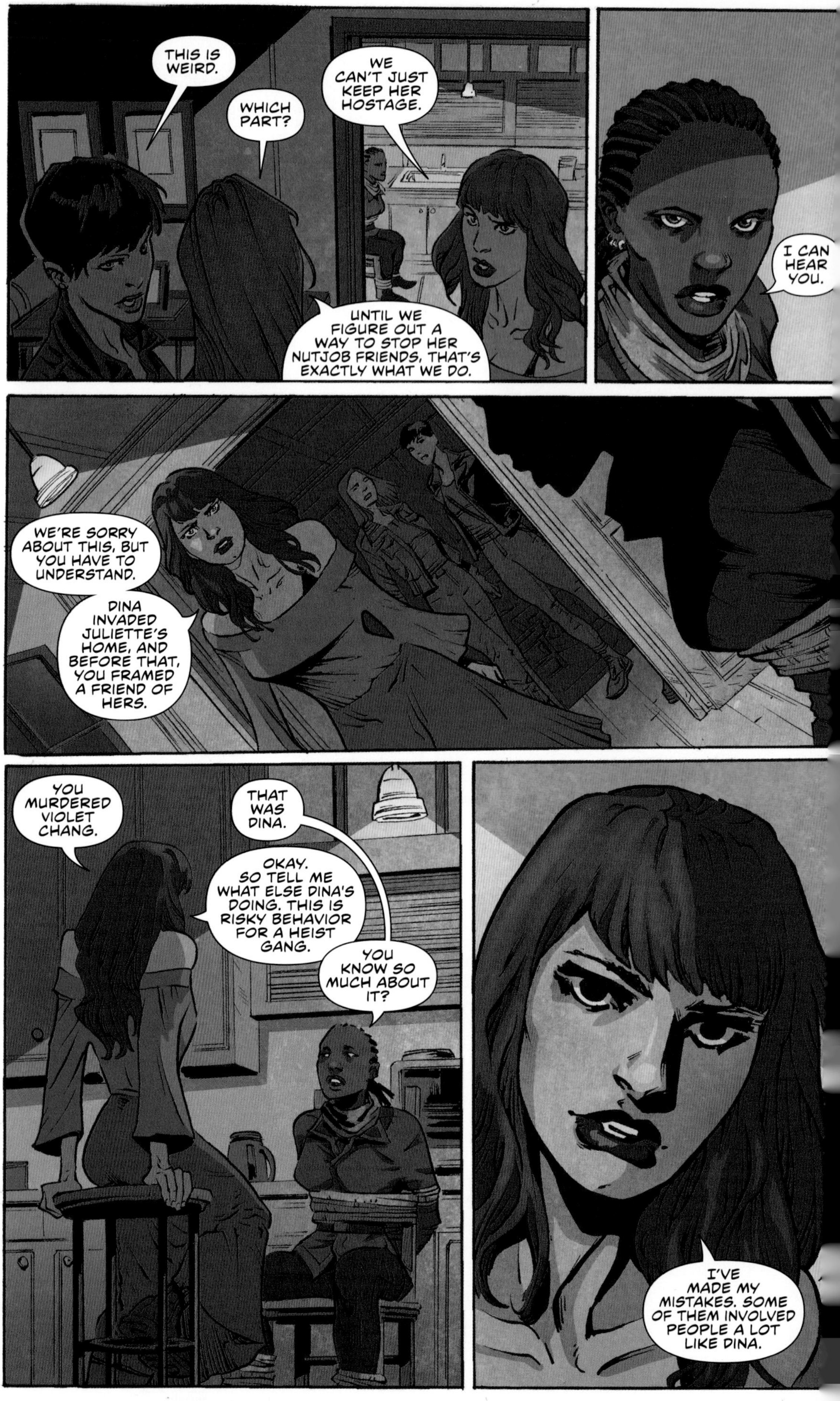
THIS IS WEIRD.
WHICH PART?
WE CAN'T JUST KEEP HER HOSTAGE.
UNTIL WE FIGURE OUT A WAY TO STOP HER NUTJOB FRIENDS, THAT'S EXACTLY WHAT WE DO.
I CAN HEAR YOU.
WE'RE SORRY ABOUT THIS, BUT YOU HAVE TO UNDERSTAND.
DINA INVADED JULIETTE'S HOME, AND BEFORE THAT, YOU FRAMED A FRIEND OF HERS.
YOU MURDERED VIOLET CHANG.
THAT WAS DINA.
OKAY. SO TELL ME WHAT ELSE DINA'S DOING. THIS IS RISKY BEHAVIOR FOR A HEIST GANG.
YOU KNOW SO MUCH ABOUT IT?
I'VE MADE MY MISTAKES. SOME OF THEM INVOLVED PEOPLE A LOT LIKE DINA.

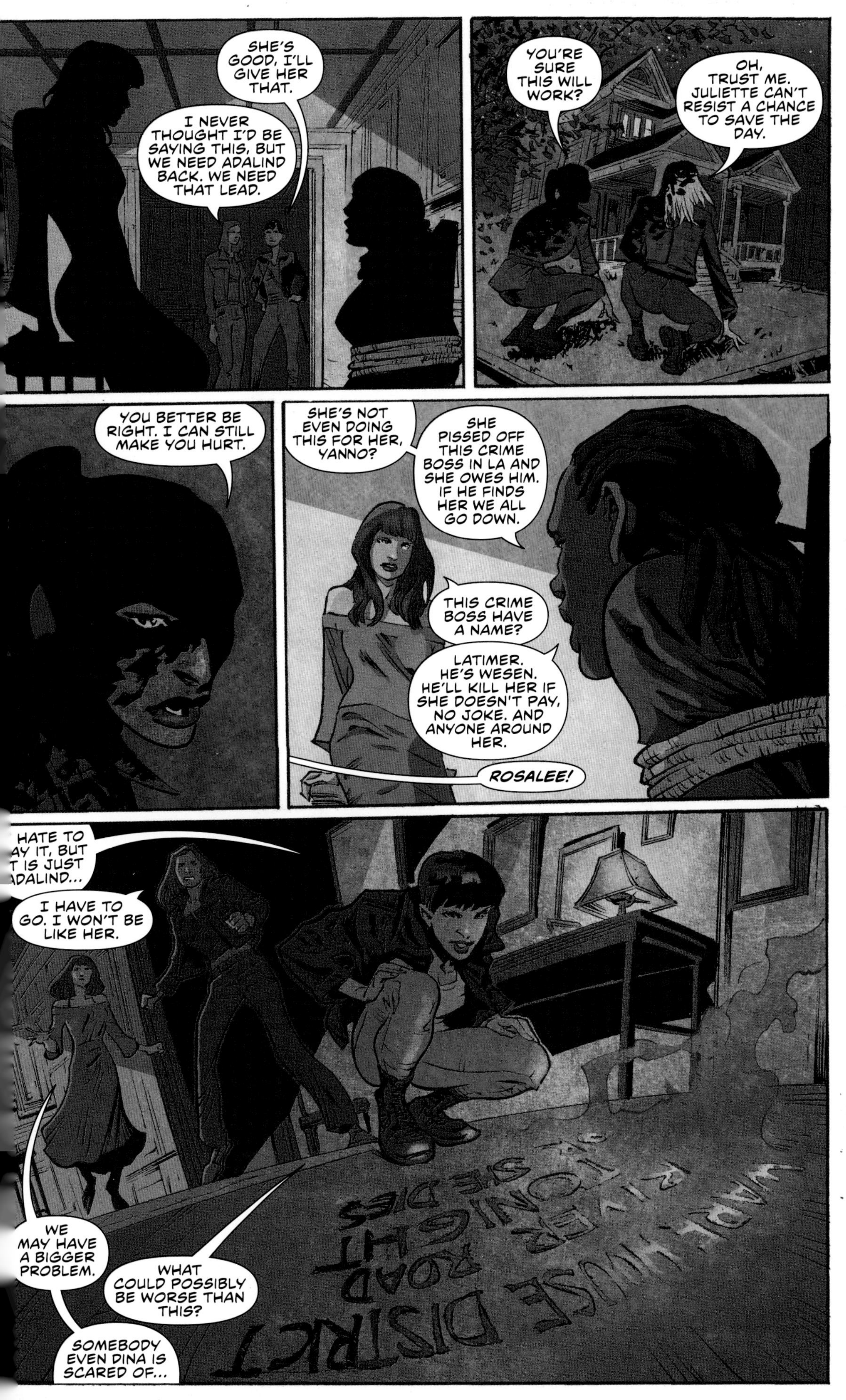

SHE'S GOOD, I'LL GIVE HER THAT.
I NEVER THOUGHT I'D BE SAYING THIS, BUT WE NEED ADALIND BACK. WE NEED THAT LEAD.
YOU'RE SURE THIS WILL WORK?
OH, TRUST ME. JULIETTE CAN'T RESIST A CHANCE TO SAVE THE DAY.
YOU BETTER BE RIGHT. I CAN STILL MAKE YOU HURT.
SHE'S NOT EVEN DOING THIS FOR HER, YANNO?
SHE PISSED OFF THIS CRIME BOSS IN LA AND SHE OWES HIM. IF HE FINDS HER WE ALL GO DOWN.
THIS CRIME BOSS HAVE A NAME?
LATIMER. HE'S WESEN. HE'LL KILL HER IF SHE DOESN'T PAY, NO JOKE. AND ANYONE AROUND HER.
ROSALEE!
HATE TO AY IT, BUT T IS JUST ADALIND...
I HAVE TO GO. I WON'T BE LIKE HER.
WE MAY HAVE A BIGGER PROBLEM.
WHAT COULD POSSIBLY BE WORSE THAN THIS?
SOMEBODY EVEN DINA IS SCARED OF...

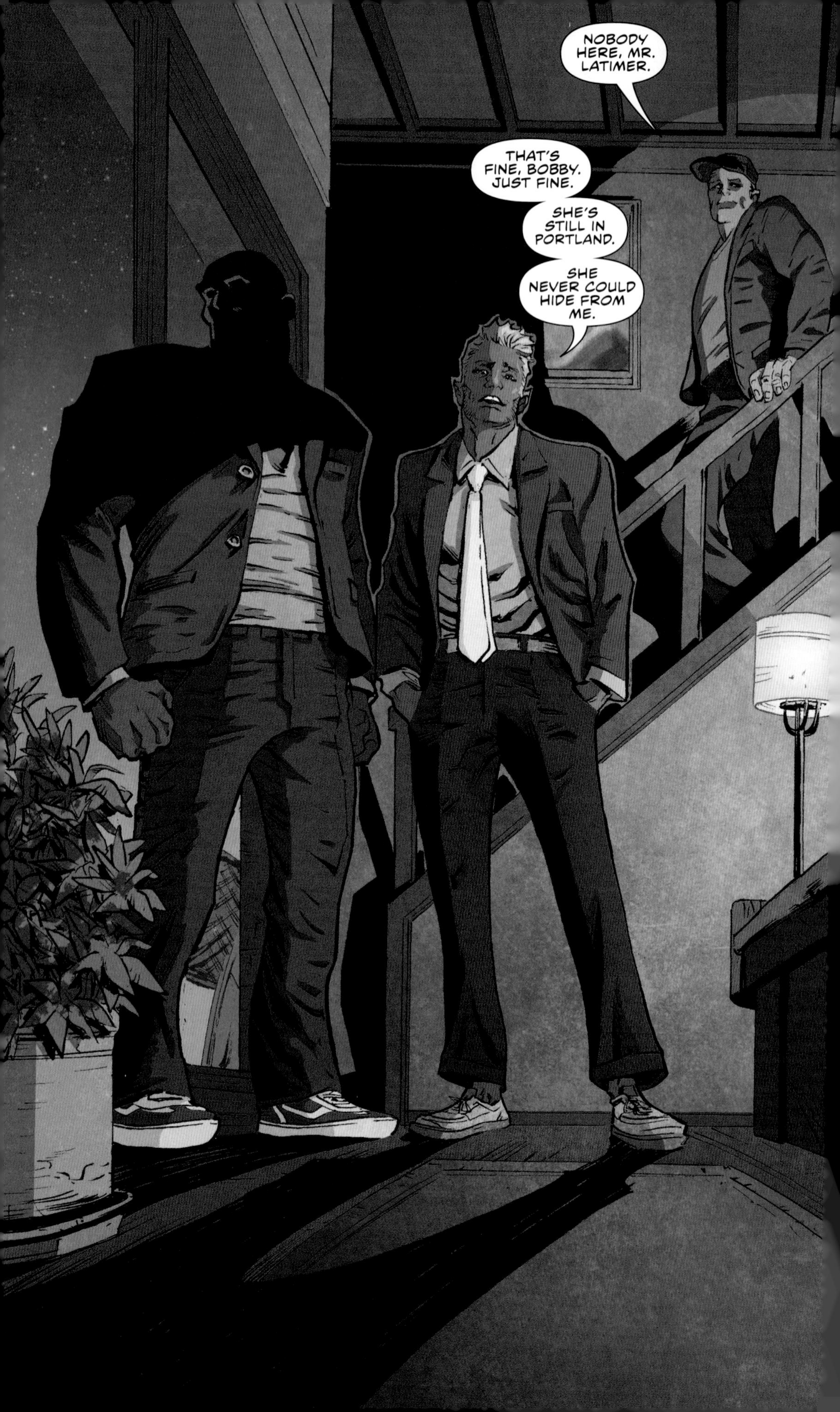
NOBODY HERE, MR. LATIMER.
THAT'S FINE, BOBBY. JUST FINE.
SHE'S STILL IN PORTLAND.
SHE NEVER COULD HIDE FROM ME.

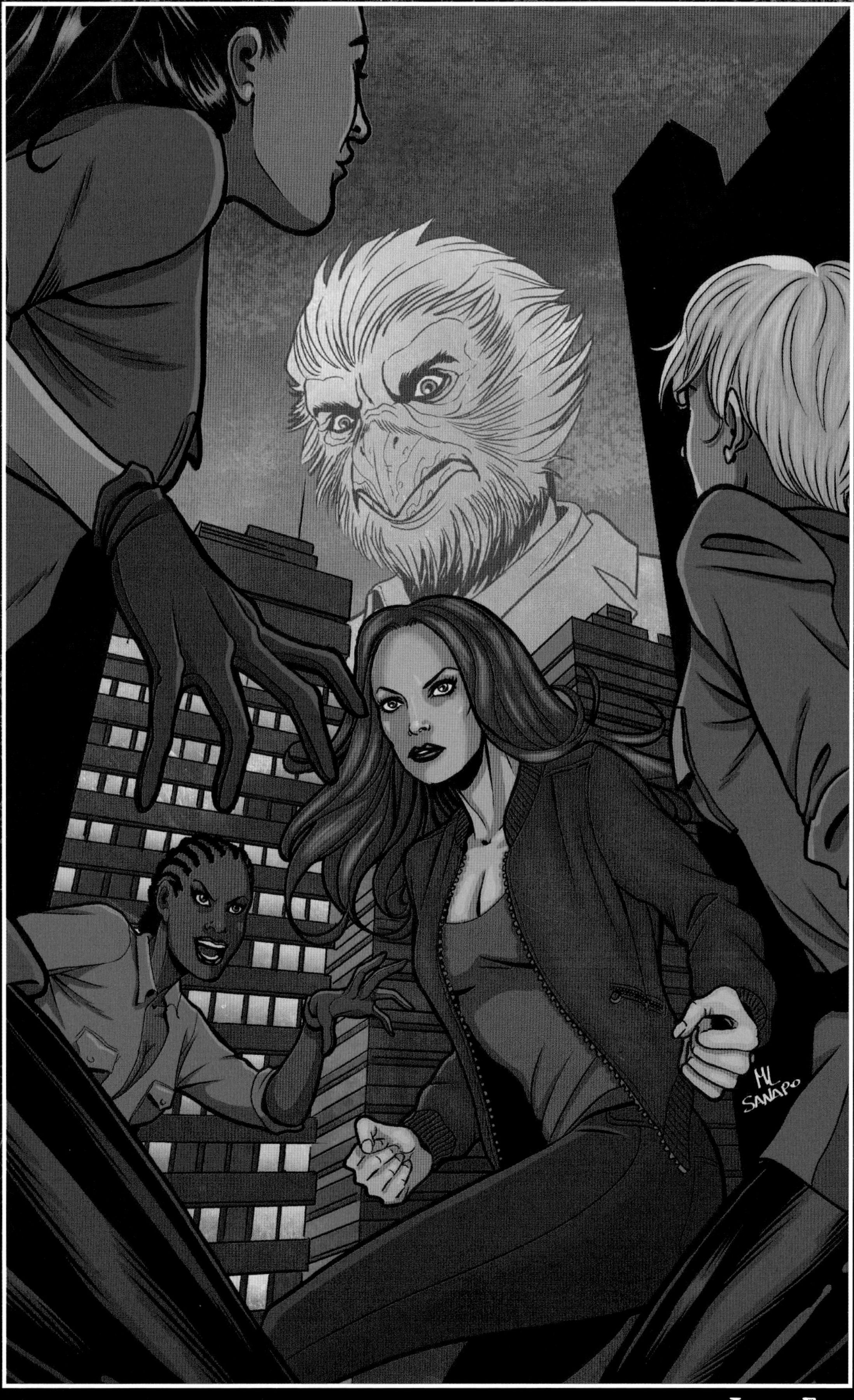
ML
SANAPO

Issue Four

Art by Maria Sanapo | Colors by Chris O'Halloran

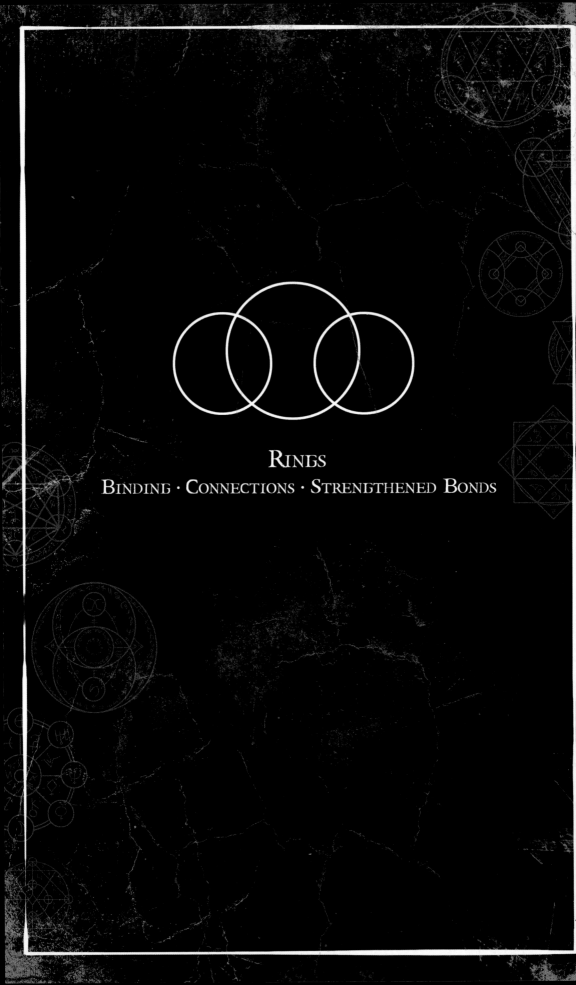

Rings

Binding · Connections · Strengthened Bonds

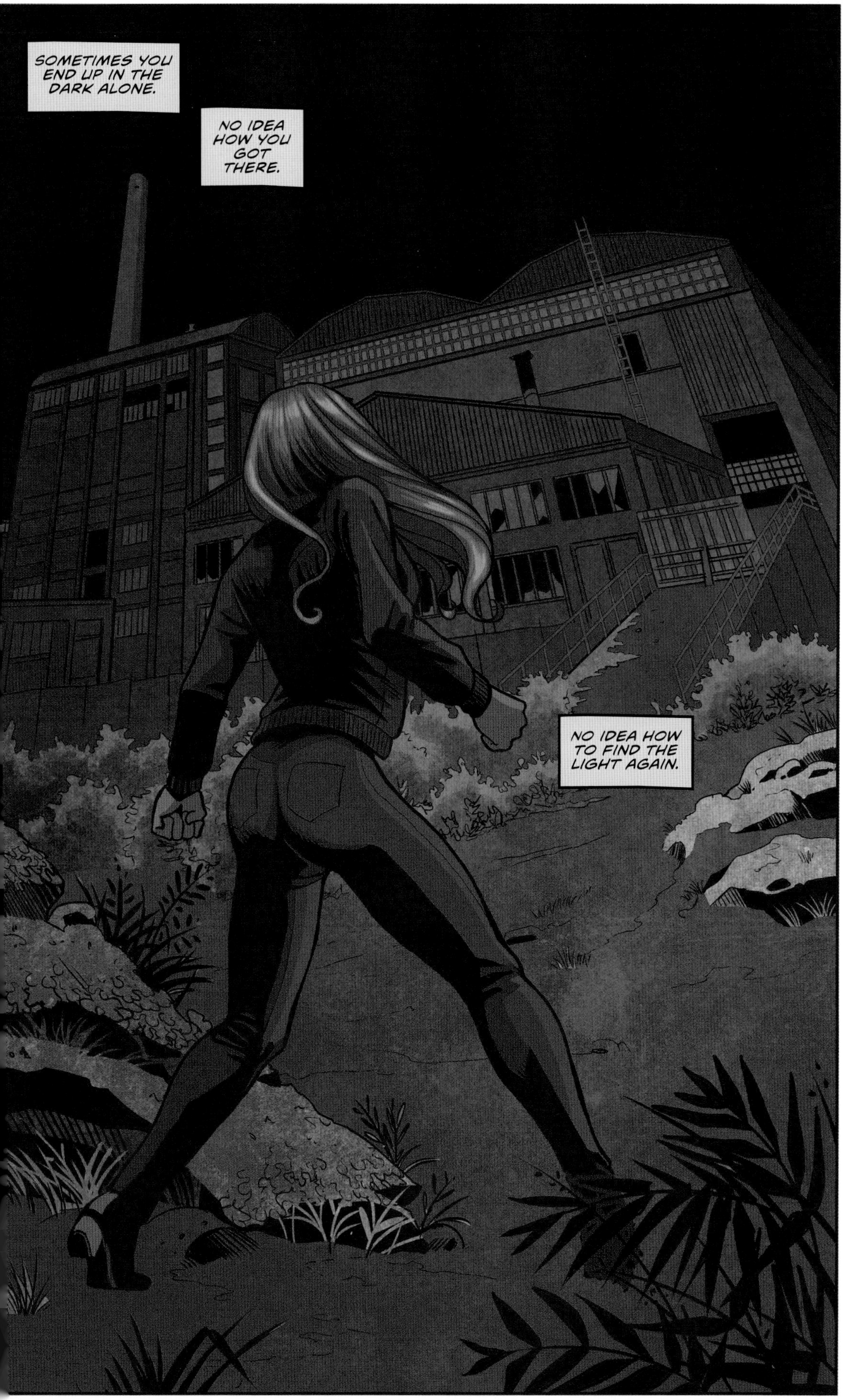

SOMETIMES YOU END UP IN THE DARK ALONE.
NO IDEA HOW YOU GOT THERE.
NO IDEA HOW TO FIND THE LIGHT AGAIN.

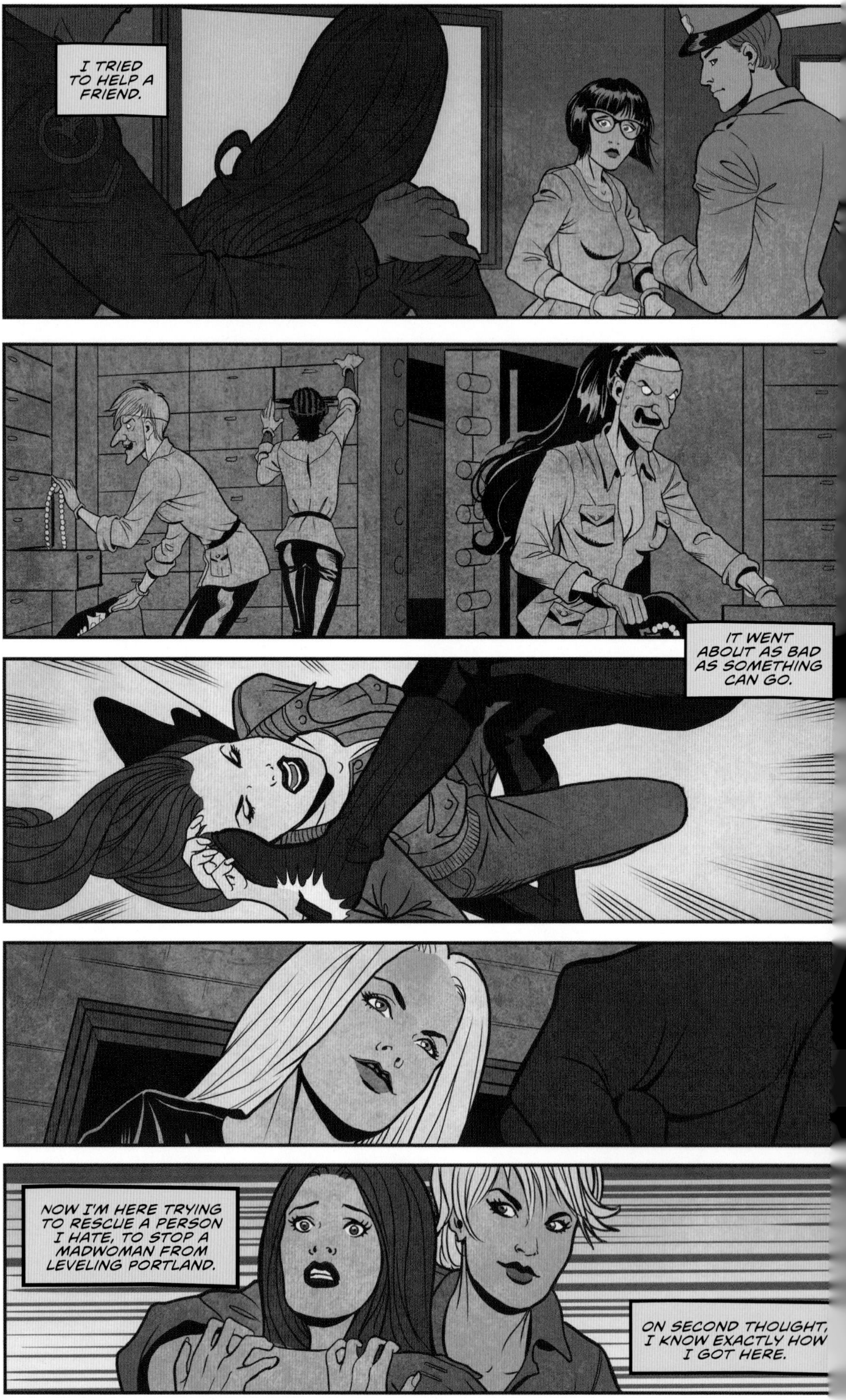
I TRIED TO HELP A FRIEND.
IT WENT ABOUT AS BAD AS SOMETHING CAN GO.
NOW I'M HERE TRYING TO RESCUE A PERSON I HATE, TO STOP A MADWOMAN FROM LEVELING PORTLAND.
ON SECOND THOUGHT, I KNOW EXACTLY HOW I GOT HERE.

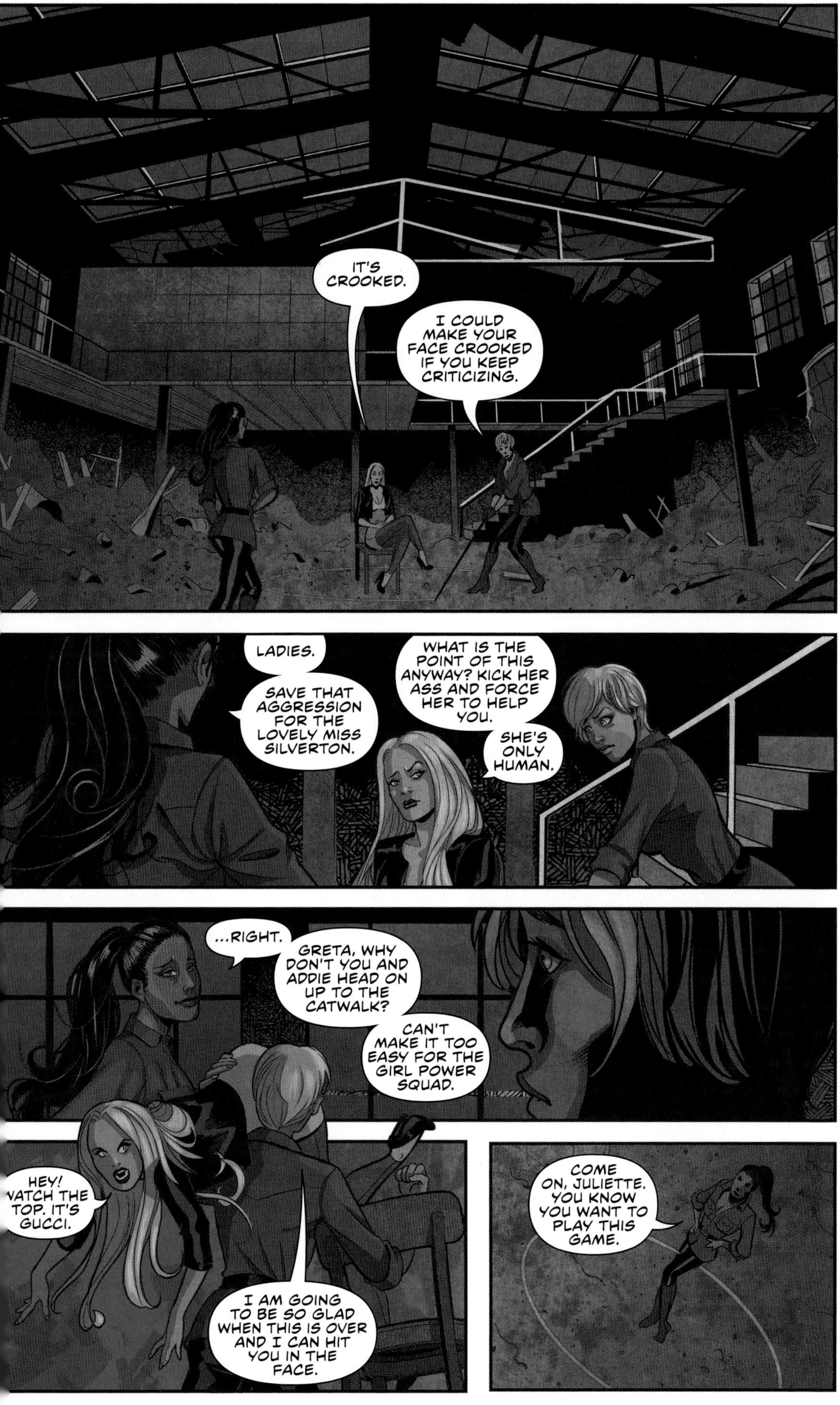
IT'S CROOKED.
I COULD MAKE YOUR FACE CROOKED IF YOU KEEP CRITICIZING.
LADIES.
SAVE THAT AGGRESSION FOR THE LOVELY MISS SILVERTON.
WHAT IS THE POINT OF THIS ANYWAY? KICK HER ASS AND FORCE HER TO HELP YOU.
SHE'S ONLY HUMAN.
...RIGHT.
GRETA, WHY DON'T YOU AND ADDIE HEAD ON UP TO THE CATWALK?
CAN'T MAKE IT TOO EASY FOR THE GIRL POWER SQUAD.
HEY! WATCH THE TOP. IT'S GUCCI.
I AM GOING TO BE SO GLAD WHEN THIS IS OVER AND I CAN HIT YOU IN THE FACE.
COME ON, JULIETTE. YOU KNOW YOU WANT TO PLAY THIS GAME.

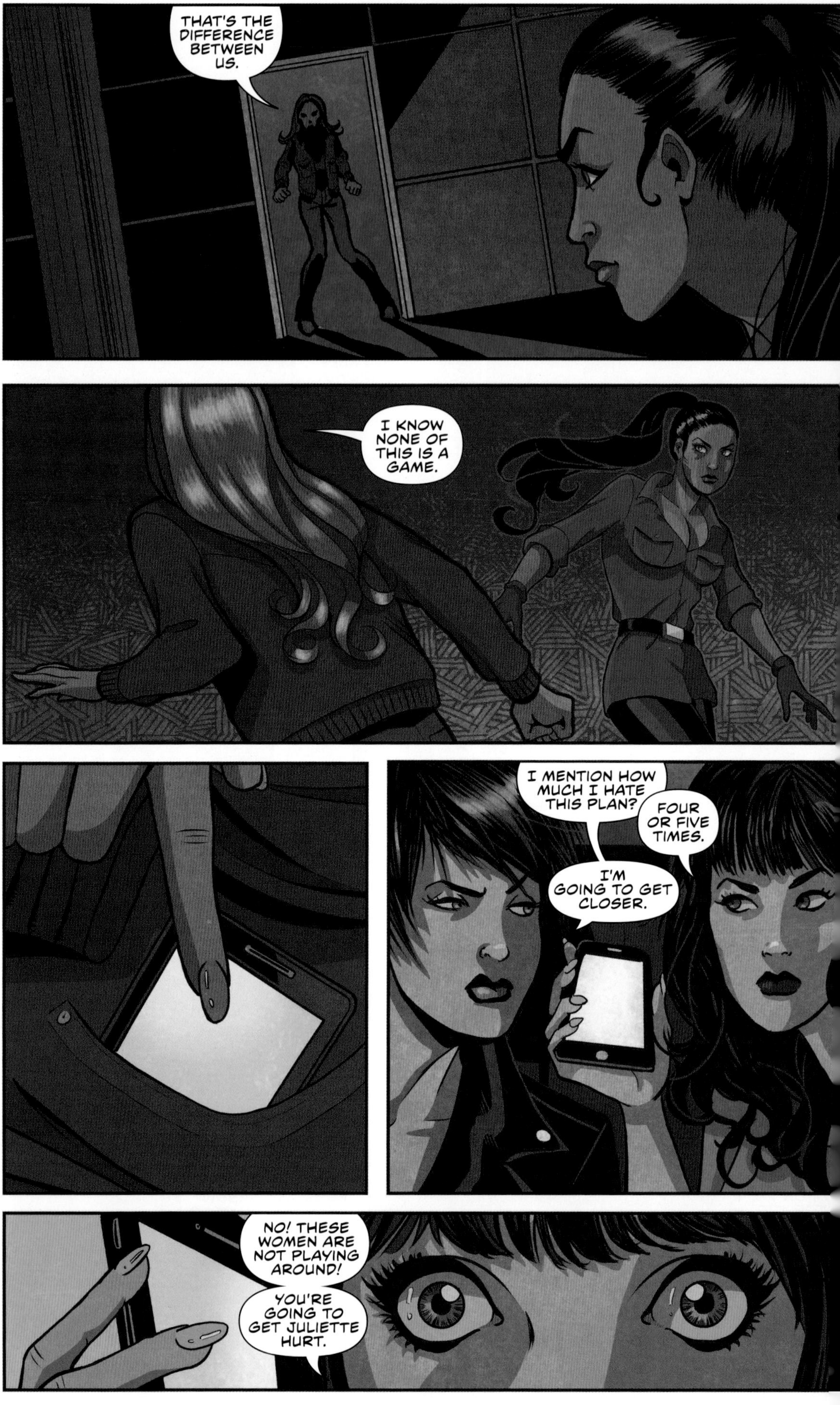
THAT'S THE DIFFERENCE BETWEEN US.
I KNOW NONE OF THIS IS A GAME.
I MENTION HOW MUCH I HATE THIS PLAN?
FOUR OR FIVE TIMES.
I'M GOING TO GET CLOSER.
NO! THESE WOMEN ARE NOT PLAYING AROUND!
YOU'RE GOING TO GET JULIETTE HURT.

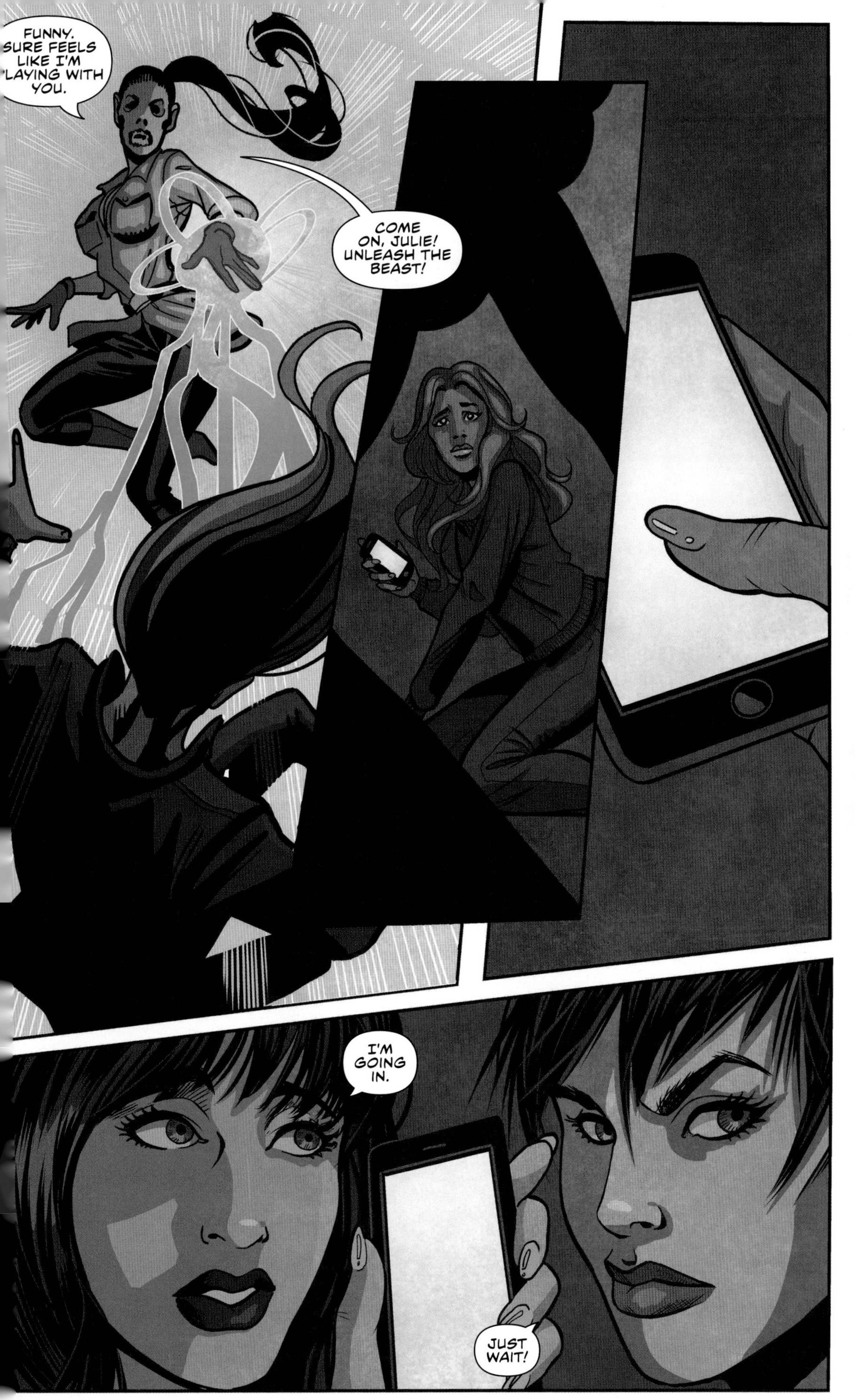
FUNNY. SURE FEELS LIKE I'M 'LAYING WITH YOU.
COME ON, JULIE! UNLEASH THE BEAST!
I'M GOING IN.
JUST WAIT!

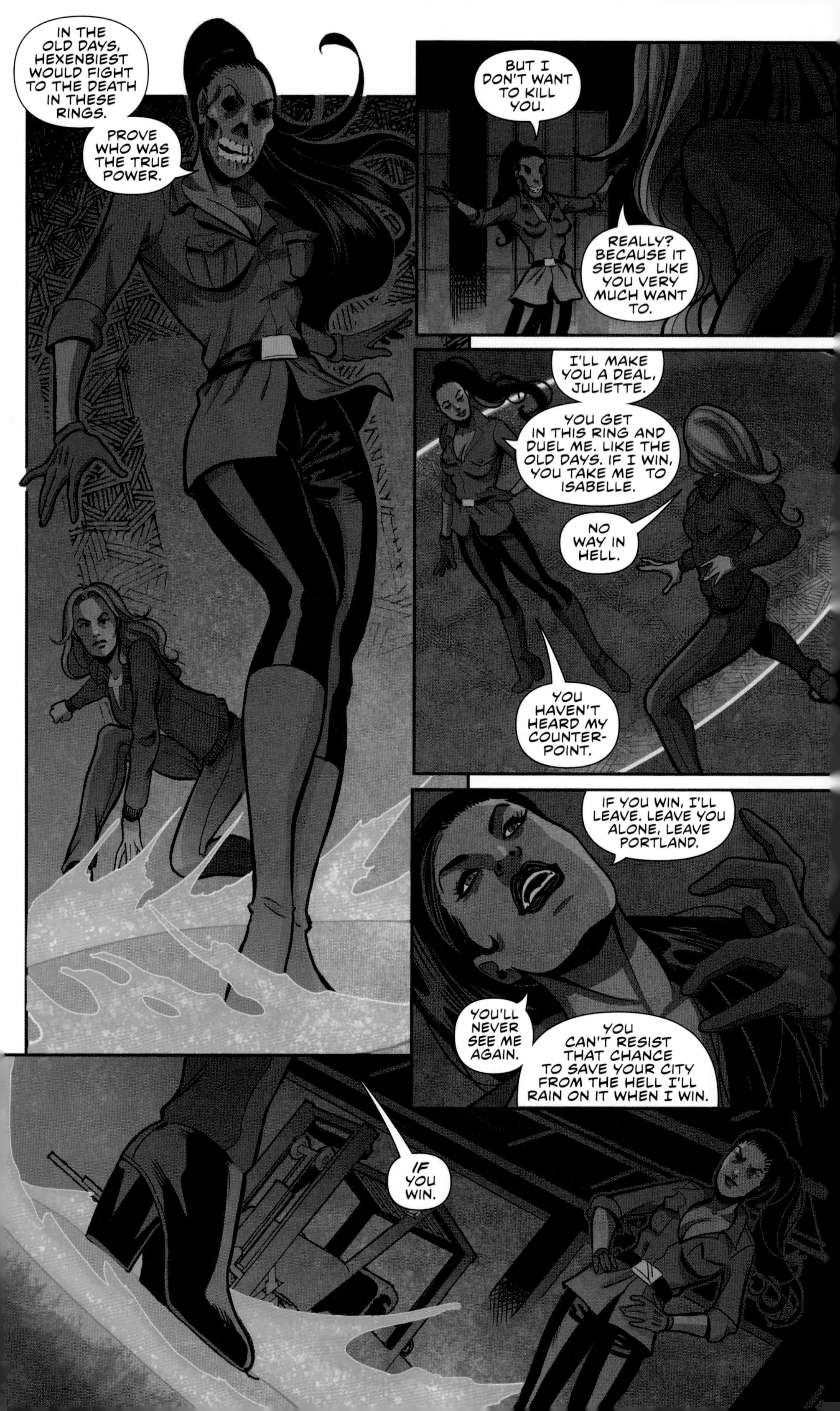
IN THE OLD DAYS, HEXENBIEST WOULD FIGHT TO THE DEATH IN THESE RINGS.
PROVE WHO WAS THE TRUE POWER.
BUT I DON'T WANT TO KILL YOU.
REALLY? BECAUSE IT SEEMS LIKE YOU VERY MUCH WANT TO.
I'LL MAKE YOU A DEAL, JULIETTE.
YOU GET IN THIS RING AND DUEL ME. LIKE THE OLD DAYS. IF I WIN, YOU TAKE ME TO ISABELLE.
NO WAY IN HELL.
YOU HAVEN'T HEARD MY COUNTER-POINT.
IF YOU WIN, I'LL LEAVE. LEAVE YOU ALONE, LEAVE PORTLAND.
YOU'LL NEVER SEE ME AGAIN.
YOU CAN'T RESIST THAT CHANCE TO SAVE YOUR CITY FROM THE HELL I'LL RAIN ON IT WHEN I WIN.
IF YOU WIN.

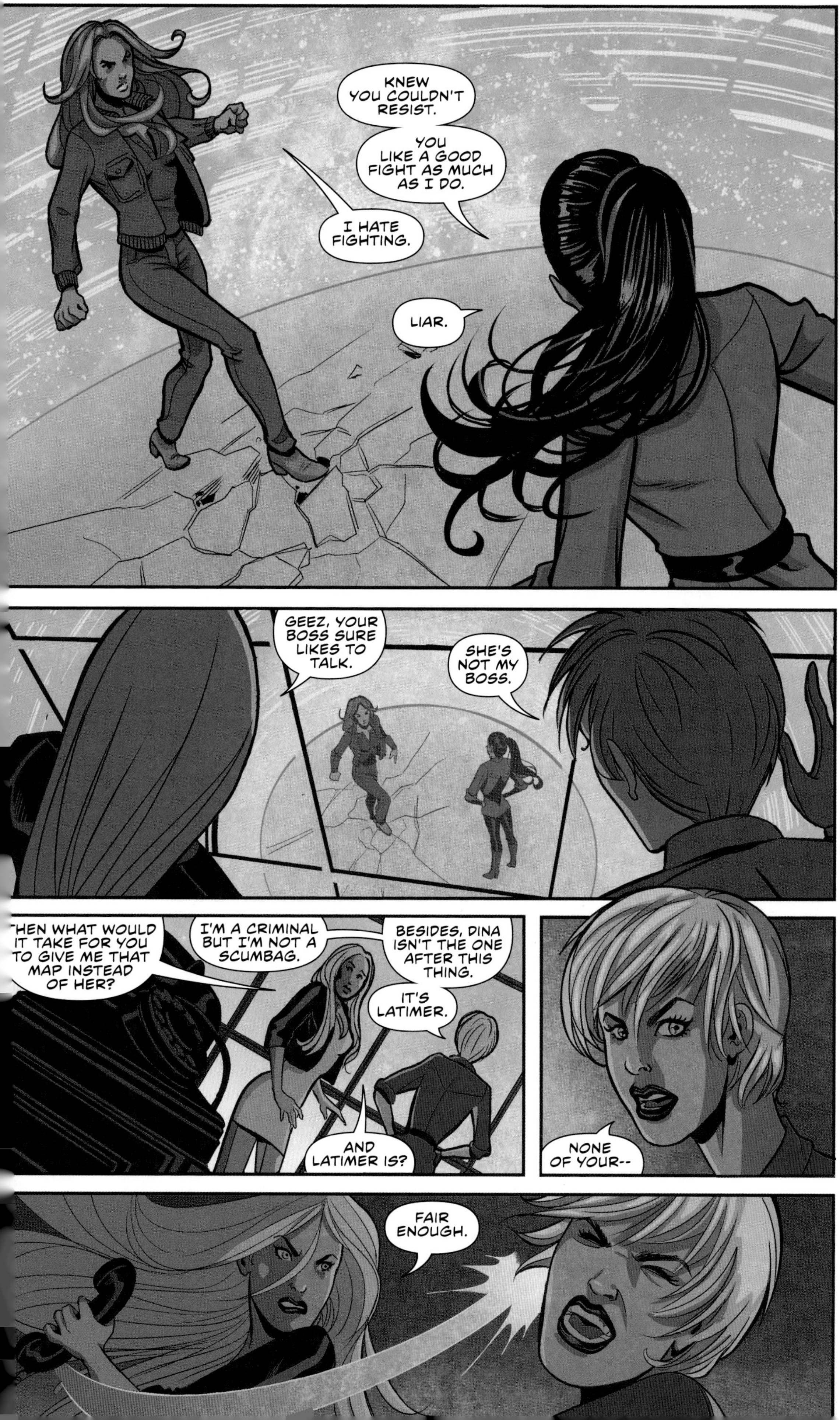
KNEW YOU COULDN'T RESIST.
YOU LIKE A GOOD FIGHT AS MUCH AS I DO.
I HATE FIGHTING.
LIAR.
GEEZ, YOUR BOSS SURE LIKES TO TALK.
SHE'S NOT MY BOSS.
THEN WHAT WOULD IT TAKE FOR YOU TO GIVE ME THAT MAP INSTEAD OF HER?
I'M A CRIMINAL BUT I'M NOT A SCUMBAG.
BESIDES, DINA ISN'T THE ONE AFTER THIS THING.
IT'S LATIMER.
AND LATIMER IS?
NONE OF YOUR--
FAIR ENOUGH.

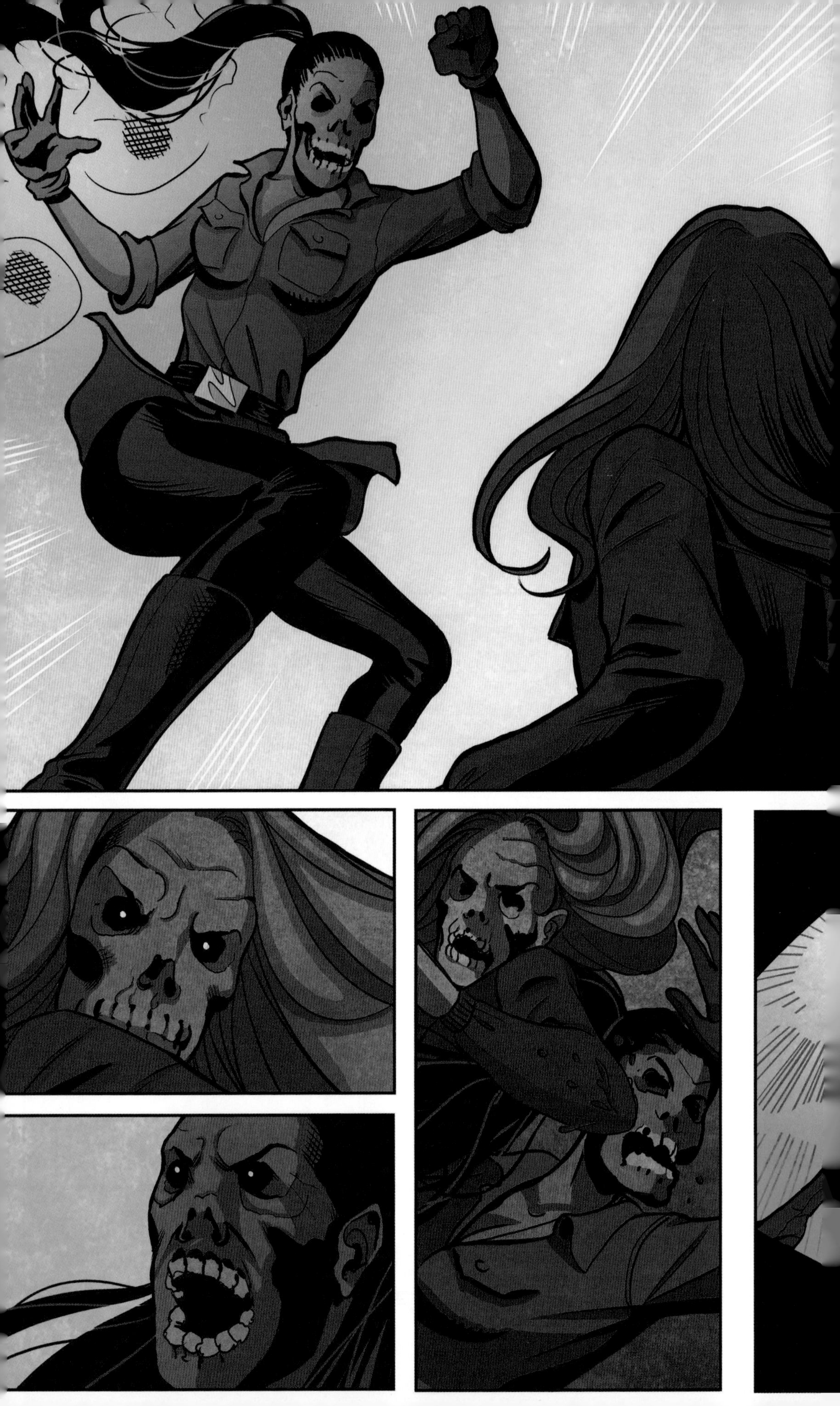

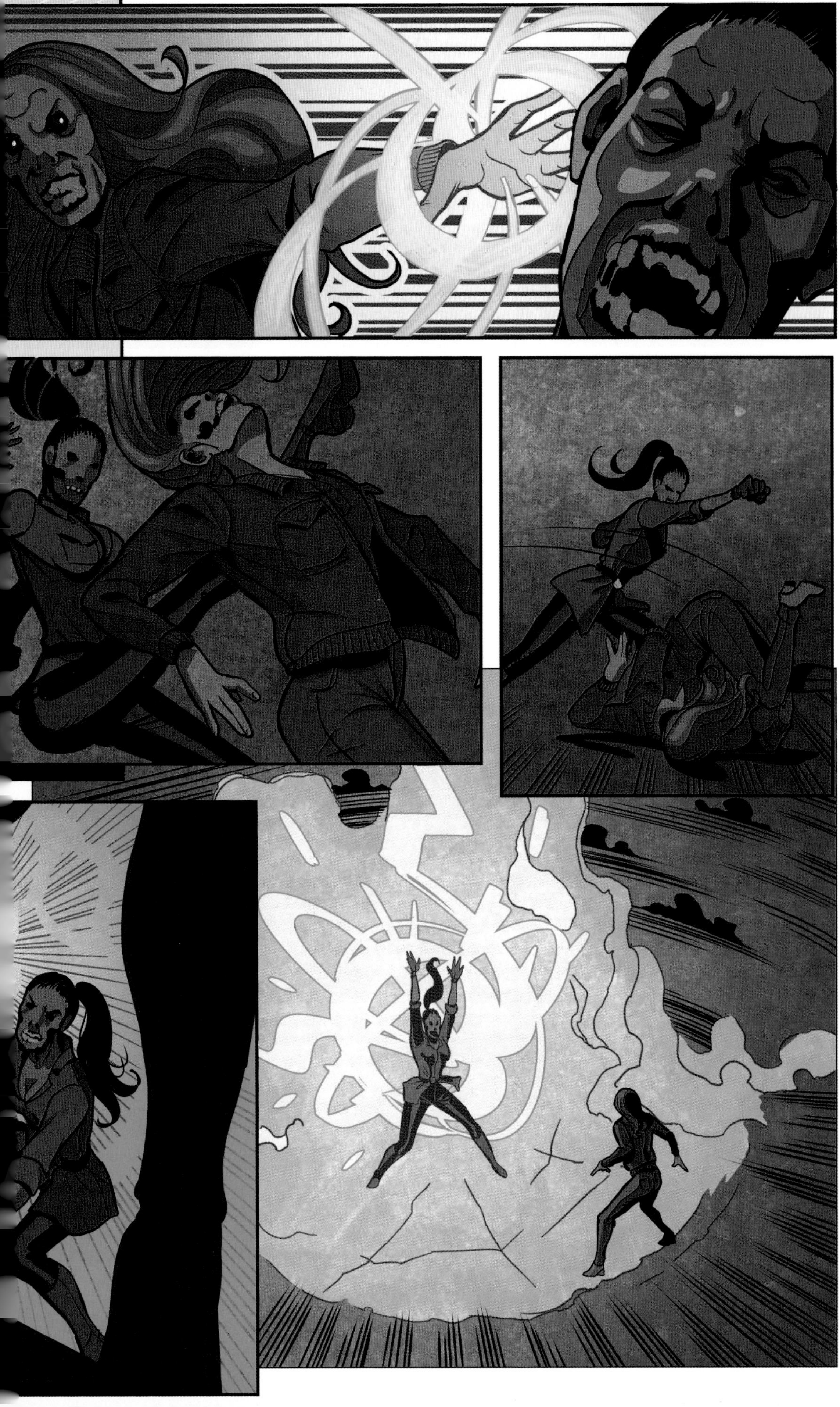

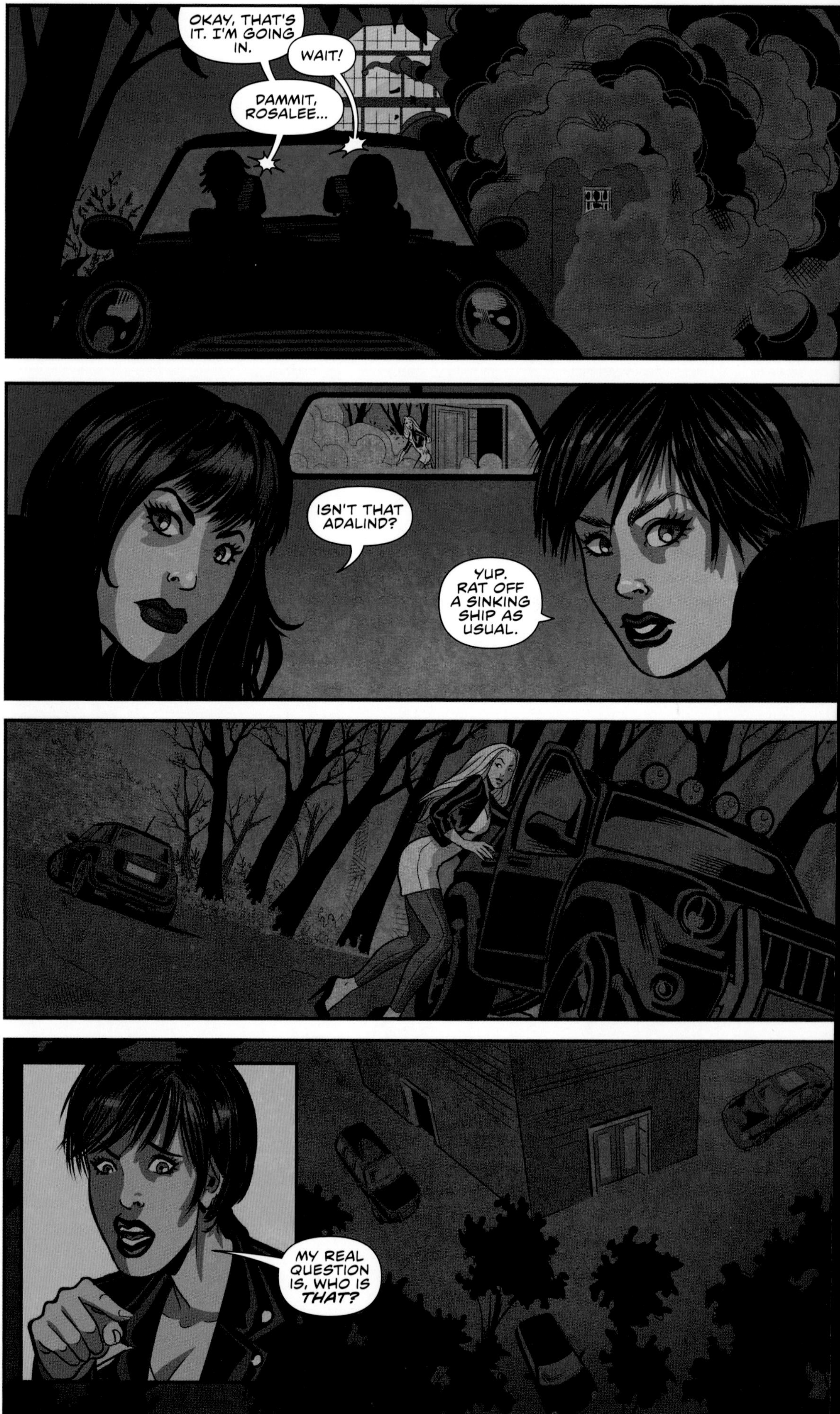
OKAY, THAT'S IT. I'M GOING IN.
WAIT!
DAMMIT, ROSALEE...
ISN'T THAT ADALIND?
YUP. RAT OFF A SINKING SHIP AS USUAL.
MY REAL QUESTION IS, WHO IS *THAT?*

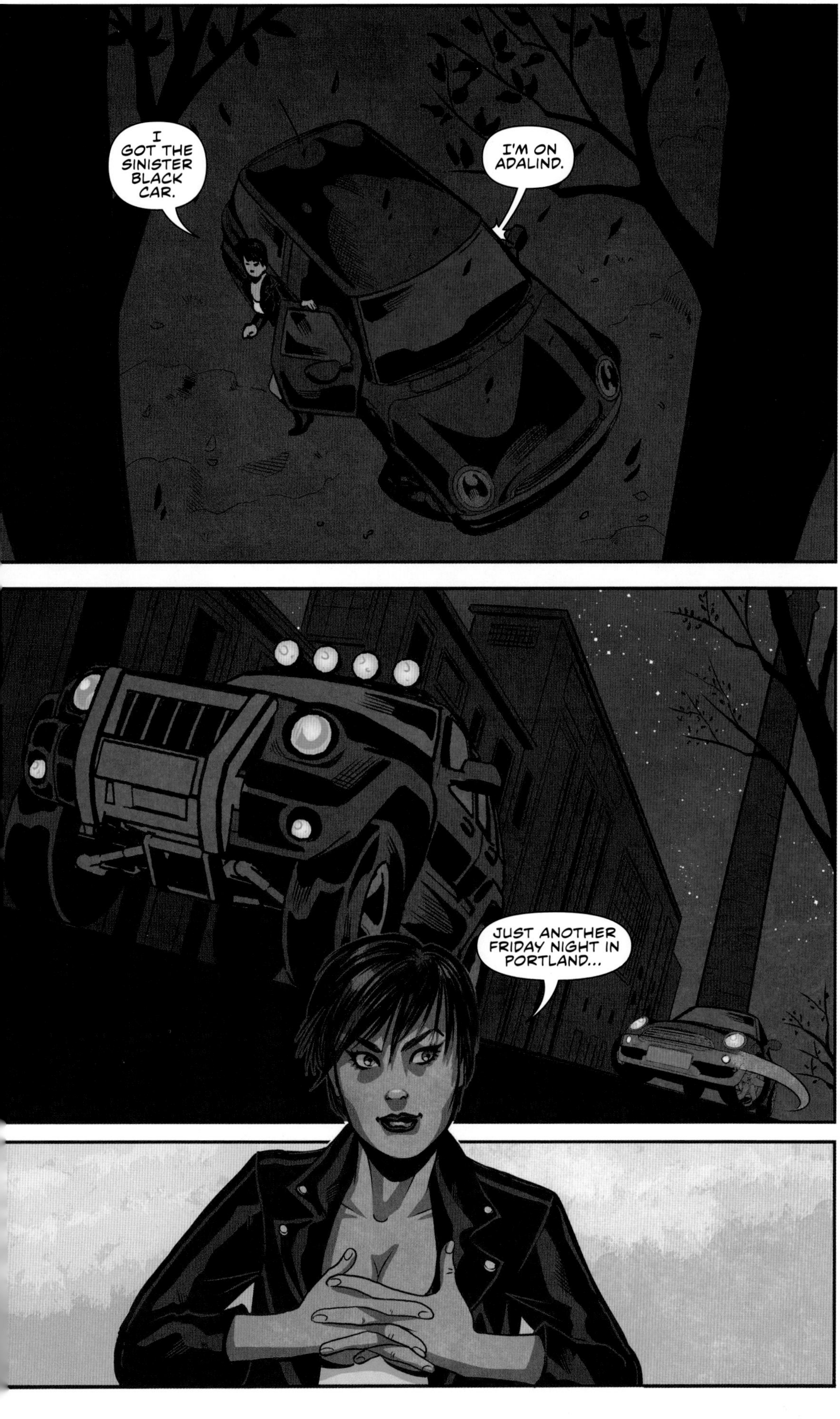
I GOT THE SINISTER BLACK CAR.
I'M ON ADALIND.
JUST ANOTHER FRIDAY NIGHT IN PORTLAND...

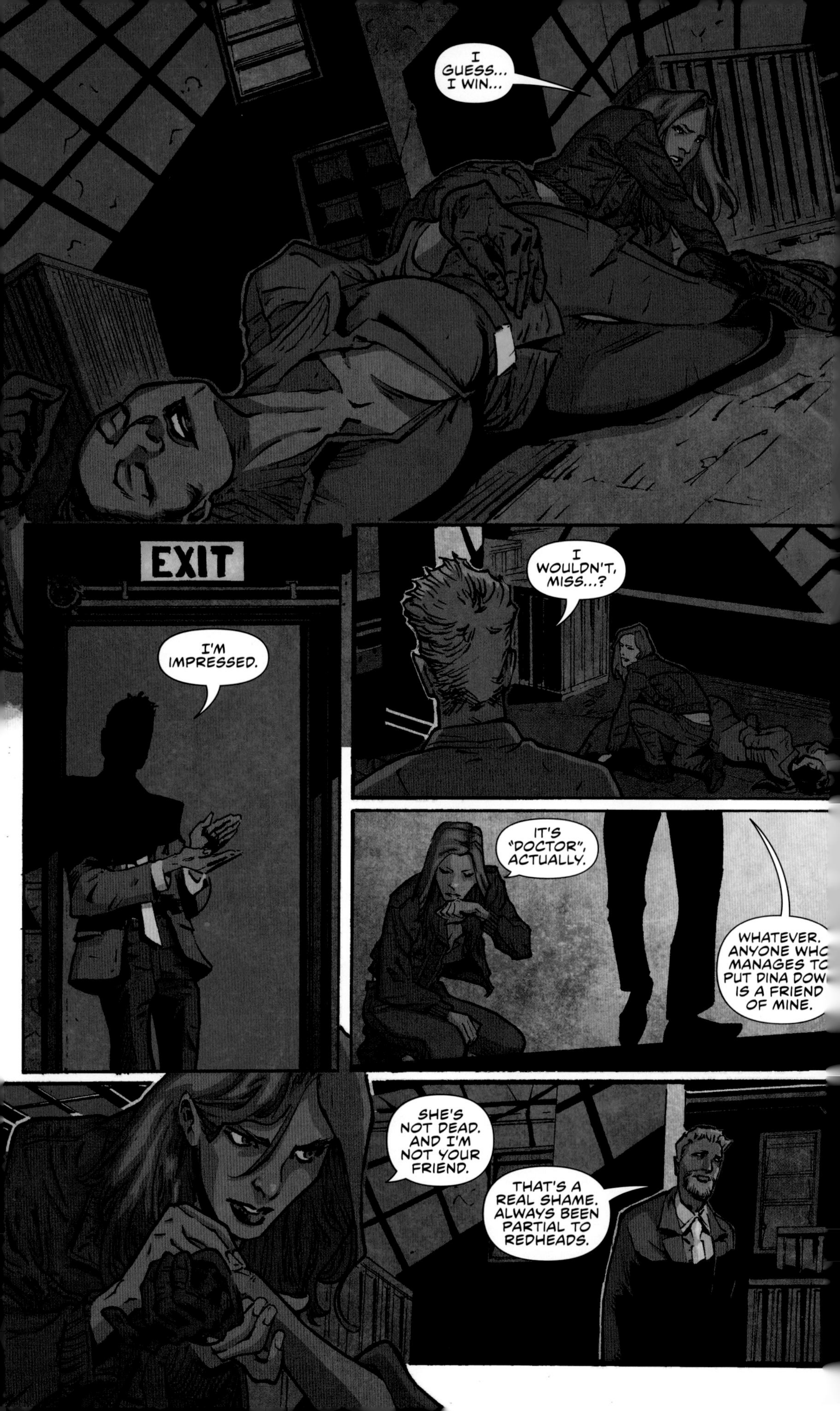
I GUESS... I WIN...
EXIT
I'M IMPRESSED.
I WOULDN'T, MISS...?
IT'S "DOCTOR", ACTUALLY.
WHATEVER. ANYONE WHO MANAGES TO PUT DINA DOWN IS A FRIEND OF MINE.
SHE'S NOT DEAD. AND I'M NOT YOUR FRIEND.
THAT'S A REAL SHAME. ALWAYS BEEN PARTIAL TO REDHEADS.

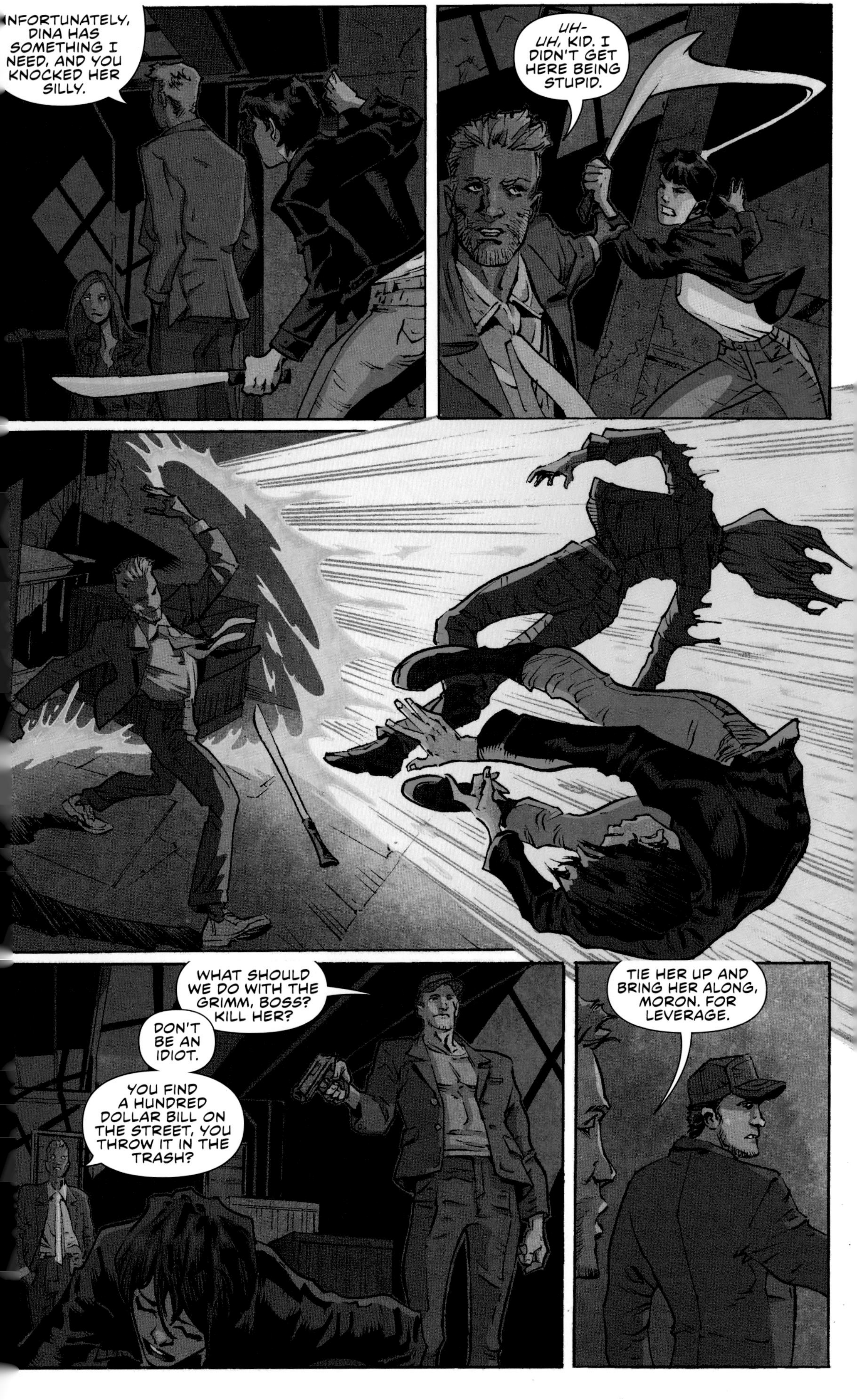

UNFORTUNATELY, DINA HAS SOMETHING I NEED, AND YOU KNOCKED HER SILLY.
UH-UH, KID. I DIDN'T GET HERE BEING STUPID.
WHAT SHOULD WE DO WITH THE GRIMM, BOSS? KILL HER?
DON'T BE AN IDIOT.
YOU FIND A HUNDRED DOLLAR BILL ON THE STREET, YOU THROW IT IN THE TRASH?
TIE HER UP AND BRING HER ALONG, MORON. FOR LEVERAGE.

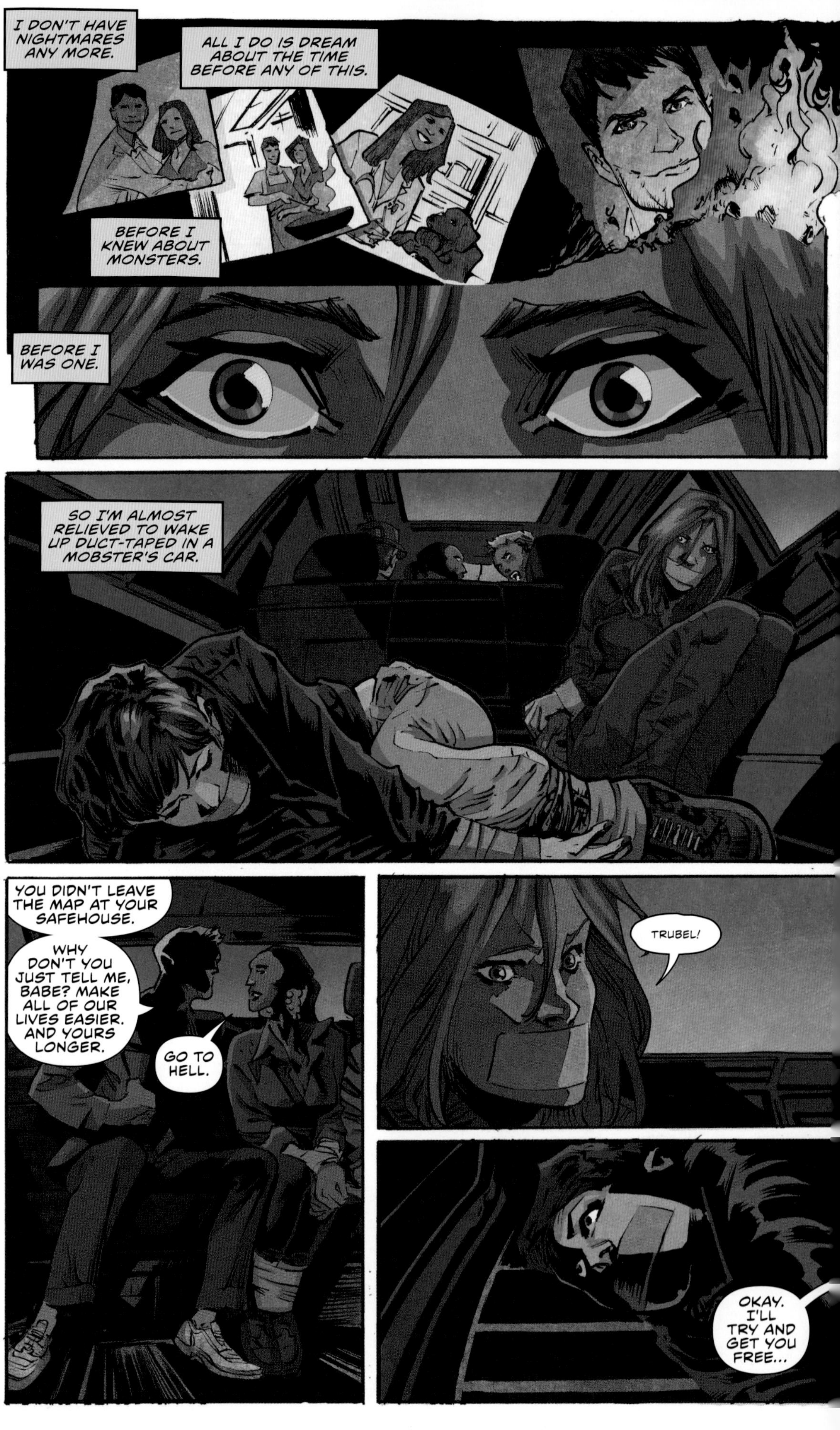
I DON'T HAVE NIGHTMARES ANY MORE.
ALL I DO IS DREAM ABOUT THE TIME BEFORE ANY OF THIS.
BEFORE I KNEW ABOUT MONSTERS.
BEFORE I WAS ONE.
SO I'M ALMOST RELIEVED TO WAKE UP DUCT-TAPED IN A MOBSTER'S CAR.
YOU DIDN'T LEAVE THE MAP AT YOUR SAFEHOUSE.
WHY DON'T YOU JUST TELL ME, BABE? MAKE ALL OF OUR LIVES EASIER. AND YOURS LONGER.
GO TO HELL.
TRUBEL!
OKAY. I'LL TRY AND GET YOU FREE...

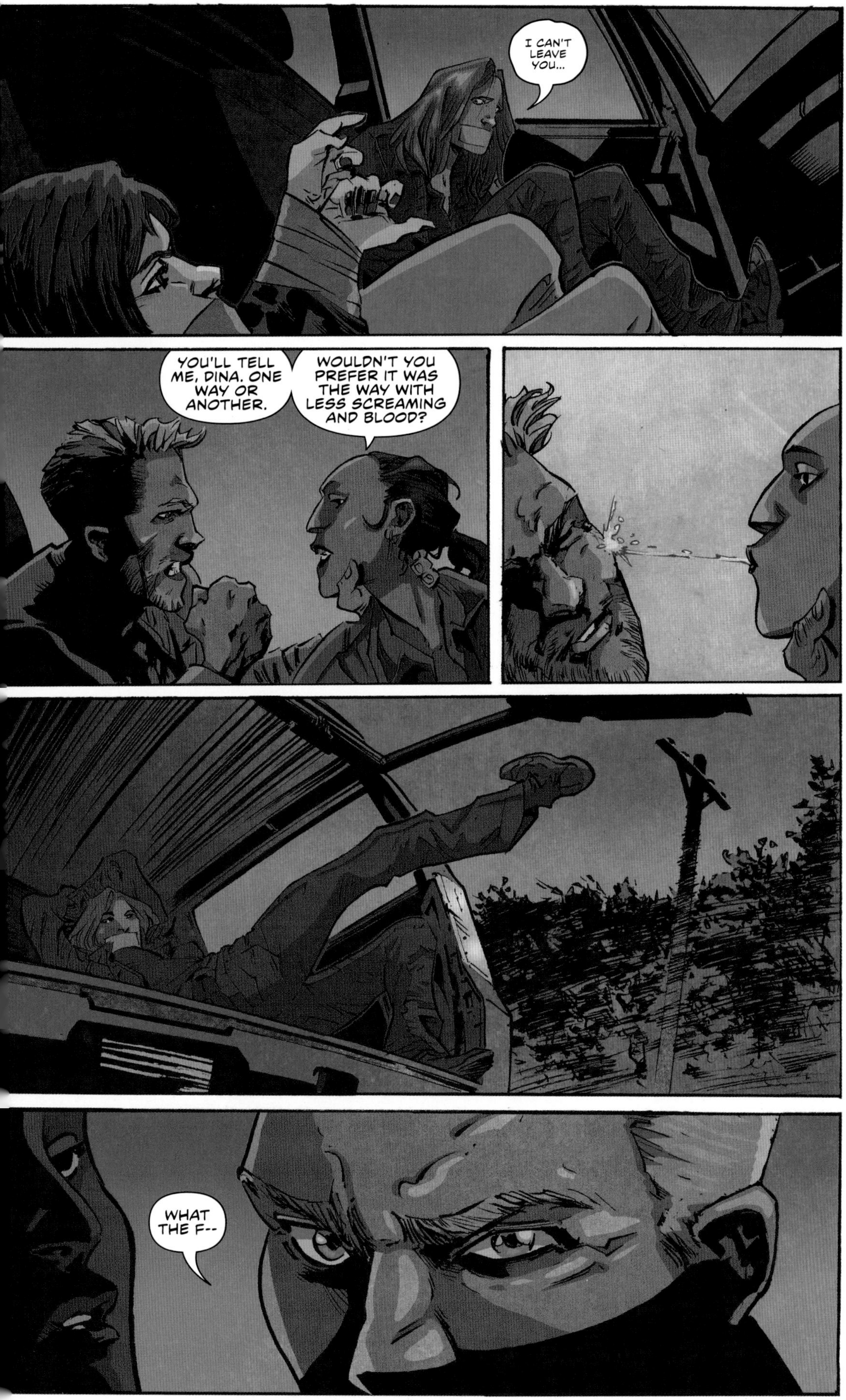

I CAN'T LEAVE YOU...
YOU'LL TELL ME, DINA. ONE WAY OR ANOTHER.
WOULDN'T YOU PREFER IT WAS THE WAY WITH LESS SCREAMING AND BLOOD?
WHAT THE F--

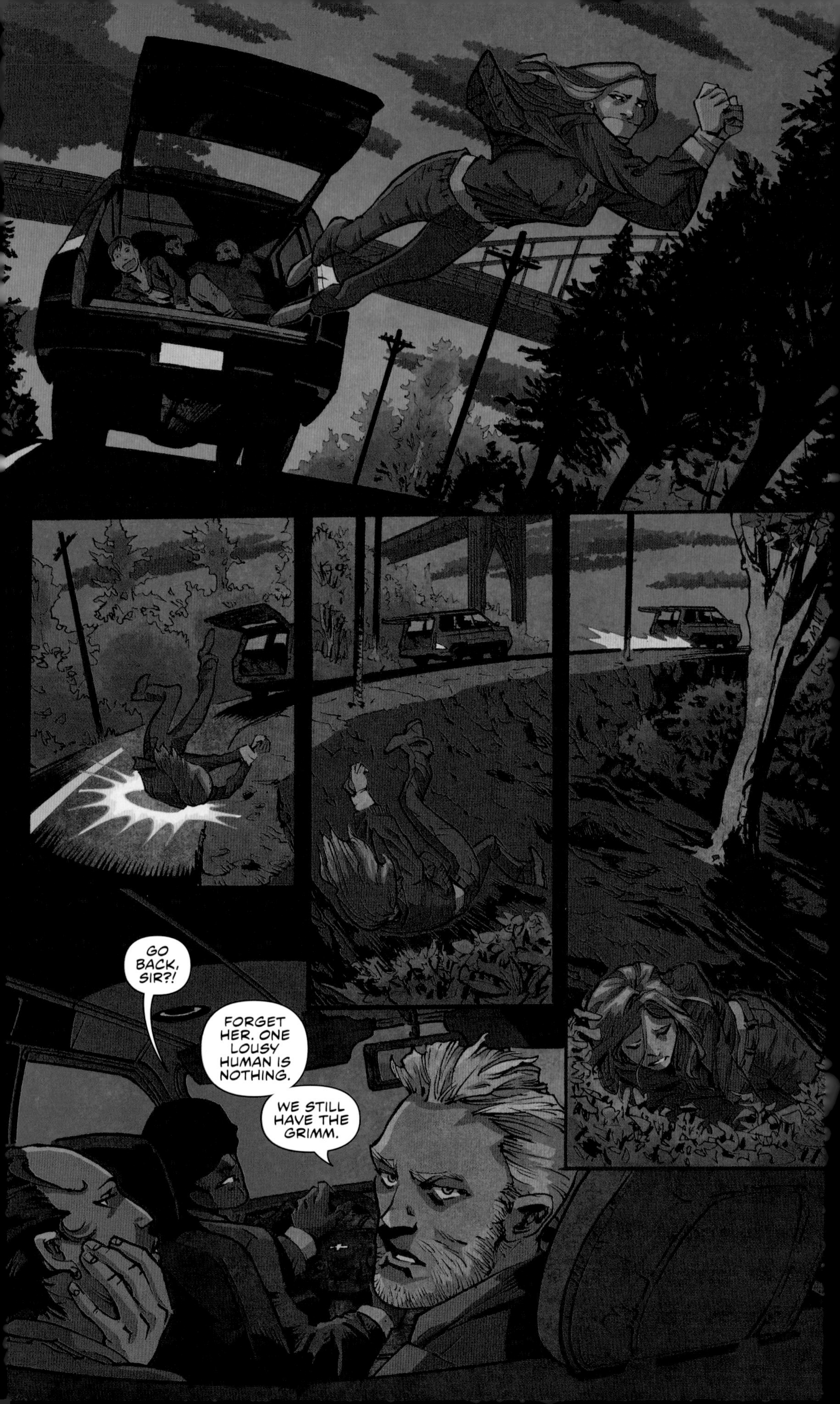
GO BACK, SIR?!
FORGET HER. ONE LOUSY HUMAN IS NOTHING.
WE STILL HAVE THE GRIMM.

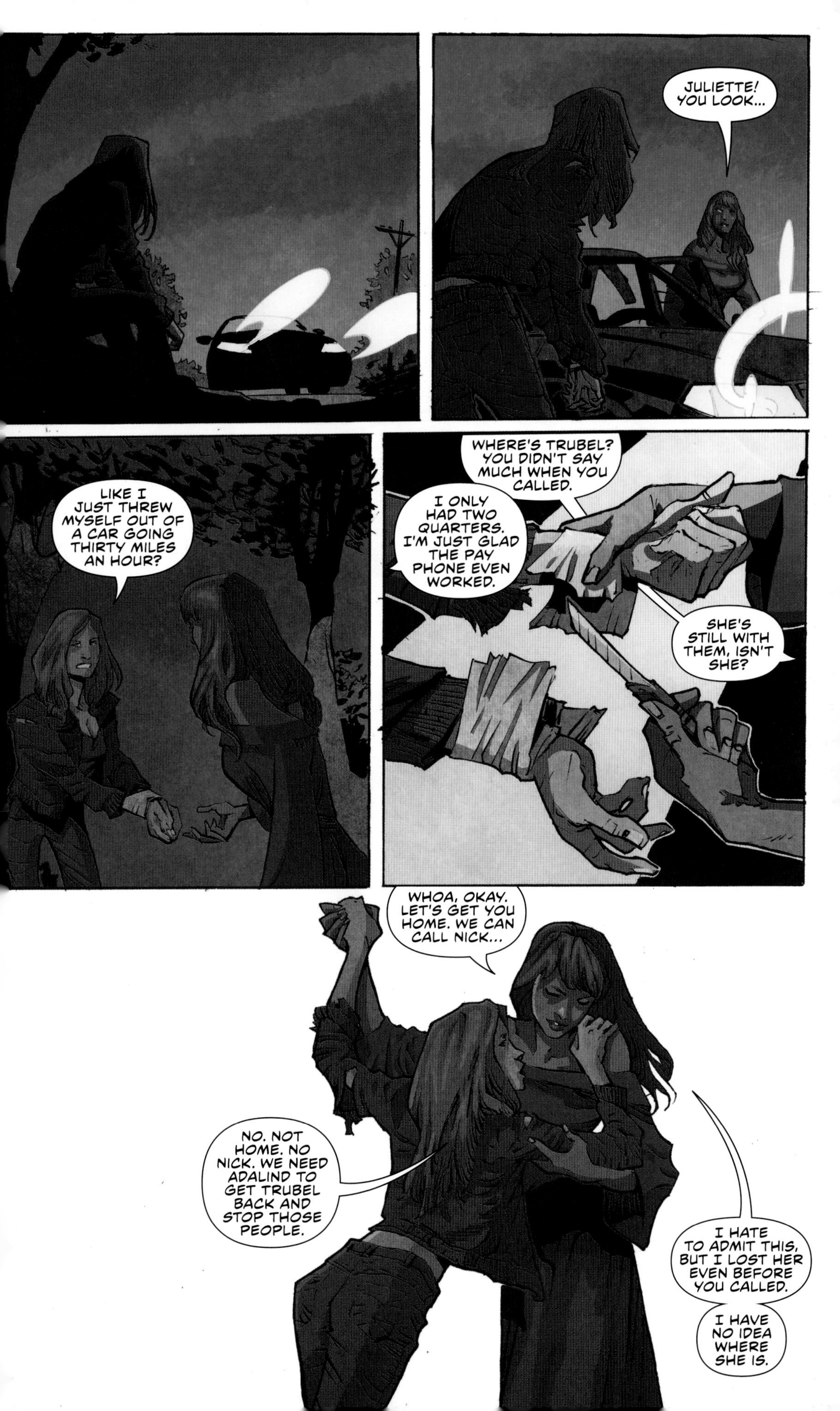
JULIETTE! YOU LOOK...
LIKE I JUST THREW MYSELF OUT OF A CAR GOING THIRTY MILES AN HOUR?
WHERE'S TRUBEL? YOU DIDN'T SAY MUCH WHEN YOU CALLED.
I ONLY HAD TWO QUARTERS. I'M JUST GLAD THE PAY PHONE EVEN WORKED.
SHE'S STILL WITH THEM, ISN'T SHE?
WHOA, OKAY. LET'S GET YOU HOME. WE CAN CALL NICK...
NO. NOT HOME. NO NICK. WE NEED ADALIND TO GET TRUBEL BACK AND STOP THOSE PEOPLE.
I HATE TO ADMIT THIS, BUT I LOST HER EVEN BEFORE YOU CALLED.
I HAVE NO IDEA WHERE SHE IS.

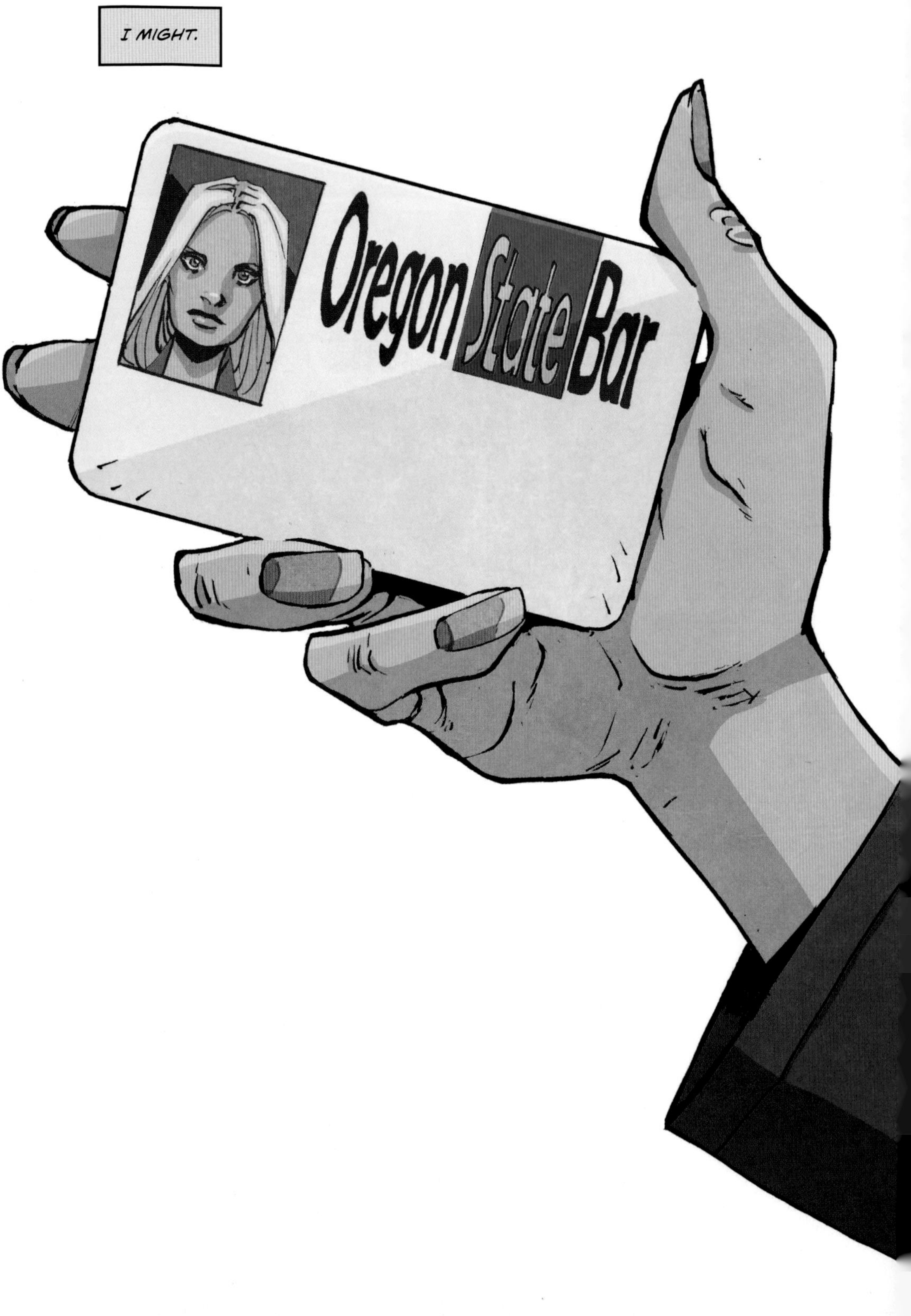
I MIGHT.
Oregon State Bar

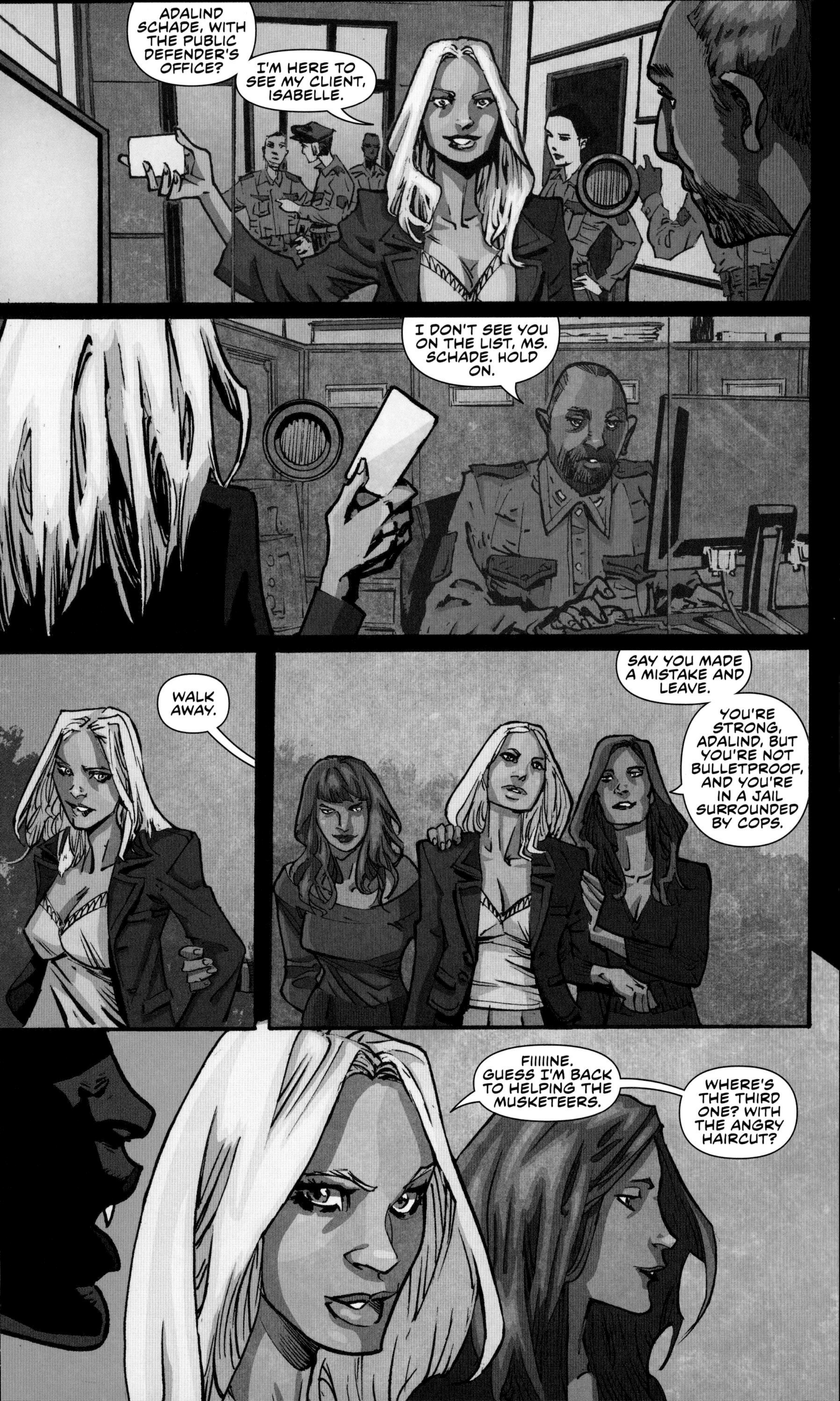
ADALIND SCHADE, WITH THE PUBLIC DEFENDER'S OFFICE?
I'M HERE TO SEE MY CLIENT, ISABELLE.
I DON'T SEE YOU ON THE LIST, MS. SCHADE. HOLD ON.
WALK AWAY.
SAY YOU MADE A MISTAKE AND LEAVE.
YOU'RE STRONG, ADALIND, BUT YOU'RE NOT BULLETPROOF, AND YOU'RE IN A JAIL SURROUNDED BY COPS.
FIIIIINE. GUESS I'M BACK TO HELPING THE MUSKETEERS.
WHERE'S THE THIRD ONE? WITH THE ANGRY HAIRCUT?

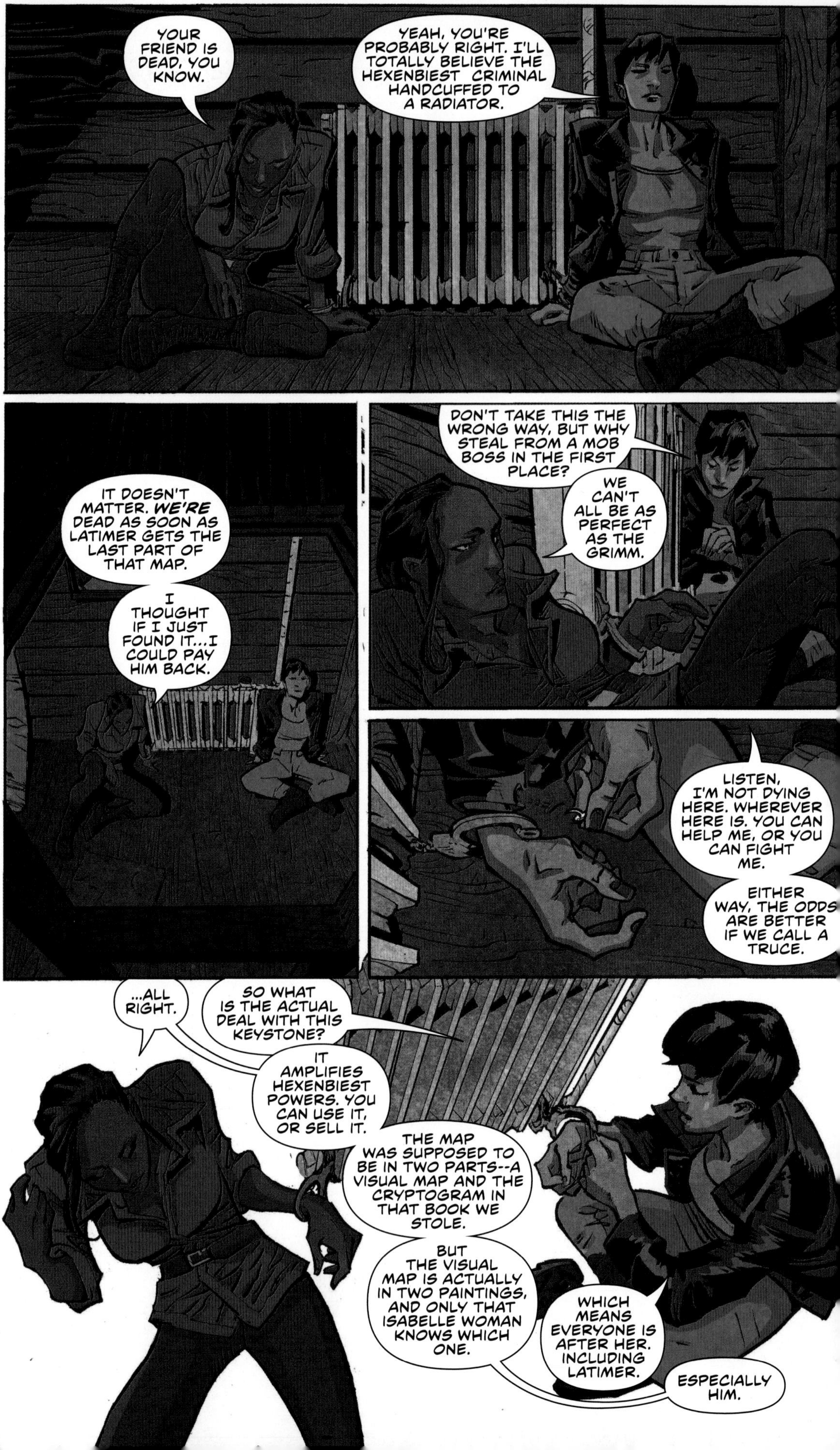
YOUR FRIEND IS DEAD, YOU KNOW.
YEAH, YOU'RE PROBABLY RIGHT. I'LL TOTALLY BELIEVE THE HEXENBIEST CRIMINAL HANDCUFFED TO A RADIATOR.
IT DOESN'T MATTER. *WE'RE* DEAD AS SOON AS LATIMER GETS THE LAST PART OF THAT MAP.
I THOUGHT IF I JUST FOUND IT...I COULD PAY HIM BACK.
DON'T TAKE THIS THE WRONG WAY, BUT WHY STEAL FROM A MOB BOSS IN THE FIRST PLACE?
WE CAN'T ALL BE AS PERFECT AS THE GRIMM.
LISTEN, I'M NOT DYING HERE. WHEREVER HERE IS. YOU CAN HELP ME, OR YOU CAN FIGHT ME.
EITHER WAY, THE ODDS ARE BETTER IF WE CALL A TRUCE.
...ALL RIGHT.
SO WHAT IS THE ACTUAL DEAL WITH THIS KEYSTONE?
IT AMPLIFIES HEXENBIEST POWERS. YOU CAN USE IT, OR SELL IT.
THE MAP WAS SUPPOSED TO BE IN TWO PARTS--A VISUAL MAP AND THE CRYPTOGRAM IN THAT BOOK WE STOLE.
BUT THE VISUAL MAP IS ACTUALLY IN TWO PAINTINGS, AND ONLY THAT ISABELLE WOMAN KNOWS WHICH ONE.
WHICH MEANS EVERYONE IS AFTER HER. INCLUDING LATIMER.
ESPECIALLY HIM.

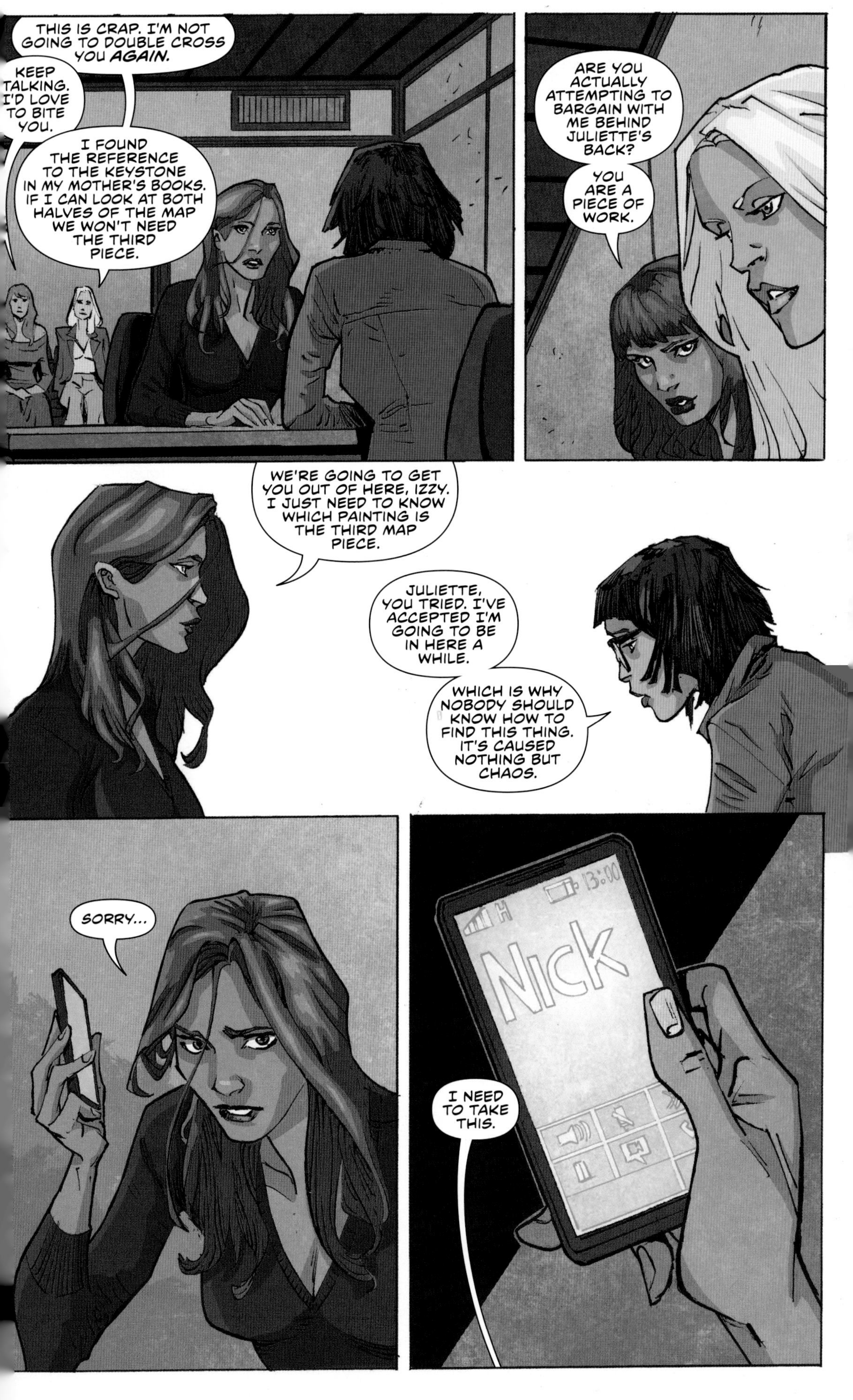
THIS IS CRAP. I'M NOT GOING TO DOUBLE CROSS YOU AGAIN.
KEEP TALKING. I'D LOVE TO BITE YOU.
I FOUND THE REFERENCE TO THE KEYSTONE IN MY MOTHER'S BOOKS. IF I CAN LOOK AT BOTH HALVES OF THE MAP WE WON'T NEED THE THIRD PIECE.
ARE YOU ACTUALLY ATTEMPTING TO BARGAIN WITH ME BEHIND JULIETTE'S BACK?
YOU ARE A PIECE OF WORK.
WE'RE GOING TO GET YOU OUT OF HERE, IZZY. I JUST NEED TO KNOW WHICH PAINTING IS THE THIRD MAP PIECE.
JULIETTE, YOU TRIED. I'VE ACCEPTED I'M GOING TO BE IN HERE A WHILE.
WHICH IS WHY NOBODY SHOULD KNOW HOW TO FIND THIS THING. IT'S CAUSED NOTHING BUT CHAOS.
SORRY...
13:00
Nick
I NEED TO TAKE THIS.

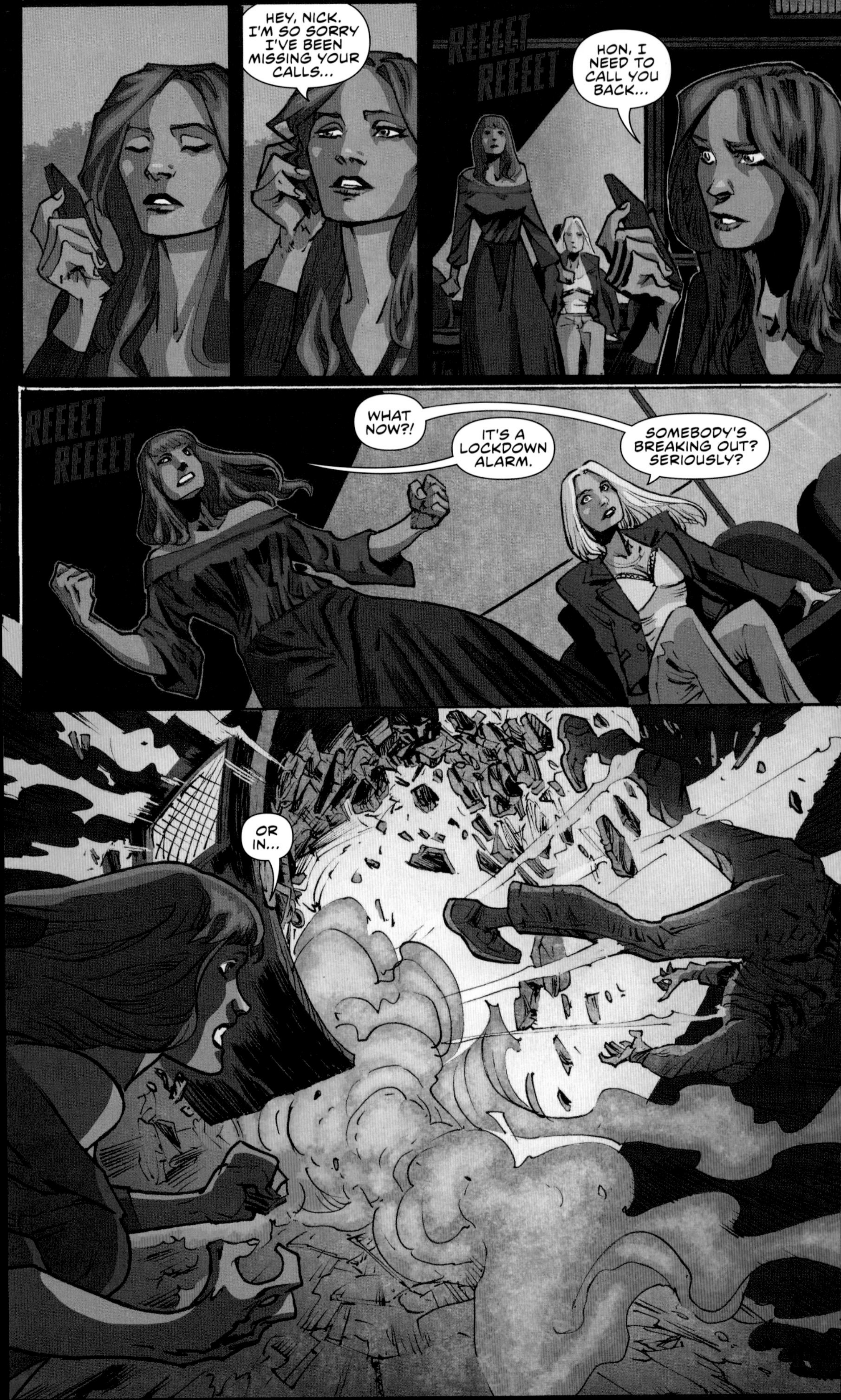
HEY, NICK. I'M SO SORRY I'VE BEEN MISSING YOUR CALLS...
REEEET
REEEET
HON, I NEED TO CALL YOU BACK...
REEEET
REEEET
WHAT NOW?!
IT'S A LOCKDOWN ALARM.
SOMEBODY'S BREAKING OUT? SERIOUSLY?
OR IN...

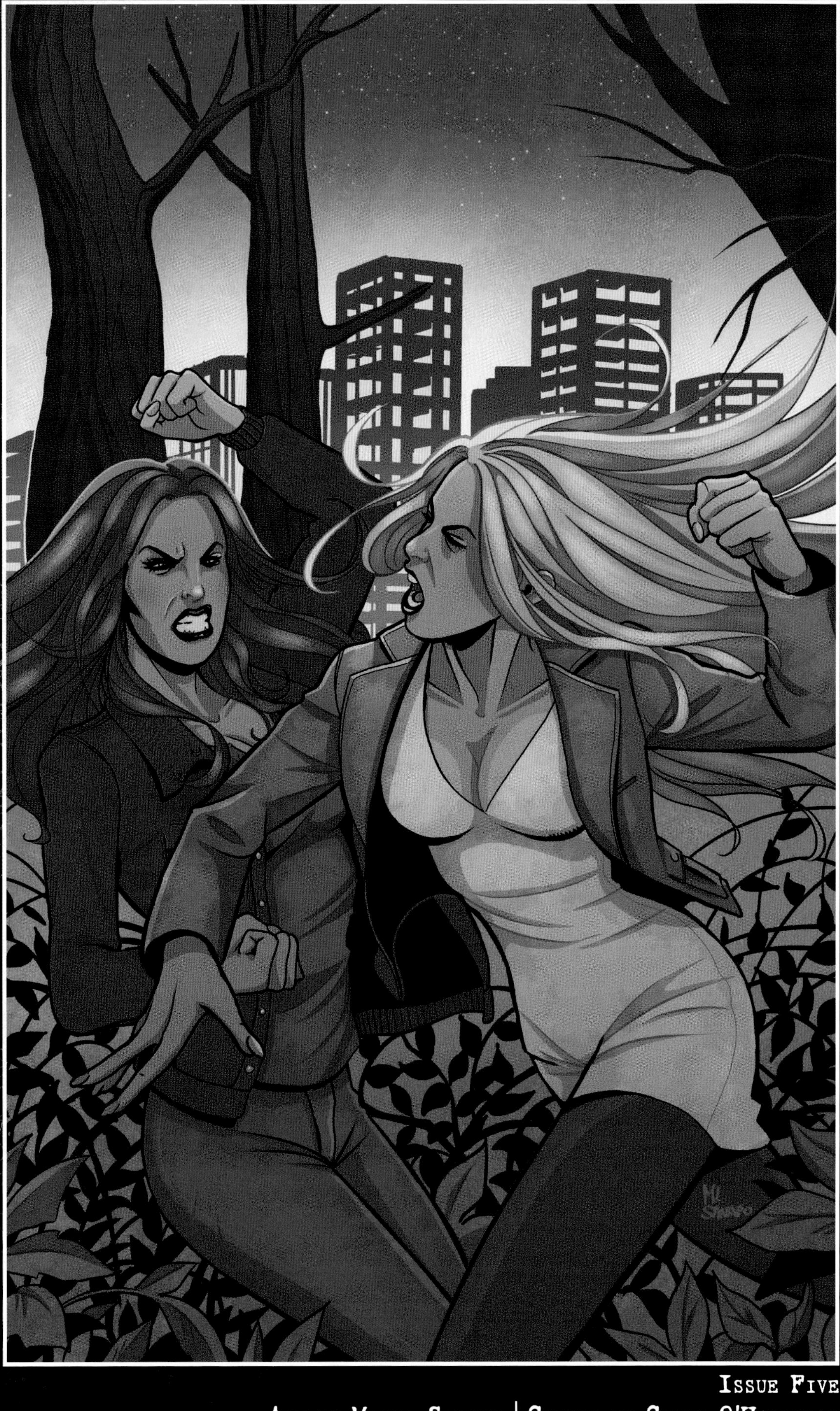

Issue Five

Art by Maria Sanapo | Colors by Chris O'Halloran

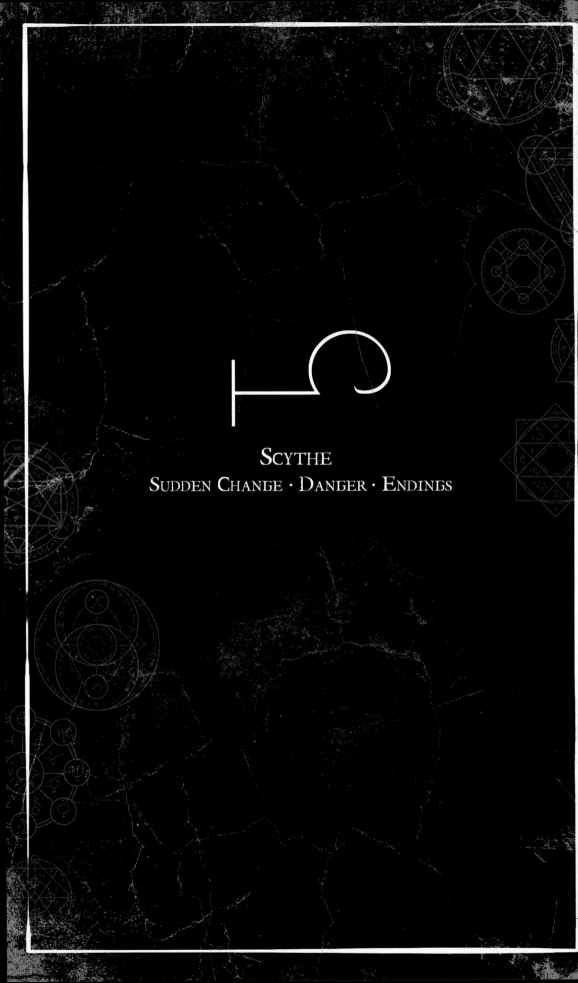

SCYTHE

SUDDEN CHANGE · DANGER · ENDINGS

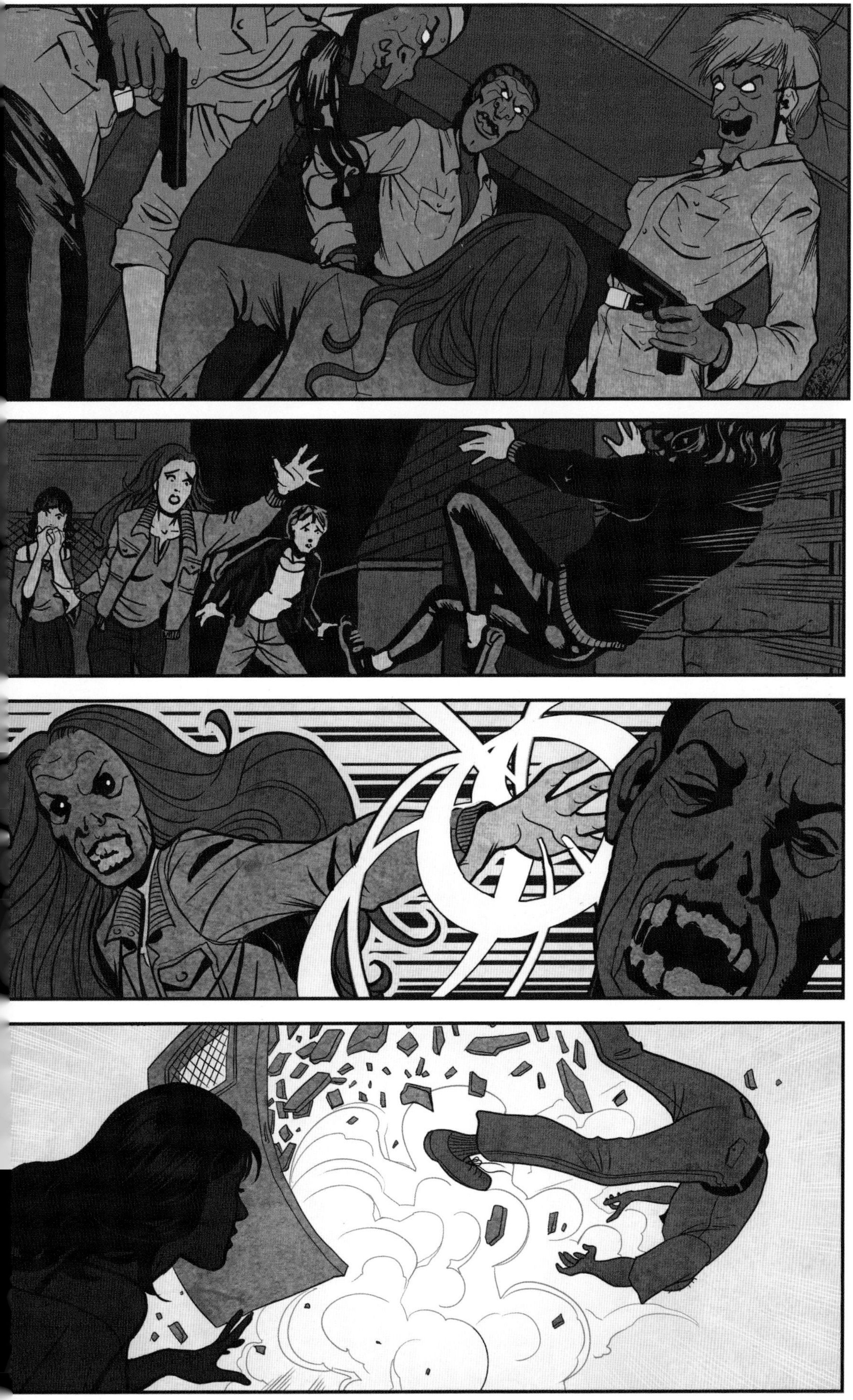

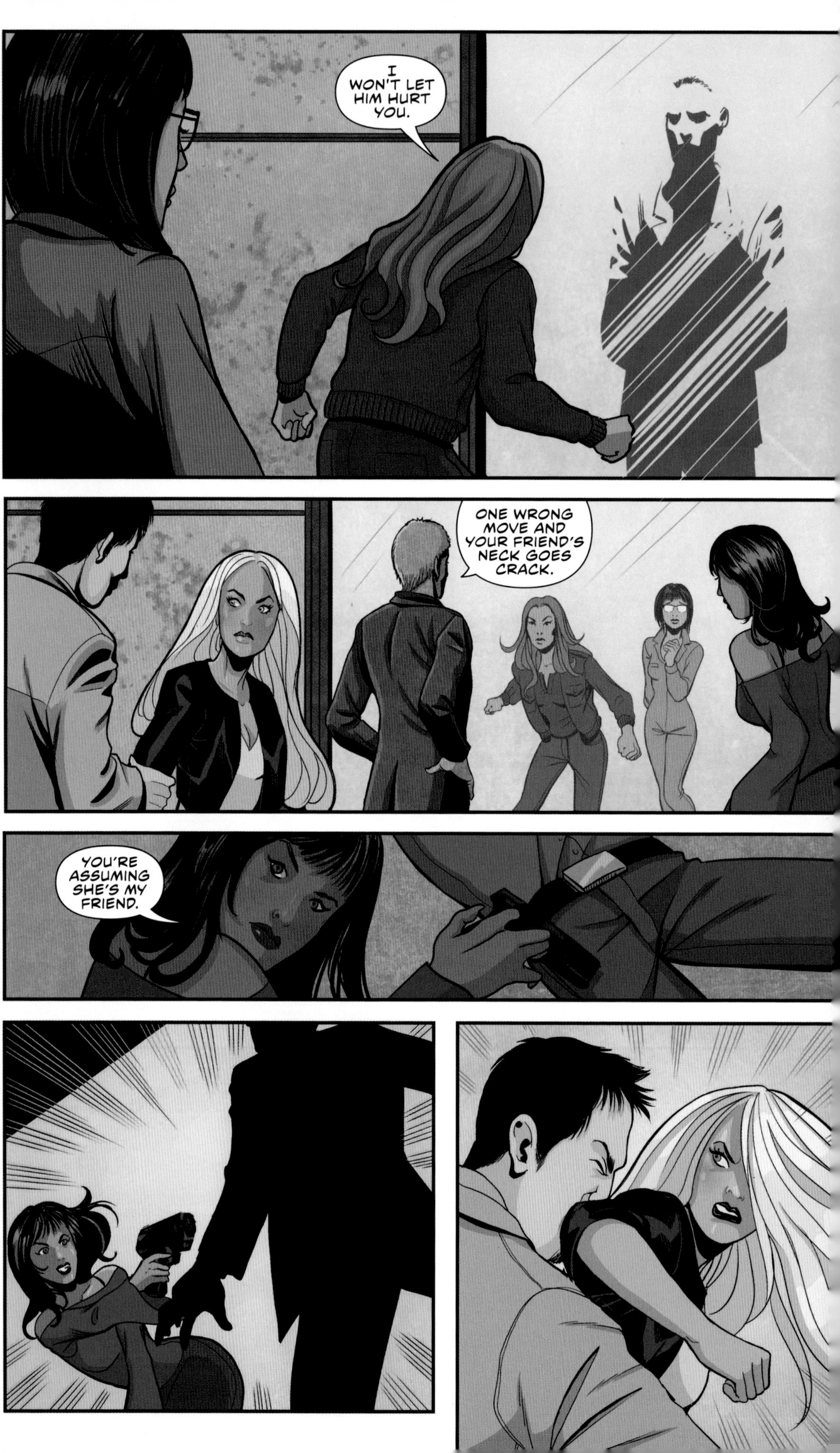
I WON'T LET HIM HURT YOU.
ONE WRONG MOVE AND YOUR FRIEND'S NECK GOES CRACK.
YOU'RE ASSUMING SHE'S MY FRIEND.

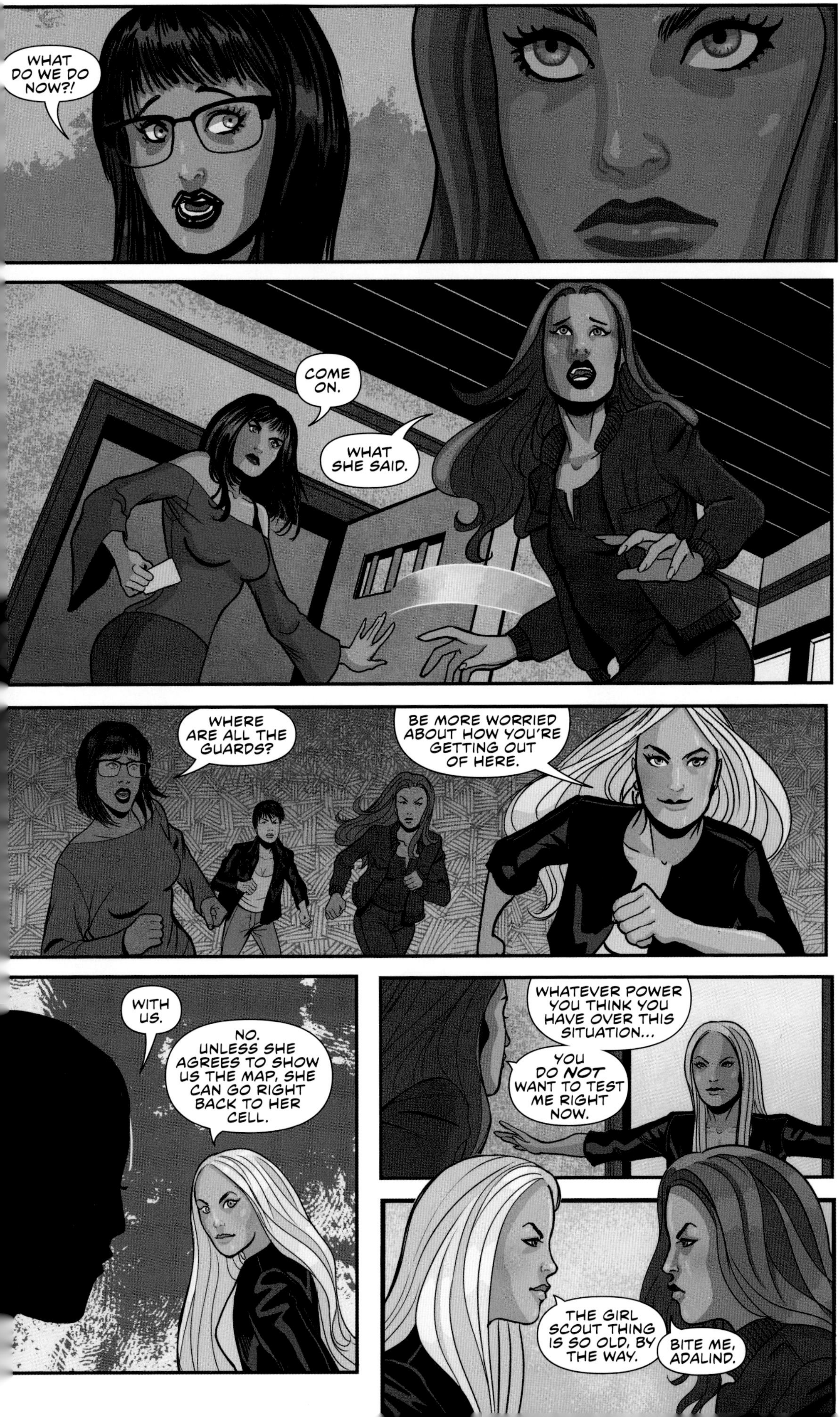
WHAT DO WE DO NOW?!
COME ON.
WHAT SHE SAID.
WHERE ARE ALL THE GUARDS?
BE MORE WORRIED ABOUT HOW YOU'RE GETTING OUT OF HERE.
WITH US.
NO. UNLESS SHE AGREES TO SHOW US THE MAP, SHE CAN GO RIGHT BACK TO HER CELL.
WHATEVER POWER YOU THINK YOU HAVE OVER THIS SITUATION...
YOU DO NOT WANT TO TEST ME RIGHT NOW.
THE GIRL SCOUT THING IS SO OLD, BY THE WAY.
BITE ME, ADALIND.

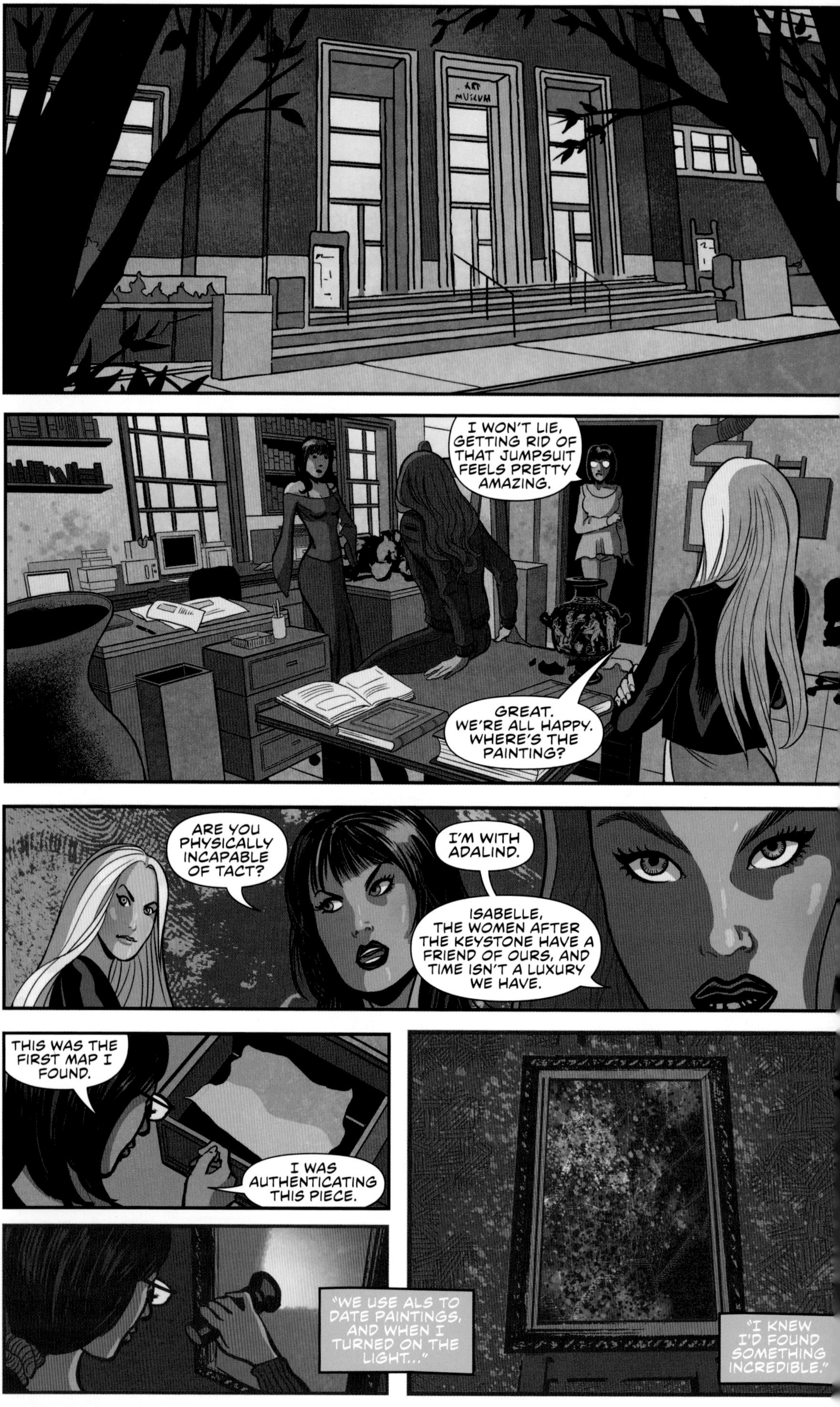
ART MUSEUM
I WON'T LIE, GETTING RID OF THAT JUMPSUIT FEELS PRETTY AMAZING.
GREAT. WE'RE ALL HAPPY. WHERE'S THE PAINTING?
ARE YOU PHYSICALLY INCAPABLE OF TACT?
I'M WITH ADALIND.
ISABELLE, THE WOMEN AFTER THE KEYSTONE HAVE A FRIEND OF OURS, AND TIME ISN'T A LUXURY WE HAVE.
THIS WAS THE FIRST MAP I FOUND.
I WAS AUTHENTICATING THIS PIECE.
"WE USE ALS TO DATE PAINTINGS, AND WHEN I TURNED ON THE LIGHT..."
"I KNEW I'D FOUND SOMETHING INCREDIBLE."

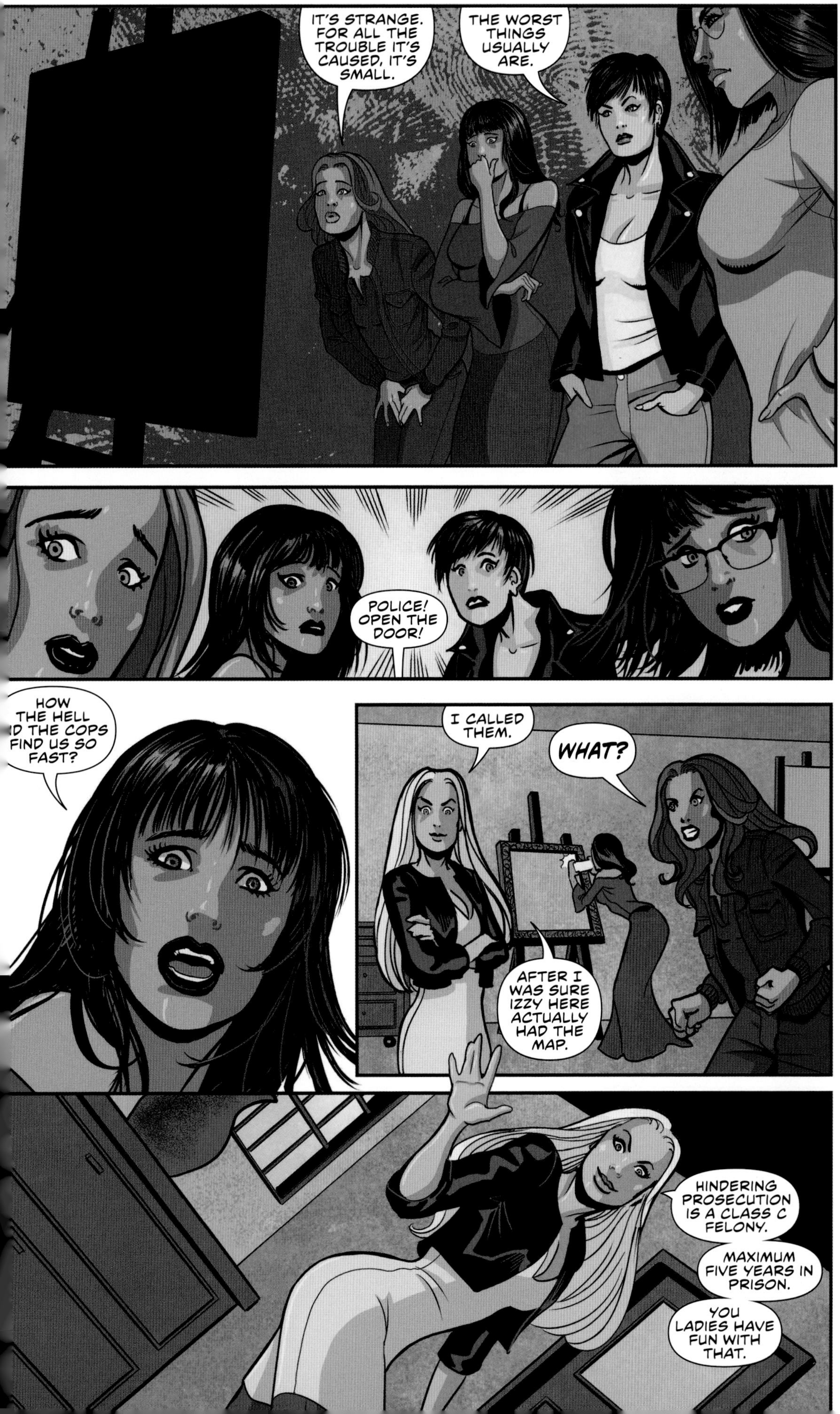
IT'S STRANGE. FOR ALL THE TROUBLE IT'S CAUSED, IT'S SMALL.
THE WORST THINGS USUALLY ARE.
POLICE! OPEN THE DOOR!
HOW THE HELL ID THE COPS FIND US SO FAST?
I CALLED THEM.
WHAT?
AFTER I WAS SURE IZZY HERE ACTUALLY HAD THE MAP.
HINDERING PROSECUTION IS A CLASS C FELONY.
MAXIMUM FIVE YEARS IN PRISON.
YOU LADIES HAVE FUN WITH THAT.

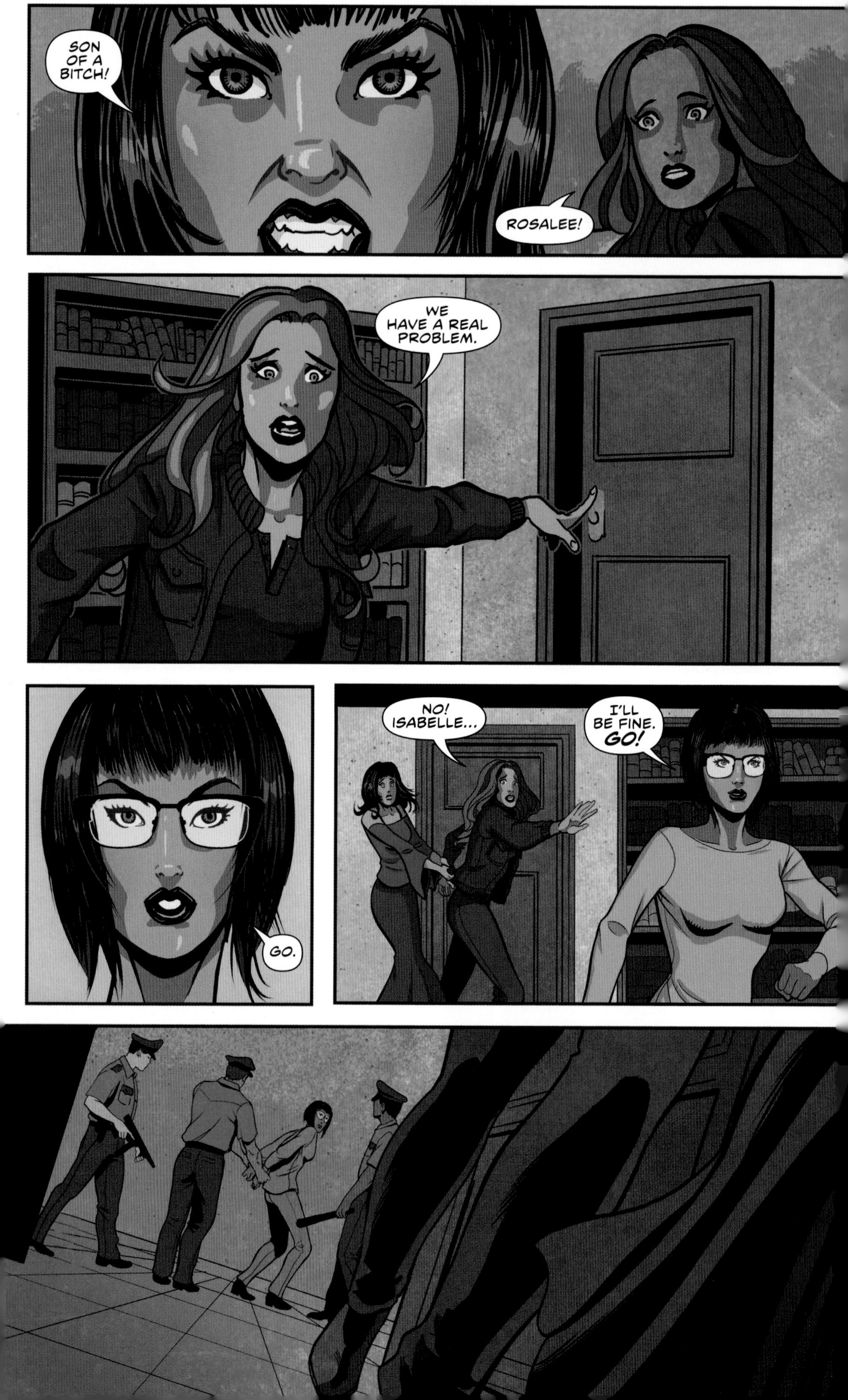
SON OF A BITCH!
ROSALEE!
WE HAVE A REAL PROBLEM.
GO.
NO! ISABELLE...
I'LL BE FINE. GO!

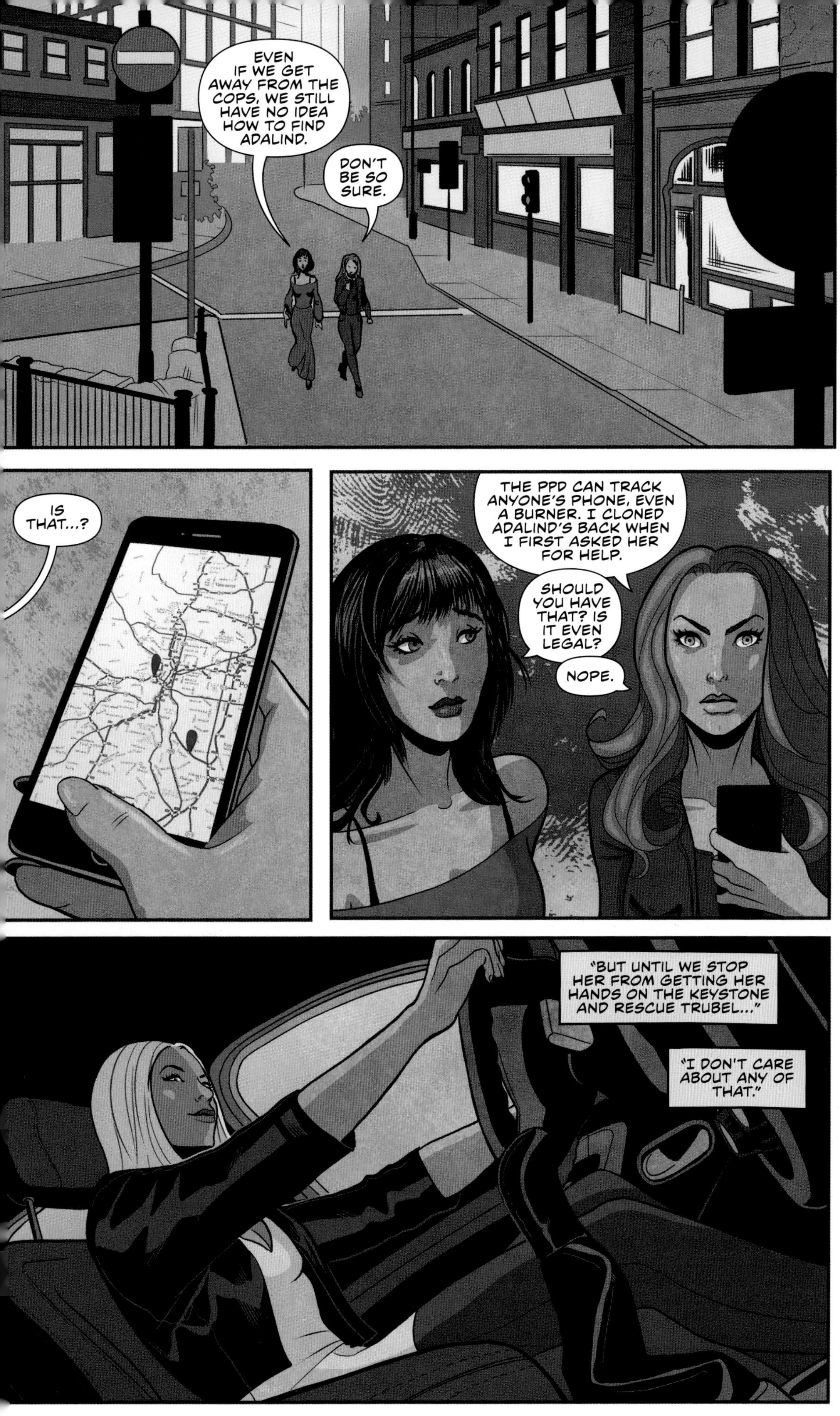

EVEN IF WE GET AWAY FROM THE COPS, WE STILL HAVE NO IDEA HOW TO FIND ADALIND.
DON'T BE SO SURE.
IS THAT...?
THE PPD CAN TRACK ANYONE'S PHONE, EVEN A BURNER. I CLONED ADALIND'S BACK WHEN I FIRST ASKED HER FOR HELP.
SHOULD YOU HAVE THAT? IS IT EVEN LEGAL?
NOPE.
"BUT UNTIL WE STOP HER FROM GETTING HER HANDS ON THE KEYSTONE AND RESCUE TRUBEL..."
"I DON'T CARE ABOUT ANY OF THAT."

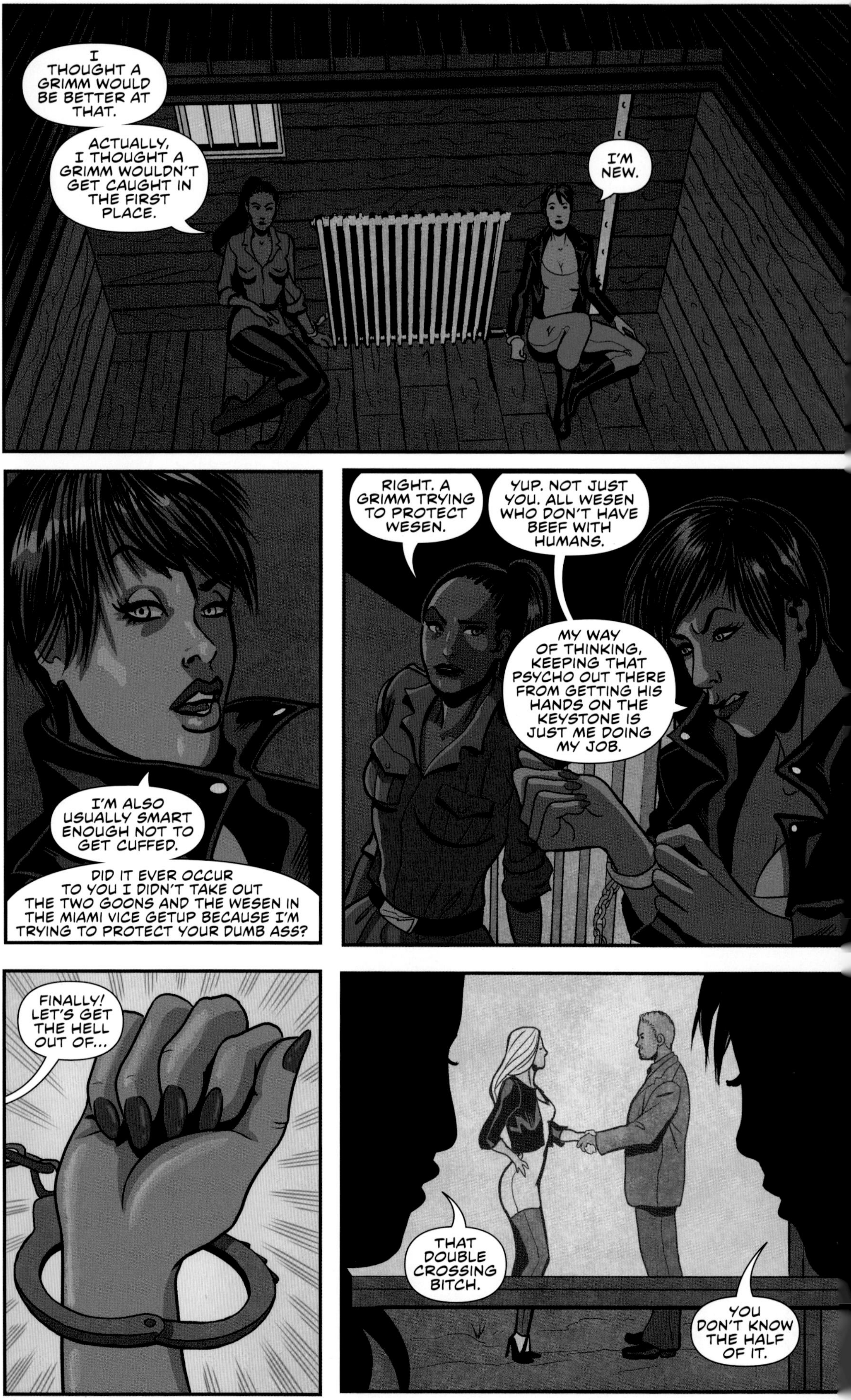
I THOUGHT A GRIMM WOULD BE BETTER AT THAT.
ACTUALLY, I THOUGHT A GRIMM WOULDN'T GET CAUGHT IN THE FIRST PLACE.
I'M NEW.
I'M ALSO USUALLY SMART ENOUGH NOT TO GET CUFFED.
DID IT EVER OCCUR TO YOU I DIDN'T TAKE OUT THE TWO GOONS AND THE WESEN IN THE MIAMI VICE GETUP BECAUSE I'M TRYING TO PROTECT YOUR DUMB ASS?
RIGHT. A GRIMM TRYING TO PROTECT WESEN.
YUP. NOT JUST YOU. ALL WESEN WHO DON'T HAVE BEEF WITH HUMANS.
MY WAY OF THINKING, KEEPING THAT PSYCHO OUT THERE FROM GETTING HIS HANDS ON THE KEYSTONE IS JUST ME DOING MY JOB.
FINALLY! LET'S GET THE HELL OUT OF...
THAT DOUBLE CROSSING BITCH.
YOU DON'T KNOW THE HALF OF IT.

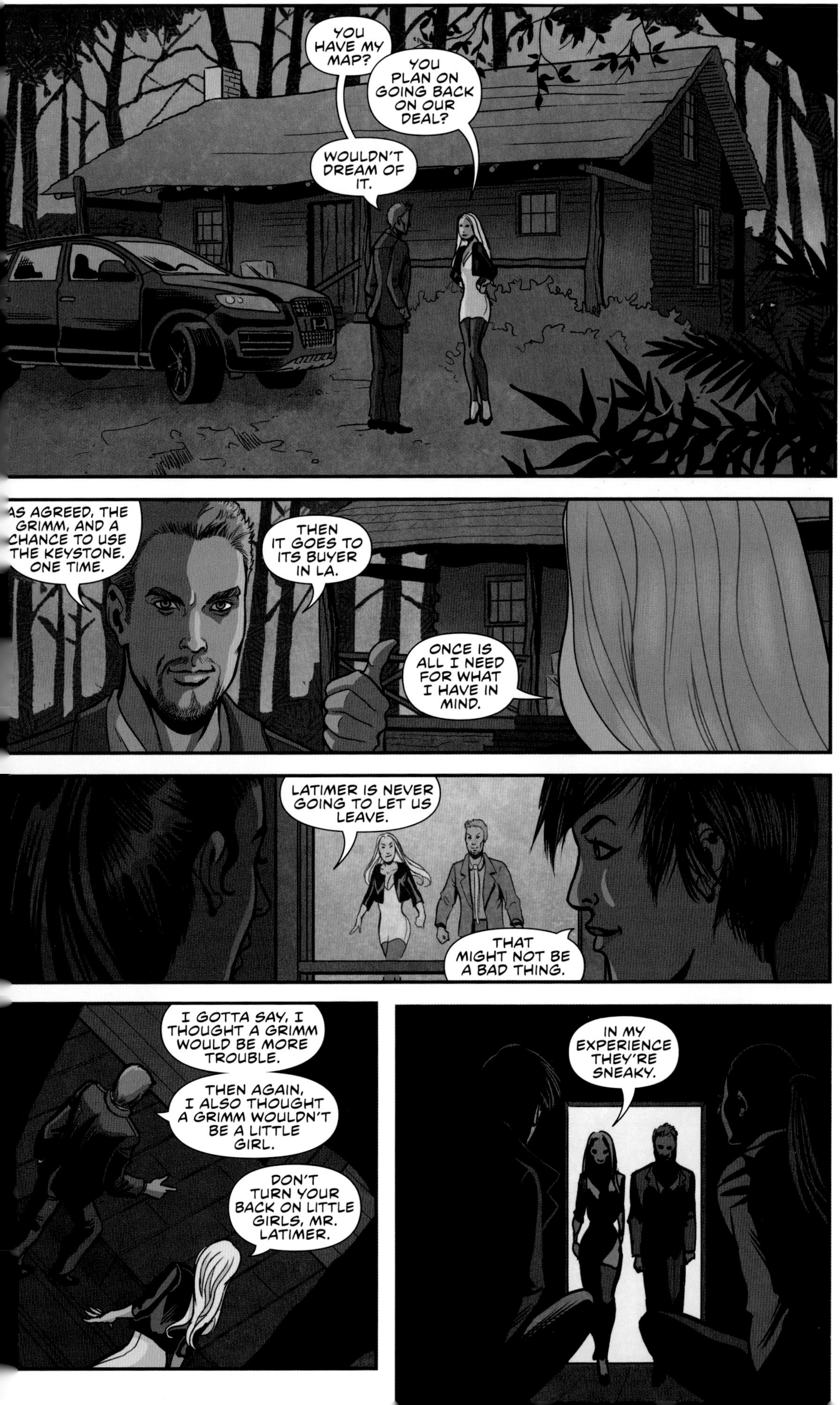
YOU HAVE MY MAP?
WOULDN'T DREAM OF IT.
YOU PLAN ON GOING BACK ON OUR DEAL?
AS AGREED, THE GRIMM, AND A CHANCE TO USE THE KEYSTONE. ONE TIME.
THEN IT GOES TO ITS BUYER IN LA.
ONCE IS ALL I NEED FOR WHAT I HAVE IN MIND.
LATIMER IS NEVER GOING TO LET US LEAVE.
THAT MIGHT NOT BE A BAD THING.
I GOTTA SAY, I THOUGHT A GRIMM WOULD BE MORE TROUBLE.
THEN AGAIN, I ALSO THOUGHT A GRIMM WOULDN'T BE A LITTLE GIRL.
DON'T TURN YOUR BACK ON LITTLE GIRLS, MR. LATIMER.
IN MY EXPERIENCE THEY'RE SNEAKY.

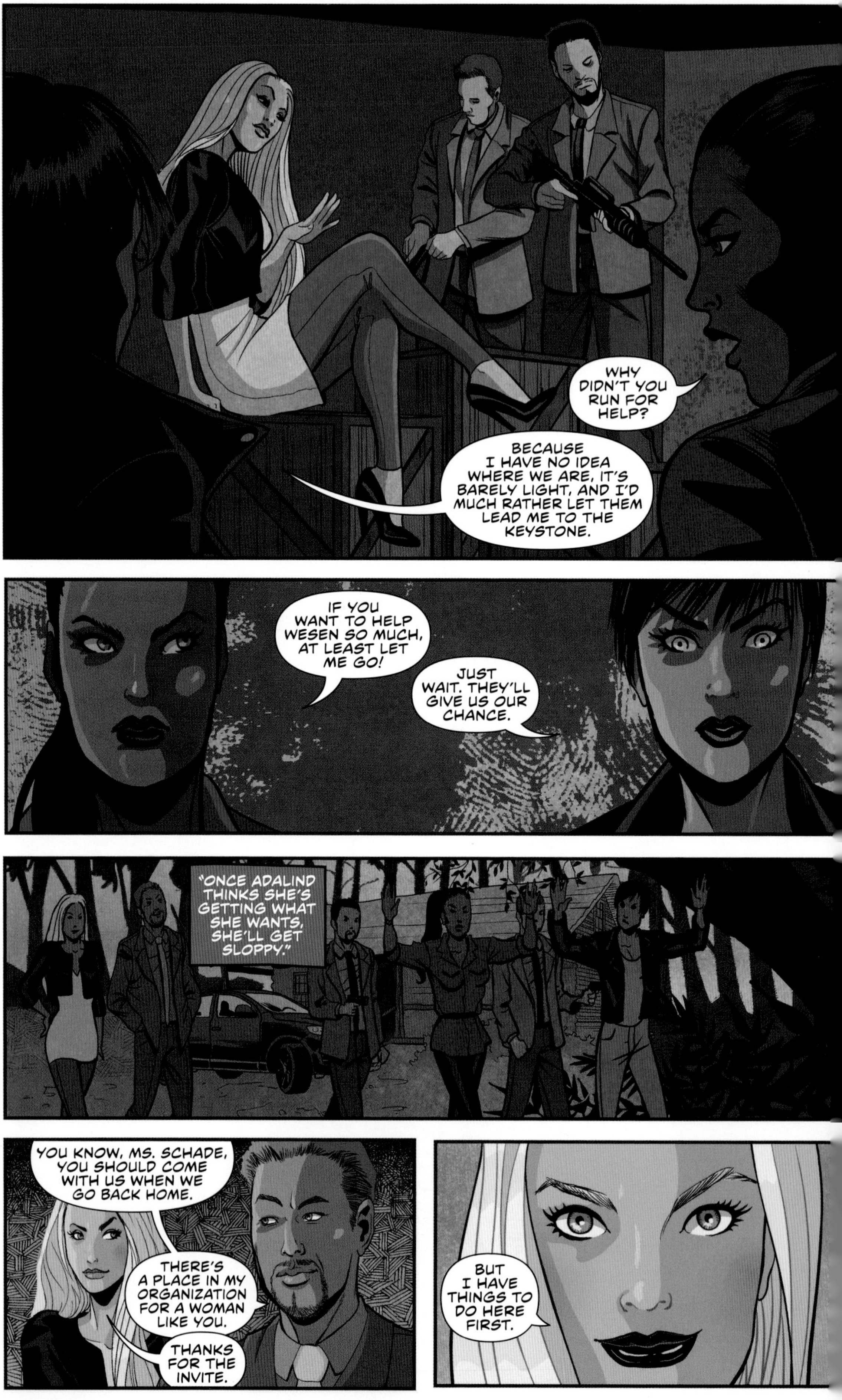

WHY DIDN'T YOU RUN FOR HELP?
BECAUSE I HAVE NO IDEA WHERE WE ARE, IT'S BARELY LIGHT, AND I'D MUCH RATHER LET THEM LEAD ME TO THE KEYSTONE.
IF YOU WANT TO HELP WESEN SO MUCH, AT LEAST LET ME GO!
JUST WAIT. THEY'LL GIVE US OUR CHANCE.
"ONCE ADALIND THINKS SHE'S GETTING WHAT SHE WANTS, SHE'LL GET SLOPPY."
YOU KNOW, MS. SCHADE, YOU SHOULD COME WITH US WHEN WE GO BACK HOME.
THERE'S A PLACE IN MY ORGANIZATION FOR A WOMAN LIKE YOU.
THANKS FOR THE INVITE.
BUT I HAVE THINGS TO DO HERE FIRST.

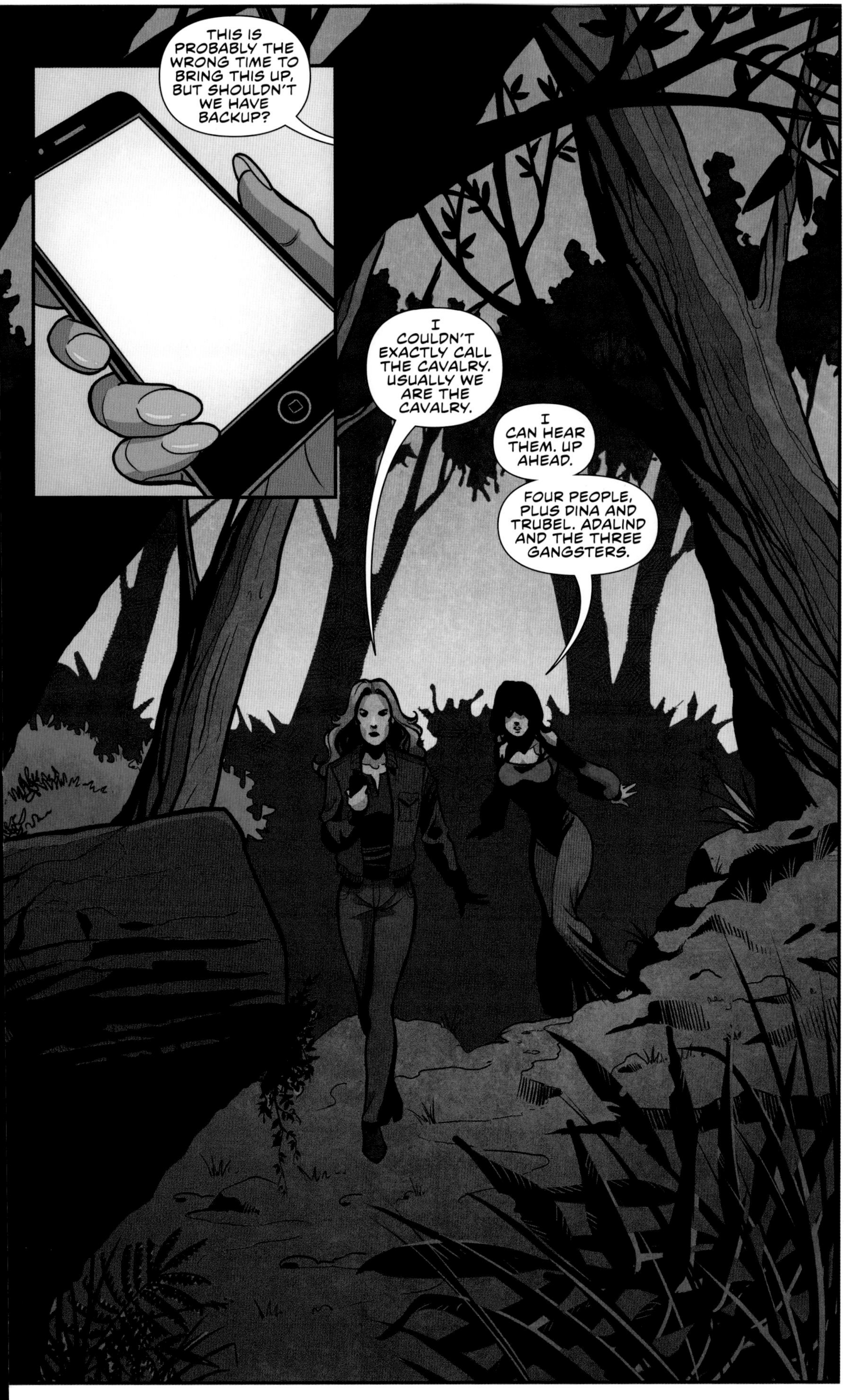
THIS IS PROBABLY THE WRONG TIME TO BRING THIS UP, BUT SHOULDN'T WE HAVE BACKUP?
I COULDN'T EXACTLY CALL THE CAVALRY. USUALLY WE ARE THE CAVALRY.
I CAN HEAR THEM. UP AHEAD.
FOUR PEOPLE, PLUS DINA AND TRUBEL. ADALIND AND THE THREE GANGSTERS.

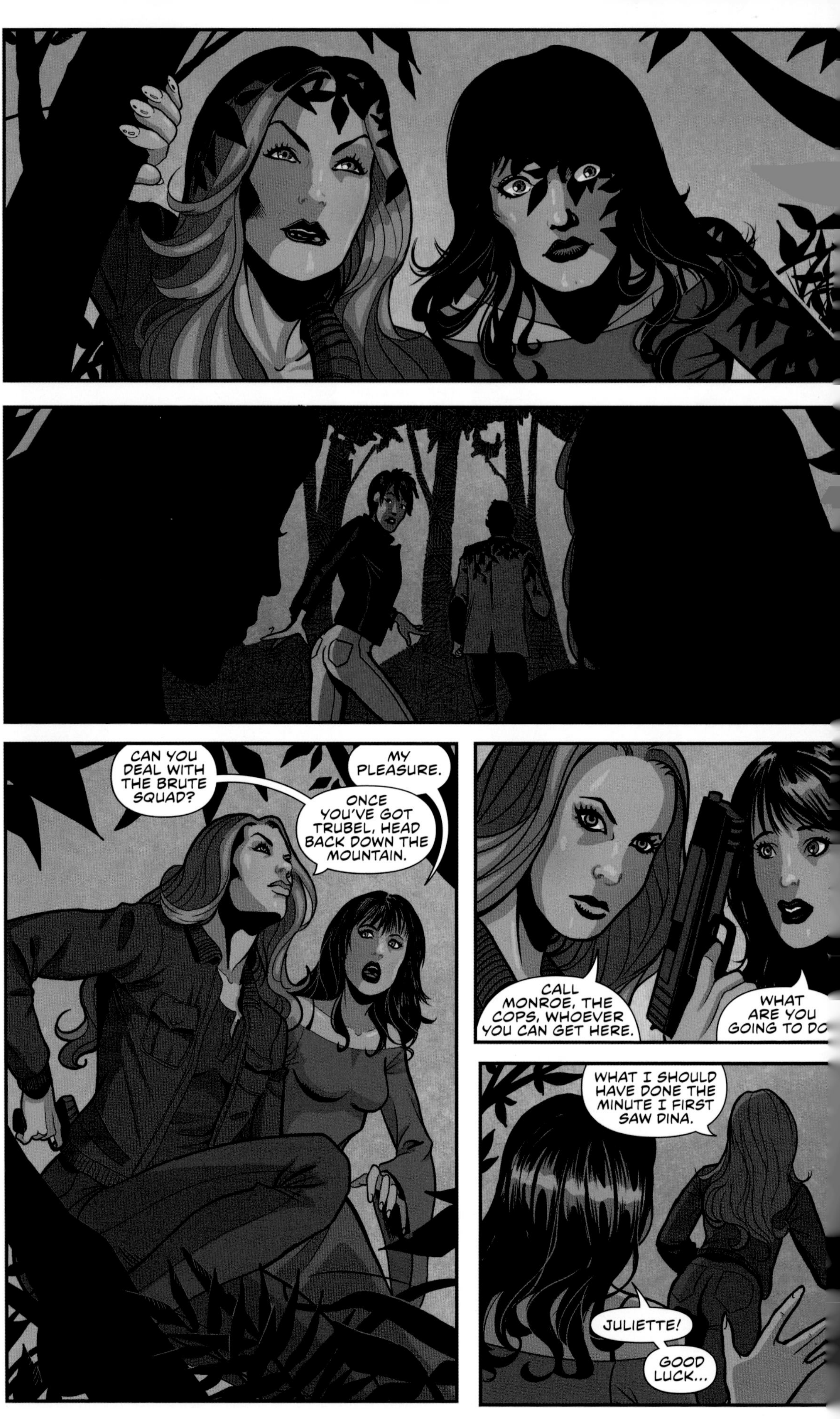

CAN YOU DEAL WITH THE BRUTE SQUAD?
MY PLEASURE.
ONCE YOU'VE GOT TRUBEL, HEAD BACK DOWN THE MOUNTAIN.
CALL MONROE, THE COPS, WHOEVER YOU CAN GET HERE.
WHAT ARE YOU GOING TO DO
WHAT I SHOULD HAVE DONE THE MINUTE I FIRST SAW DINA.
JULIETTE!
GOOD LUCK...

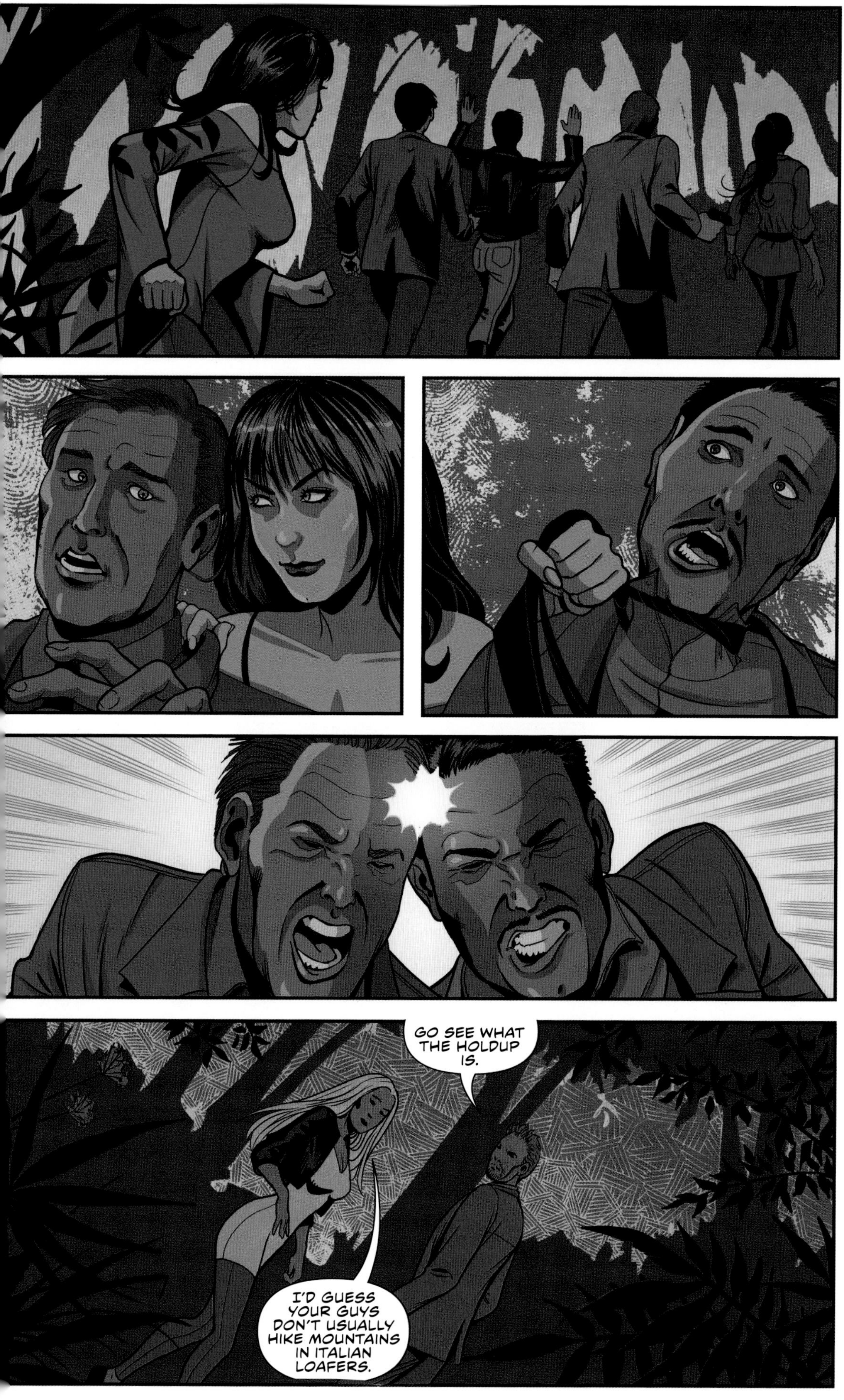
GO SEE WHAT THE HOLDUP IS.
I'D GUESS YOUR GUYS DON'T USUALLY HIKE MOUNTAINS IN ITALIAN LOAFERS.

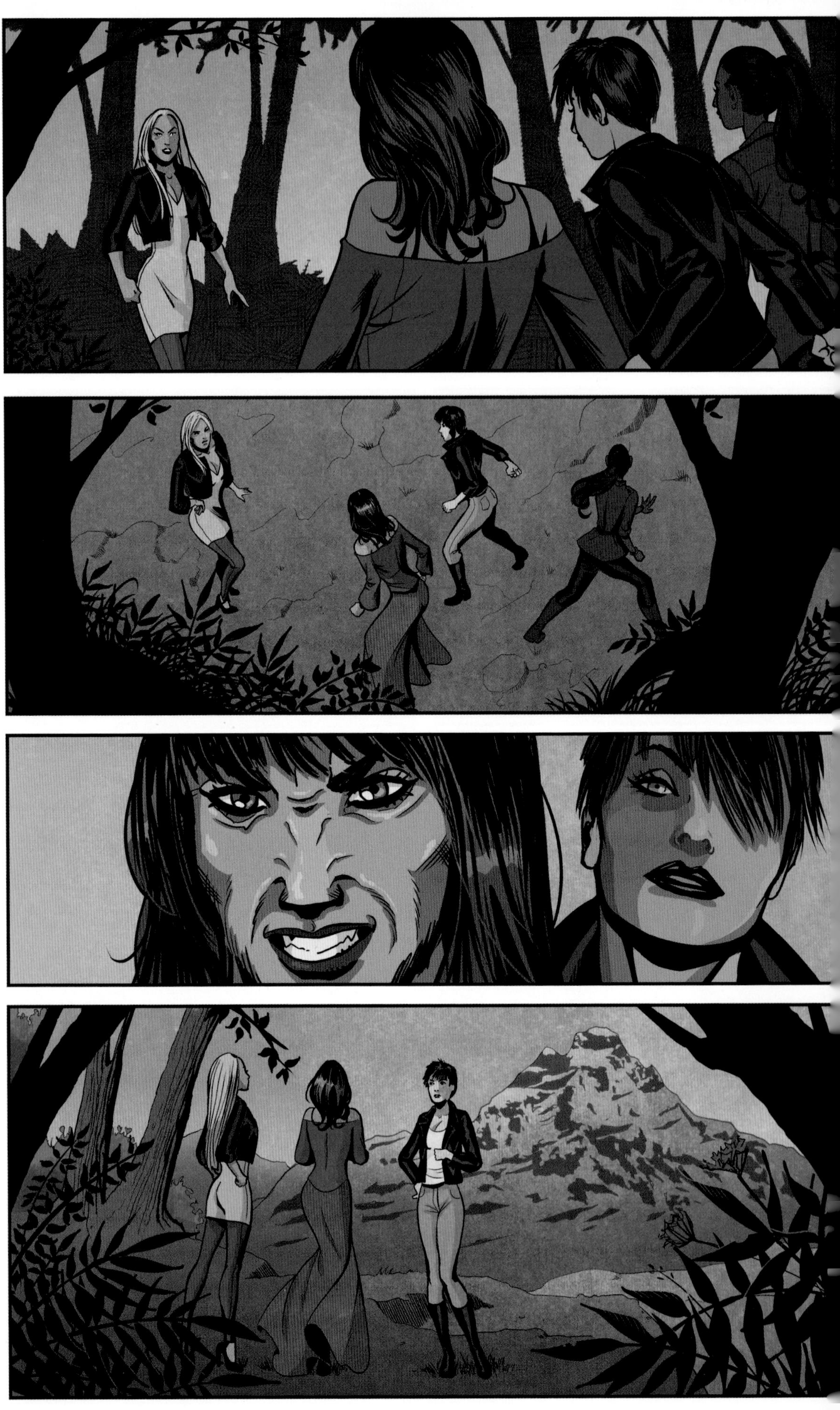

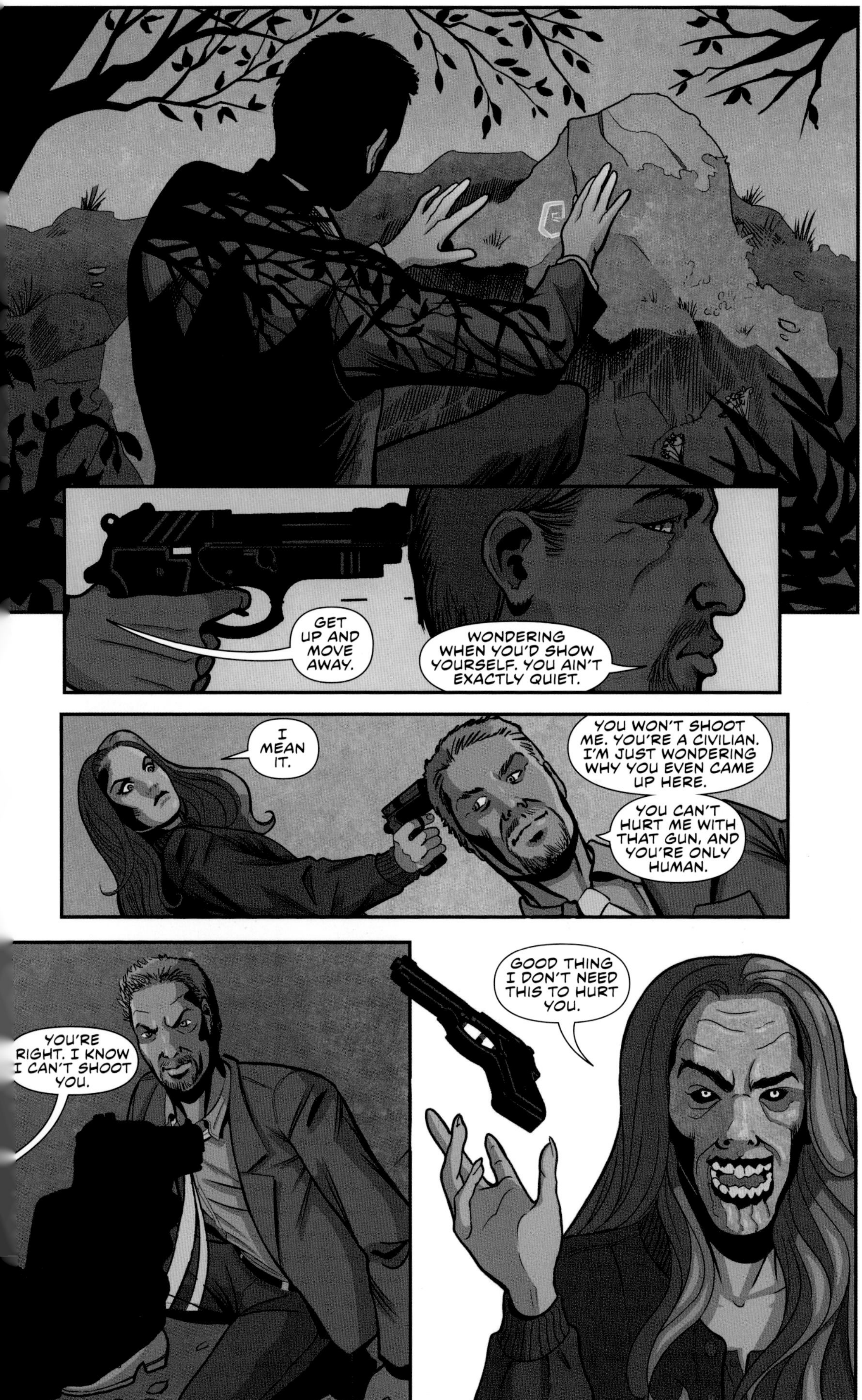
GET UP AND MOVE AWAY.
WONDERING WHEN YOU'D SHOW YOURSELF. YOU AIN'T EXACTLY QUIET.
I MEAN IT.
YOU WON'T SHOOT ME. YOU'RE A CIVILIAN. I'M JUST WONDERING WHY YOU EVEN CAME UP HERE.
YOU CAN'T HURT ME WITH THAT GUN, AND YOU'RE ONLY HUMAN.
YOU'RE RIGHT. I KNOW I CAN'T SHOOT YOU.
GOOD THING I DON'T NEED THIS TO HURT YOU.

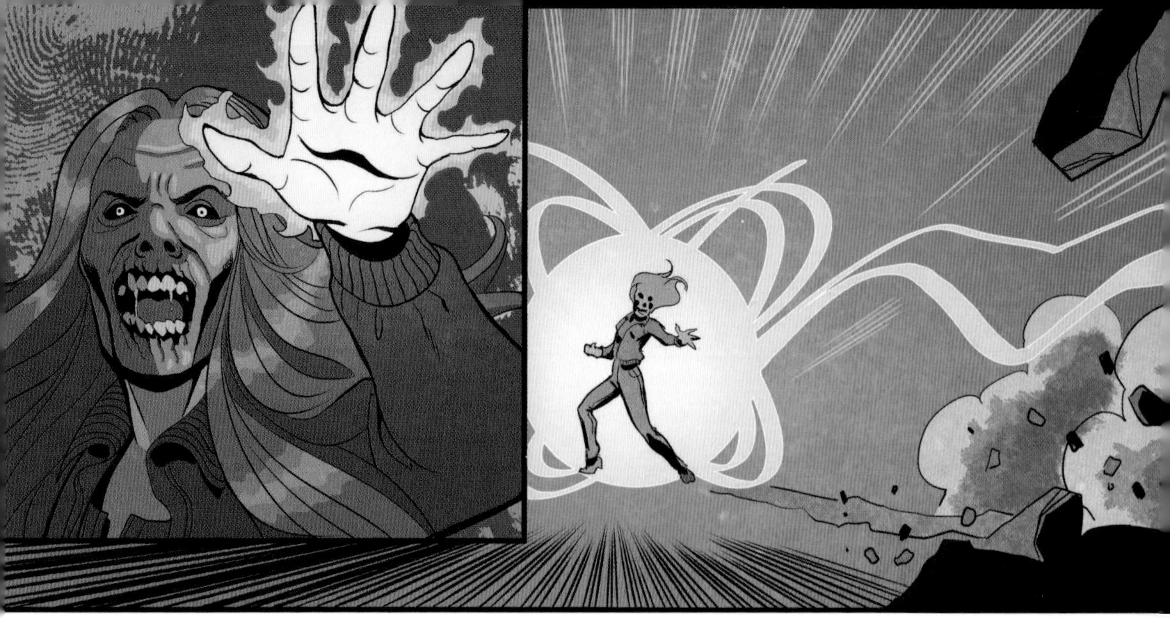

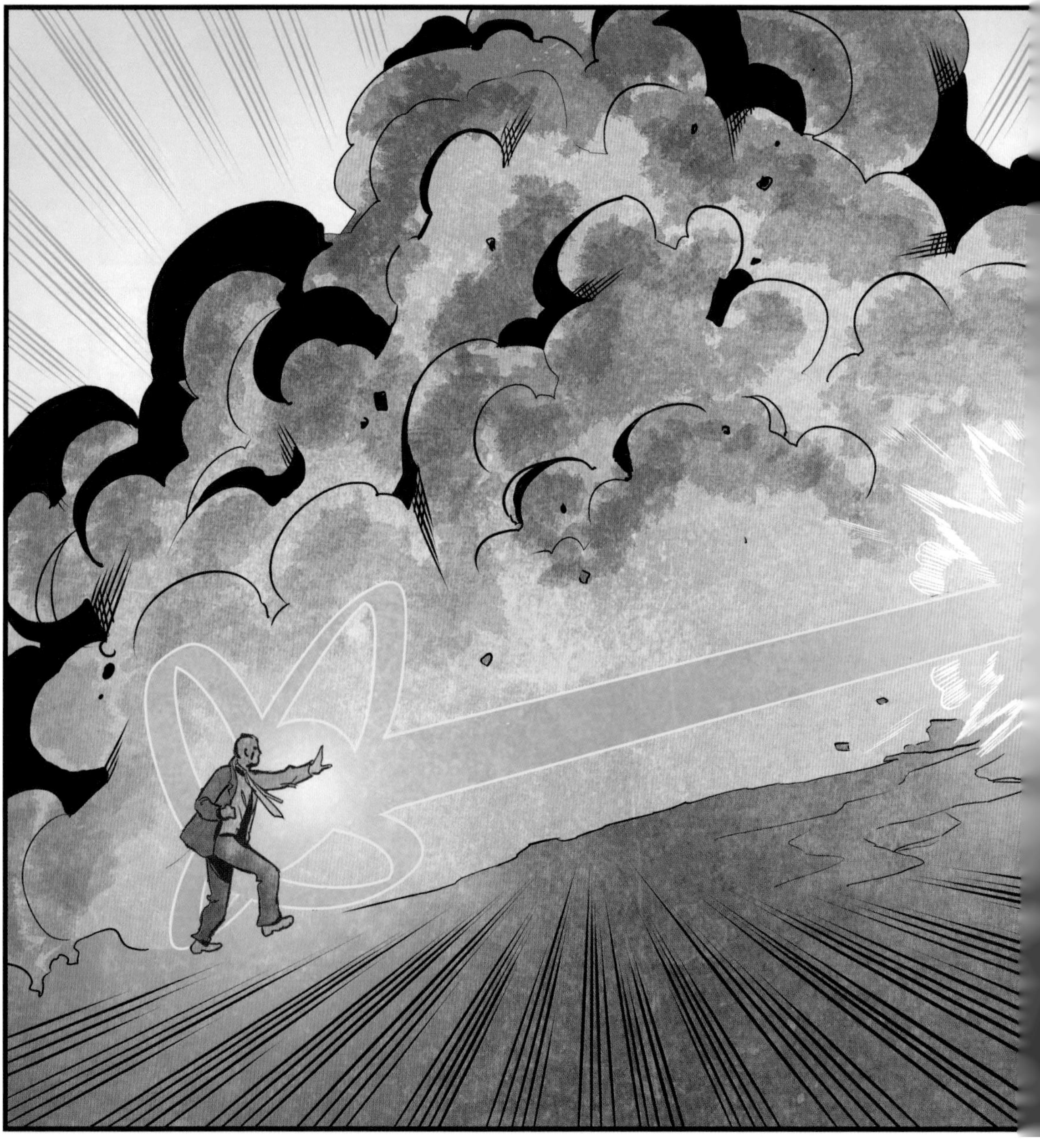

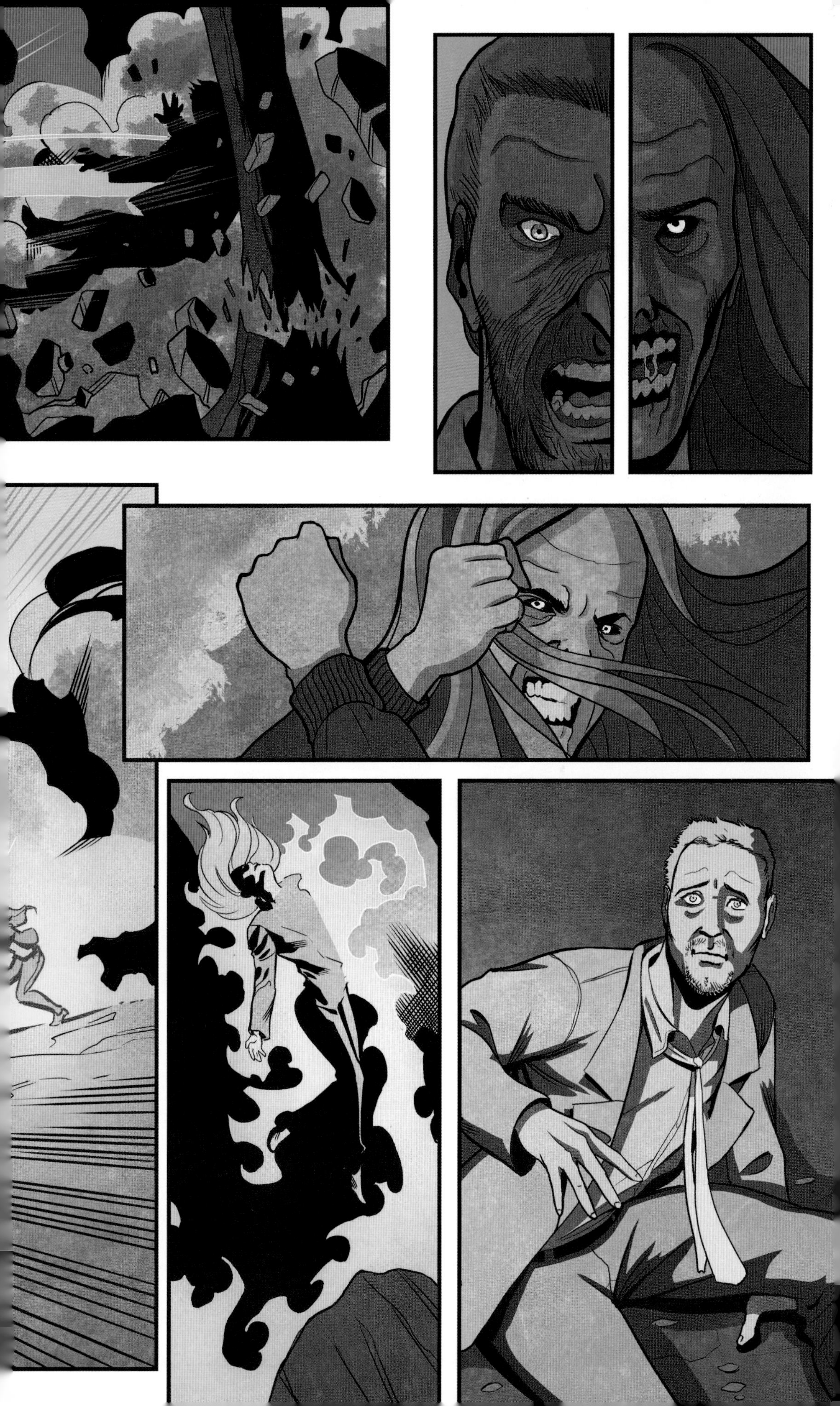

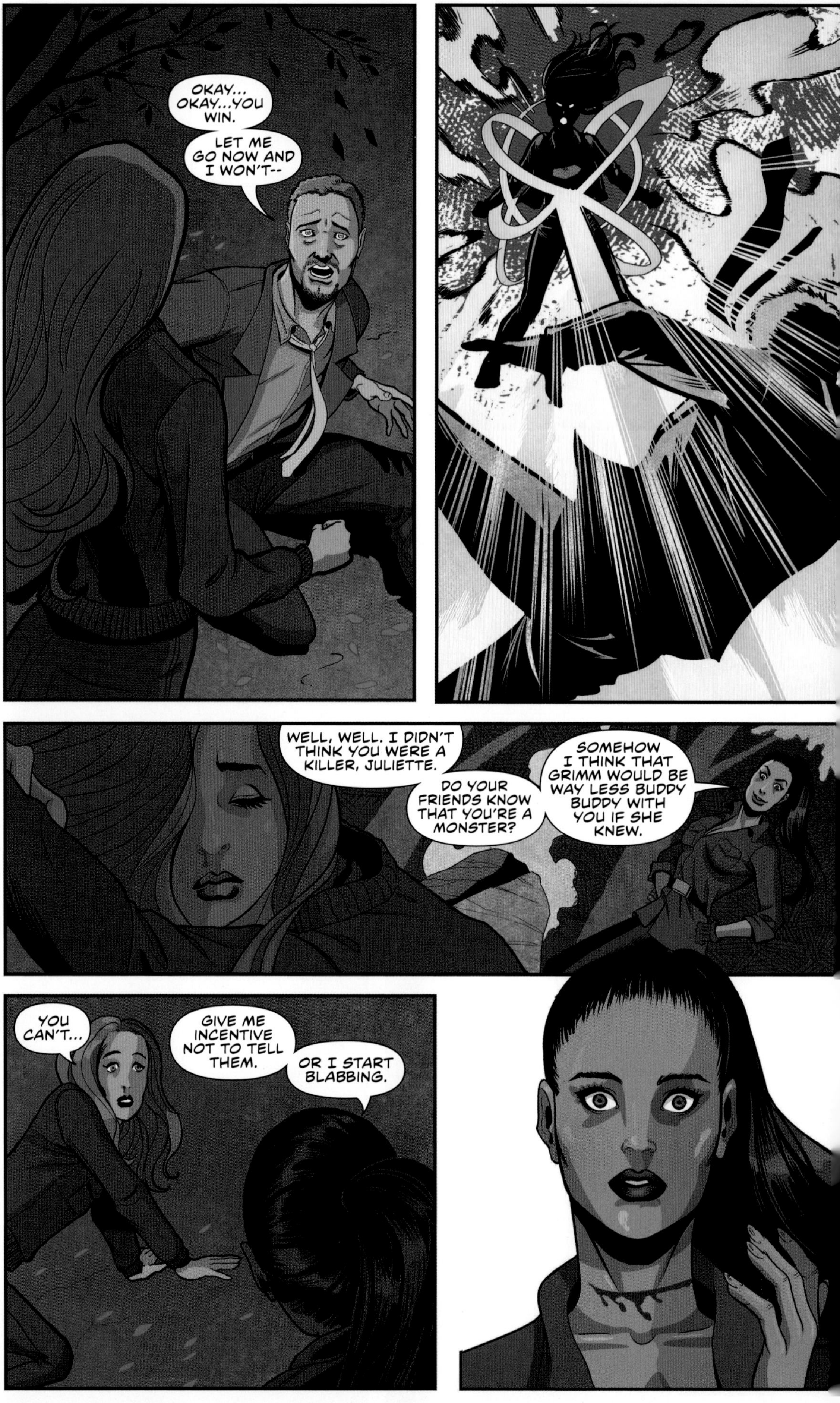
OKAY... OKAY...YOU WIN.
LET ME GO NOW AND I WON'T--
WELL, WELL. I DIDN'T THINK YOU WERE A KILLER, JULIETTE.
DO YOUR FRIENDS KNOW THAT YOU'RE A MONSTER?
SOMEHOW I THINK THAT GRIMM WOULD BE WAY LESS BUDDY BUDDY WITH YOU IF SHE KNEW.
YOU CAN'T...
GIVE ME INCENTIVE NOT TO TELL THEM.
OR I START BLABBING.

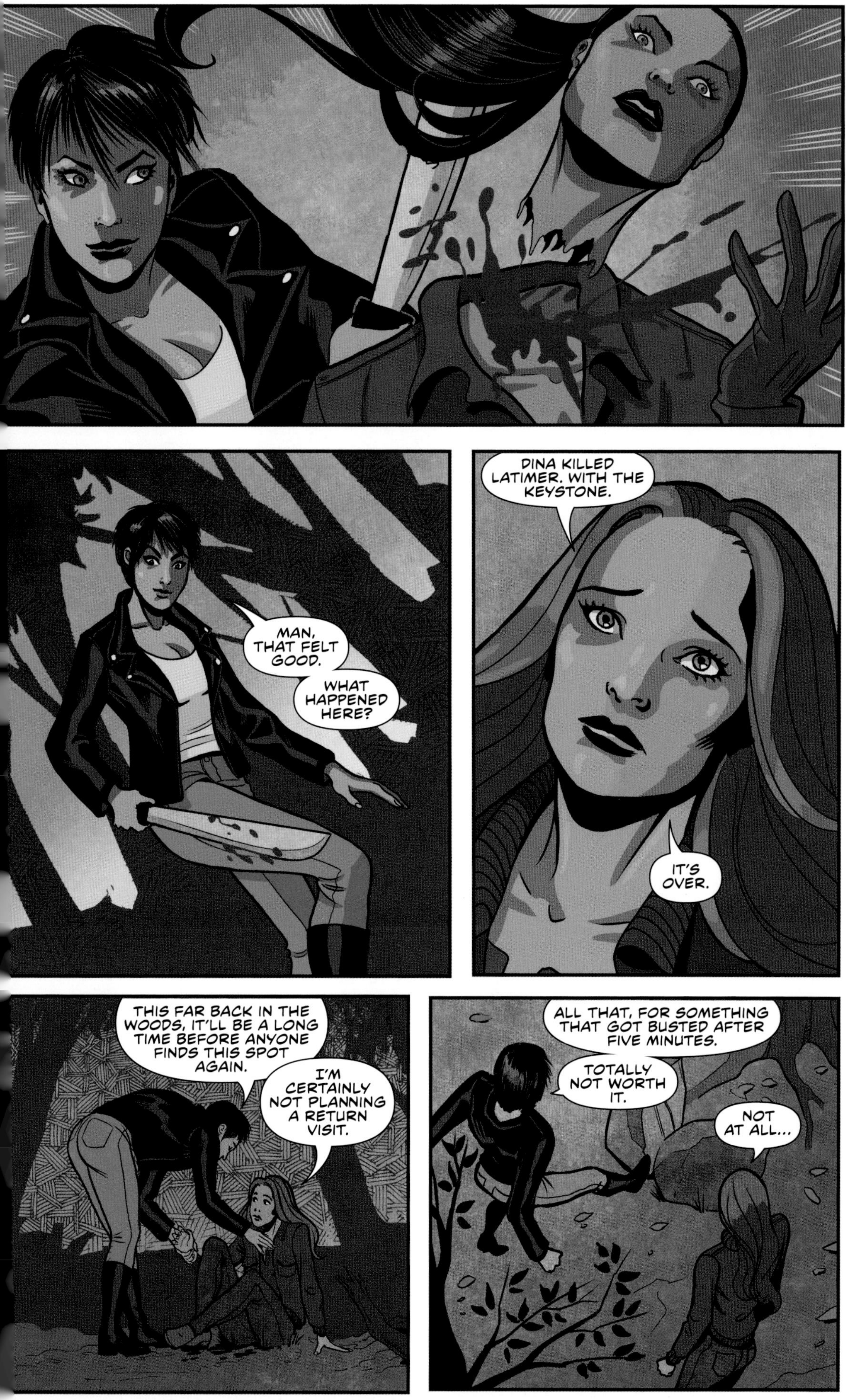
MAN, THAT FELT GOOD.
WHAT HAPPENED HERE?
DINA KILLED LATIMER. WITH THE KEYSTONE.
IT'S OVER.
THIS FAR BACK IN THE WOODS, IT'LL BE A LONG TIME BEFORE ANYONE FINDS THIS SPOT AGAIN.
I'M CERTAINLY NOT PLANNING A RETURN VISIT.
ALL THAT, FOR SOMETHING THAT GOT BUSTED AFTER FIVE MINUTES.
TOTALLY NOT WORTH IT.
NOT AT ALL...

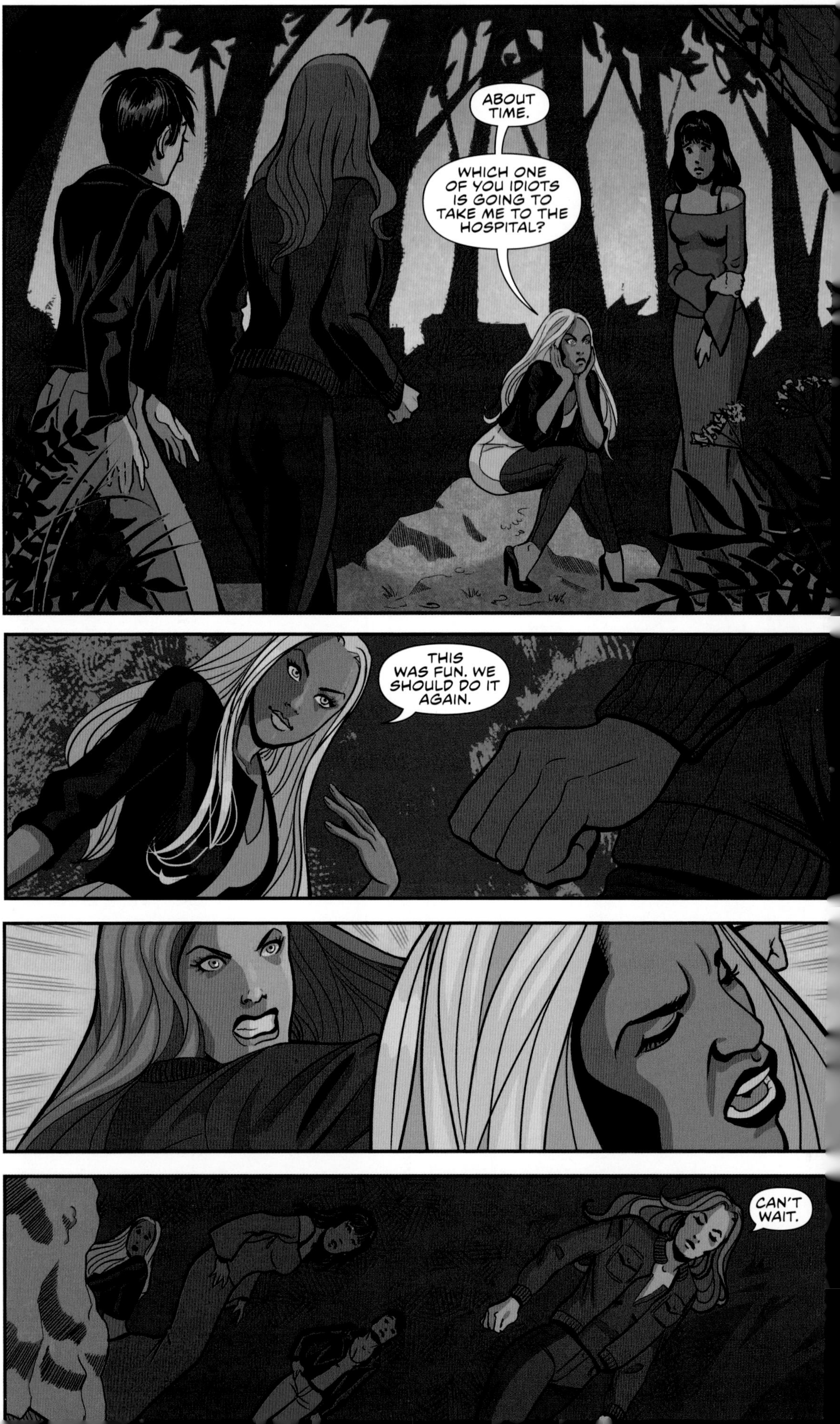
ABOUT TIME.
WHICH ONE OF YOU IDIOTS IS GOING TO TAKE ME TO THE HOSPITAL?
THIS WAS FUN. WE SHOULD DO IT AGAIN.
CAN'T WAIT.

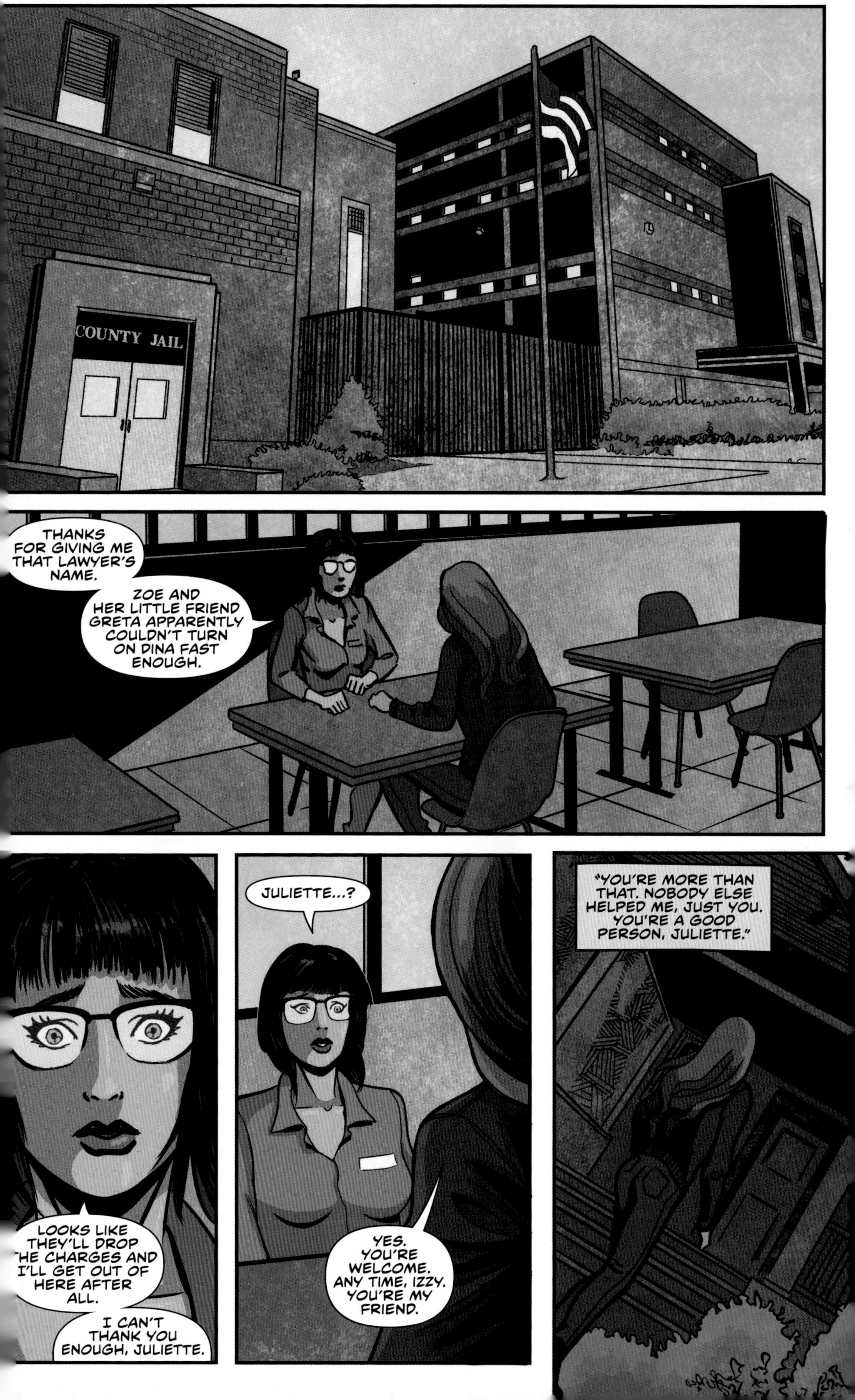
COUNTY JAIL
THANKS FOR GIVING ME THAT LAWYER'S NAME.
ZOE AND HER LITTLE FRIEND GRETA APPARENTLY COULDN'T TURN ON DINA FAST ENOUGH.
LOOKS LIKE THEY'LL DROP THE CHARGES AND I'LL GET OUT OF HERE AFTER ALL.
I CAN'T THANK YOU ENOUGH, JULIETTE.
JULIETTE...?
YES. YOU'RE WELCOME. ANY TIME, IZZY. YOU'RE MY FRIEND.
"YOU'RE MORE THAN THAT. NOBODY ELSE HELPED ME, JUST YOU. YOU'RE A GOOD PERSON, JULIETTE."

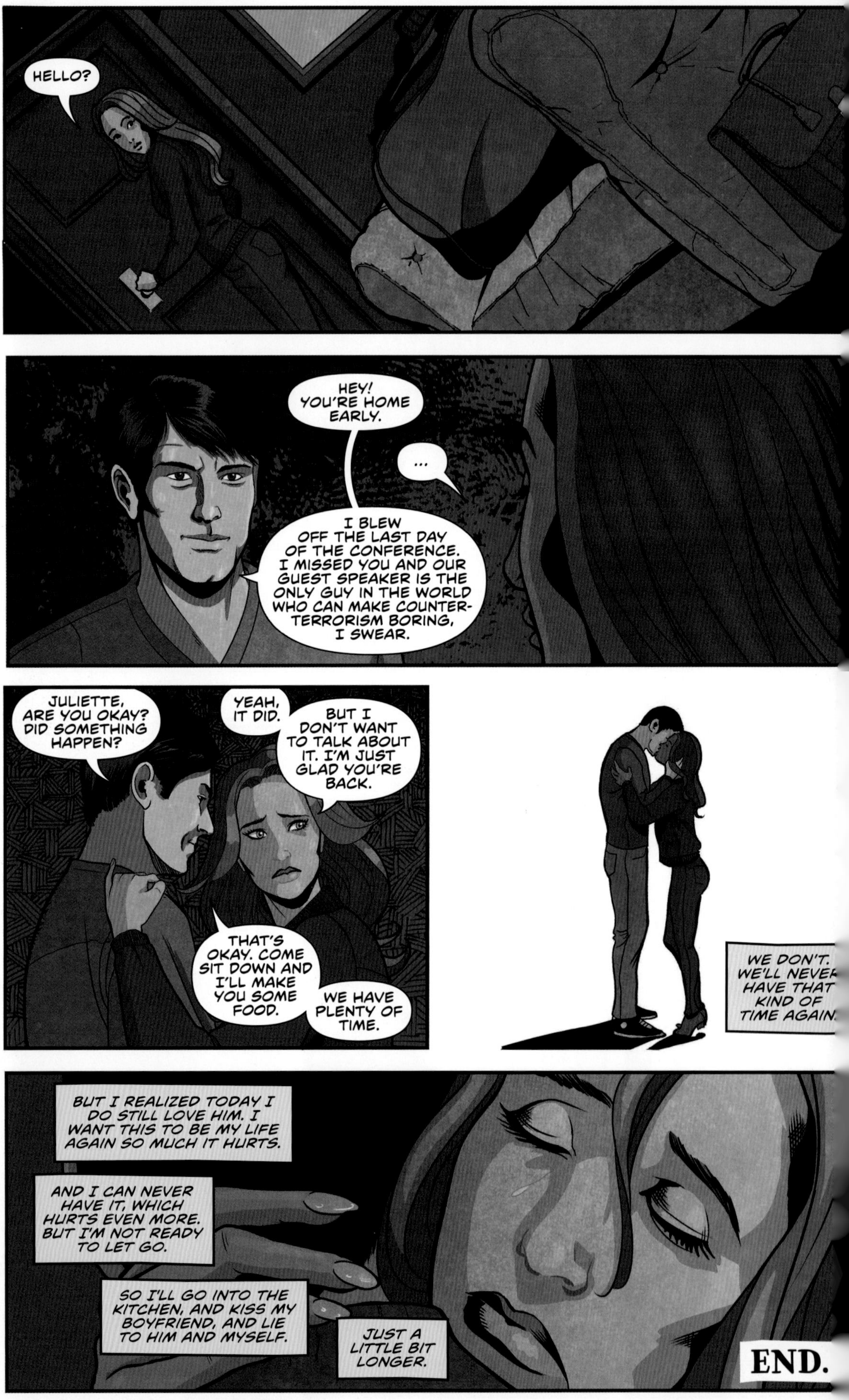
HELLO?
HEY! YOU'RE HOME EARLY.
...
I BLEW OFF THE LAST DAY OF THE CONFERENCE. I MISSED YOU AND OUR GUEST SPEAKER IS THE ONLY GUY IN THE WORLD WHO CAN MAKE COUNTER-TERRORISM BORING, I SWEAR.
JULIETTE, ARE YOU OKAY? DID SOMETHING HAPPEN?
YEAH, IT DID.
BUT I DON'T WANT TO TALK ABOUT IT. I'M JUST GLAD YOU'RE BACK.
THAT'S OKAY. COME SIT DOWN AND I'LL MAKE YOU SOME FOOD.
WE HAVE PLENTY OF TIME.
WE DON'T. WE'LL NEVER HAVE THAT KIND OF TIME AGAIN.
BUT I REALIZED TODAY I DO STILL LOVE HIM. I WANT THIS TO BE MY LIFE AGAIN SO MUCH IT HURTS.
AND I CAN NEVER HAVE IT, WHICH HURTS EVEN MORE. BUT I'M NOT READY TO LET GO.
SO I'LL GO INTO THE KITCHEN, AND KISS MY BOYFRIEND, AND LIE TO HIM AND MYSELF.
JUST A LITTLE BIT LONGER.
END.

VARIANT
COVER GALLERY

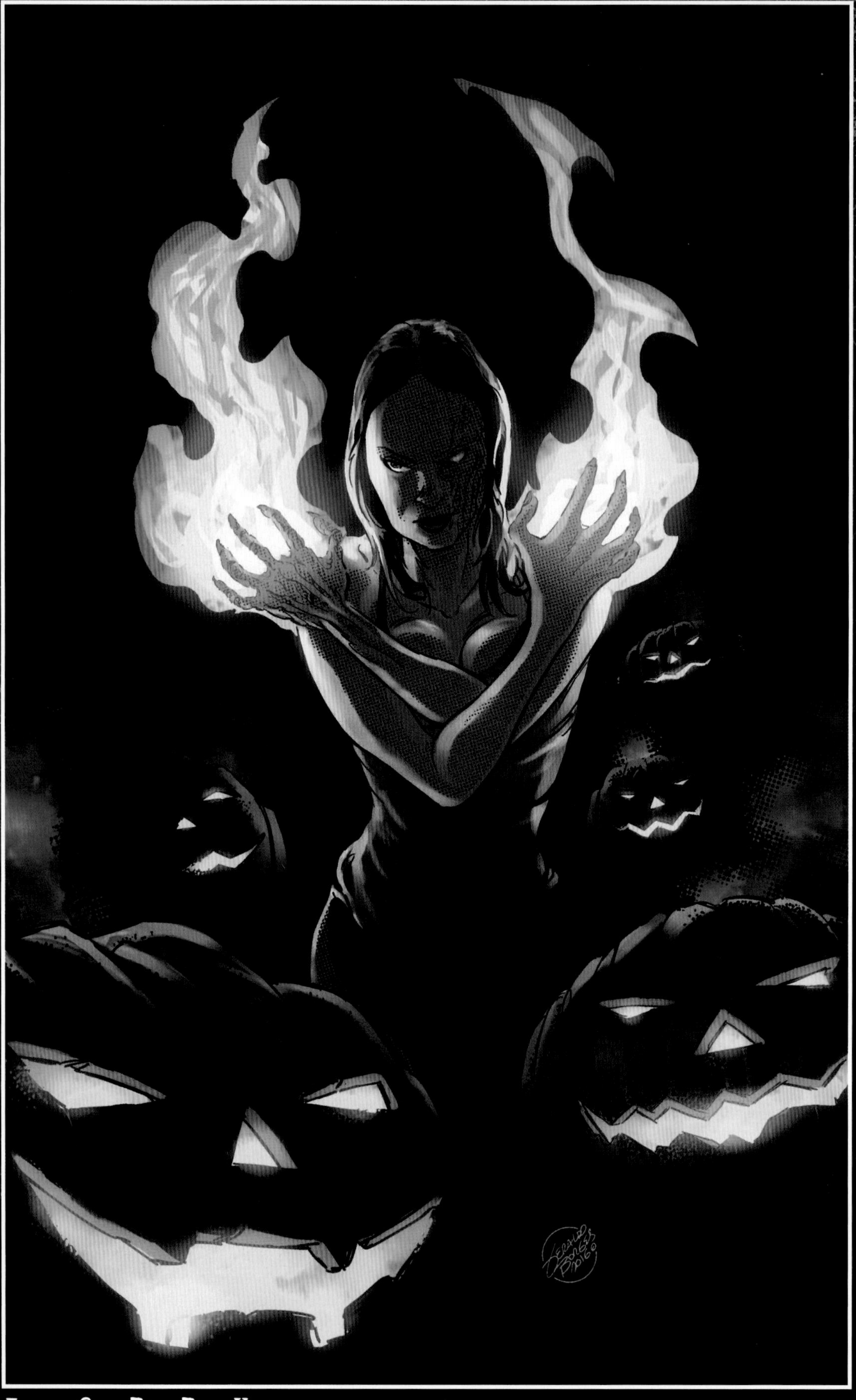

Issue One Bam Box Variant
Art by Geraldo Borges

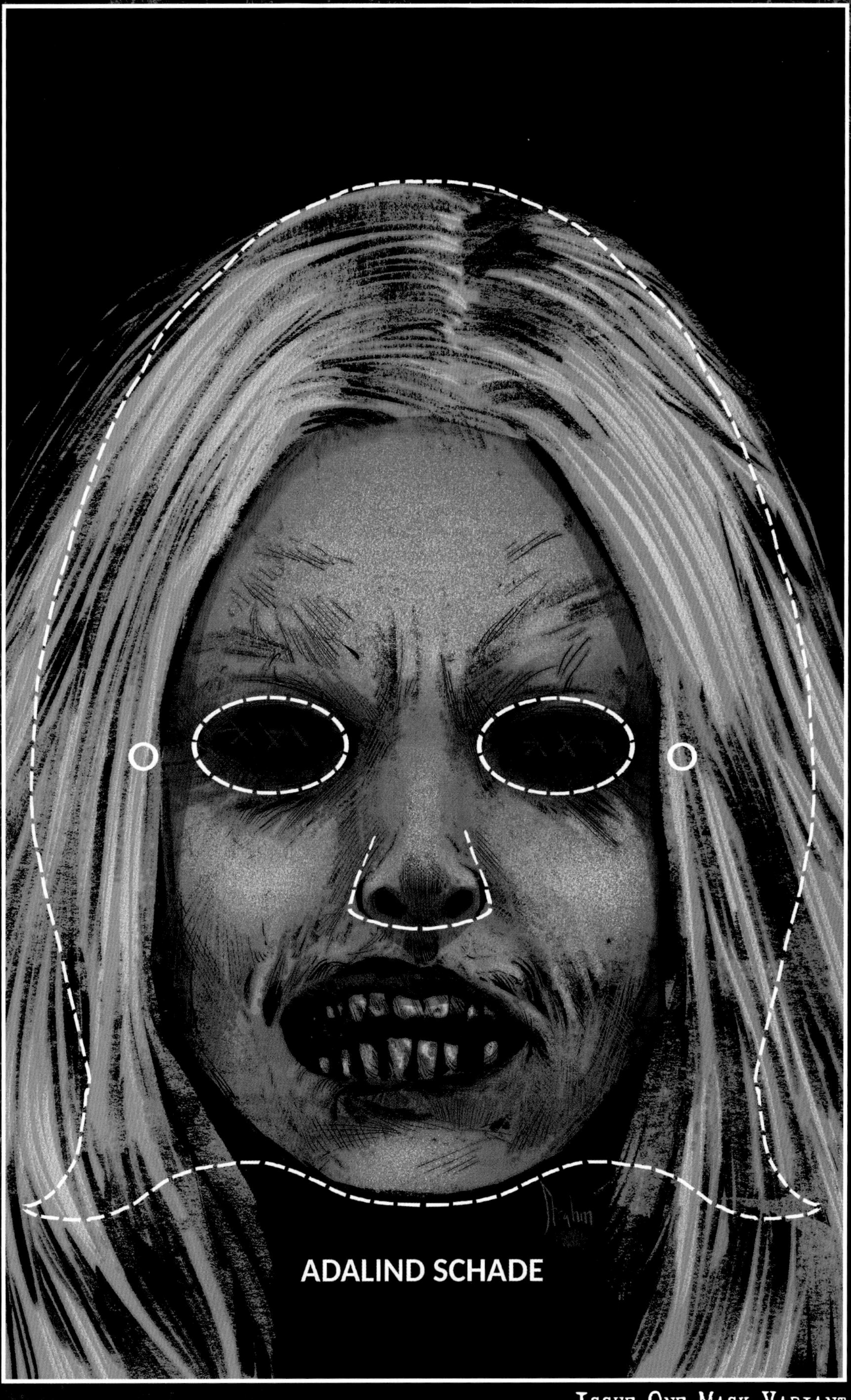
ADALIND SCHADE

Issue One Mask Variant

Art by Kyle Strahm | Colors by Greg Smallwood

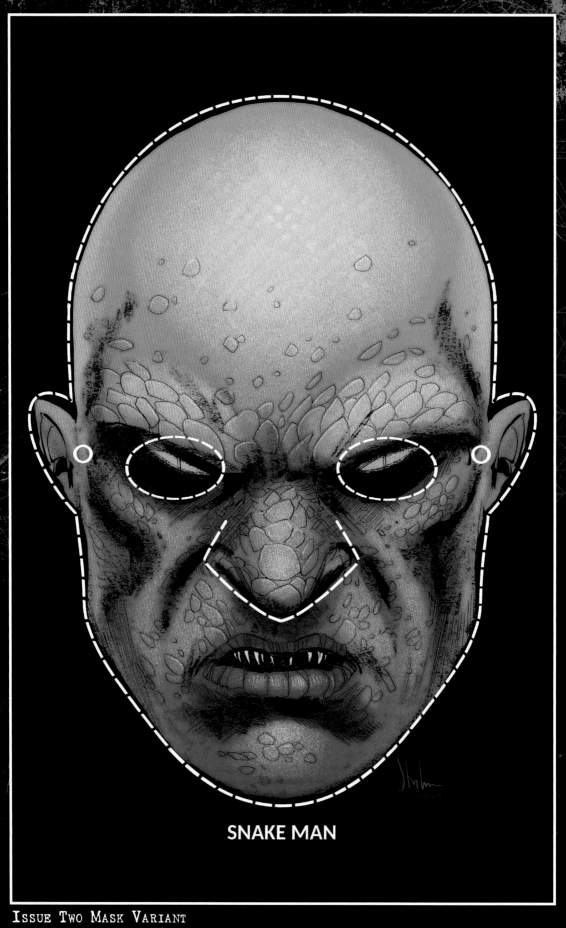

SNAKE MAN

ISSUE TWO MASK VARIANT
ART BY KYLE STRAHM | COLORS BY GREG SMALLWOOD

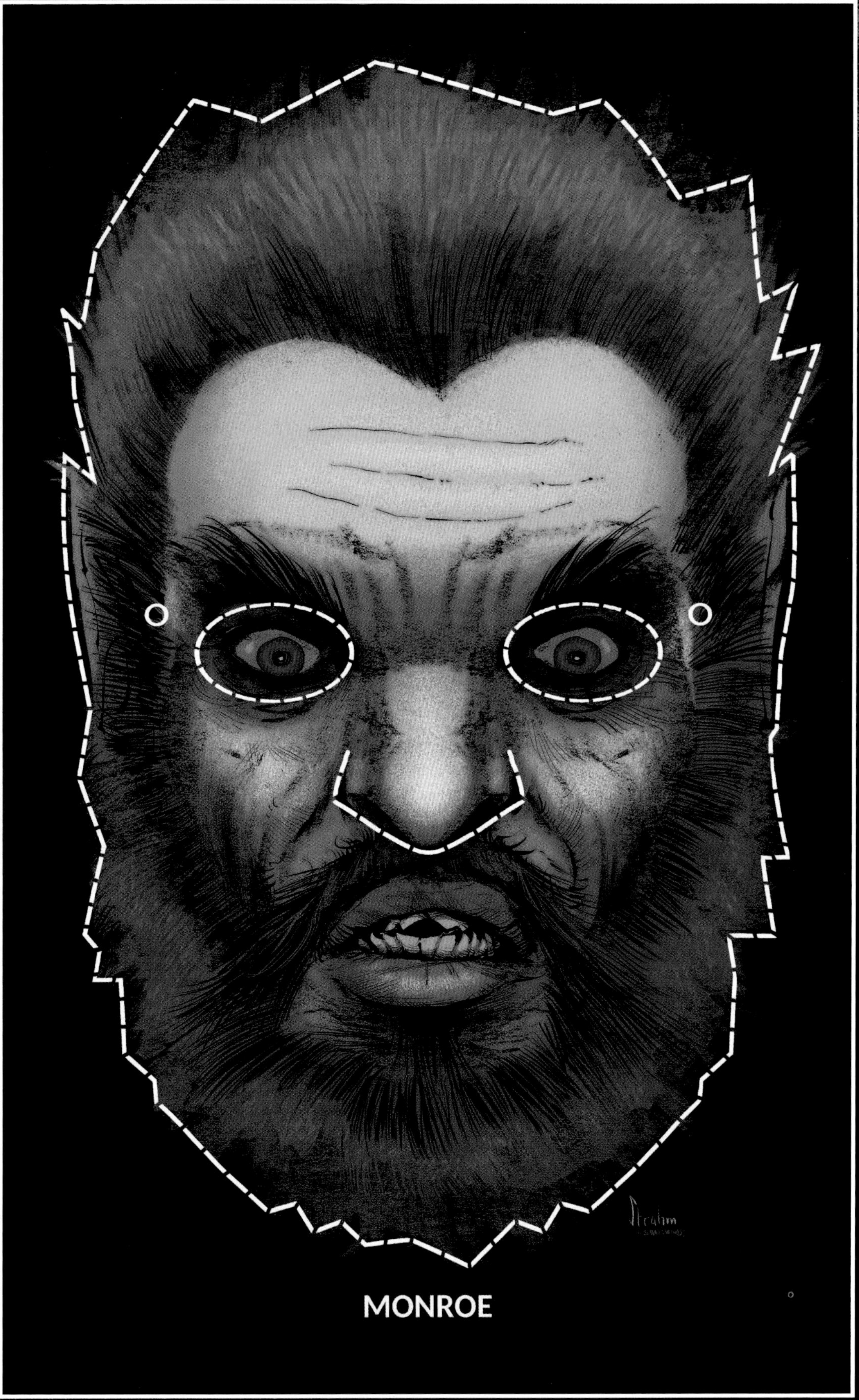

MONROE

Issue Three Mask Variant

Art by Kyle Strahm | Colors by Greg Smallwood

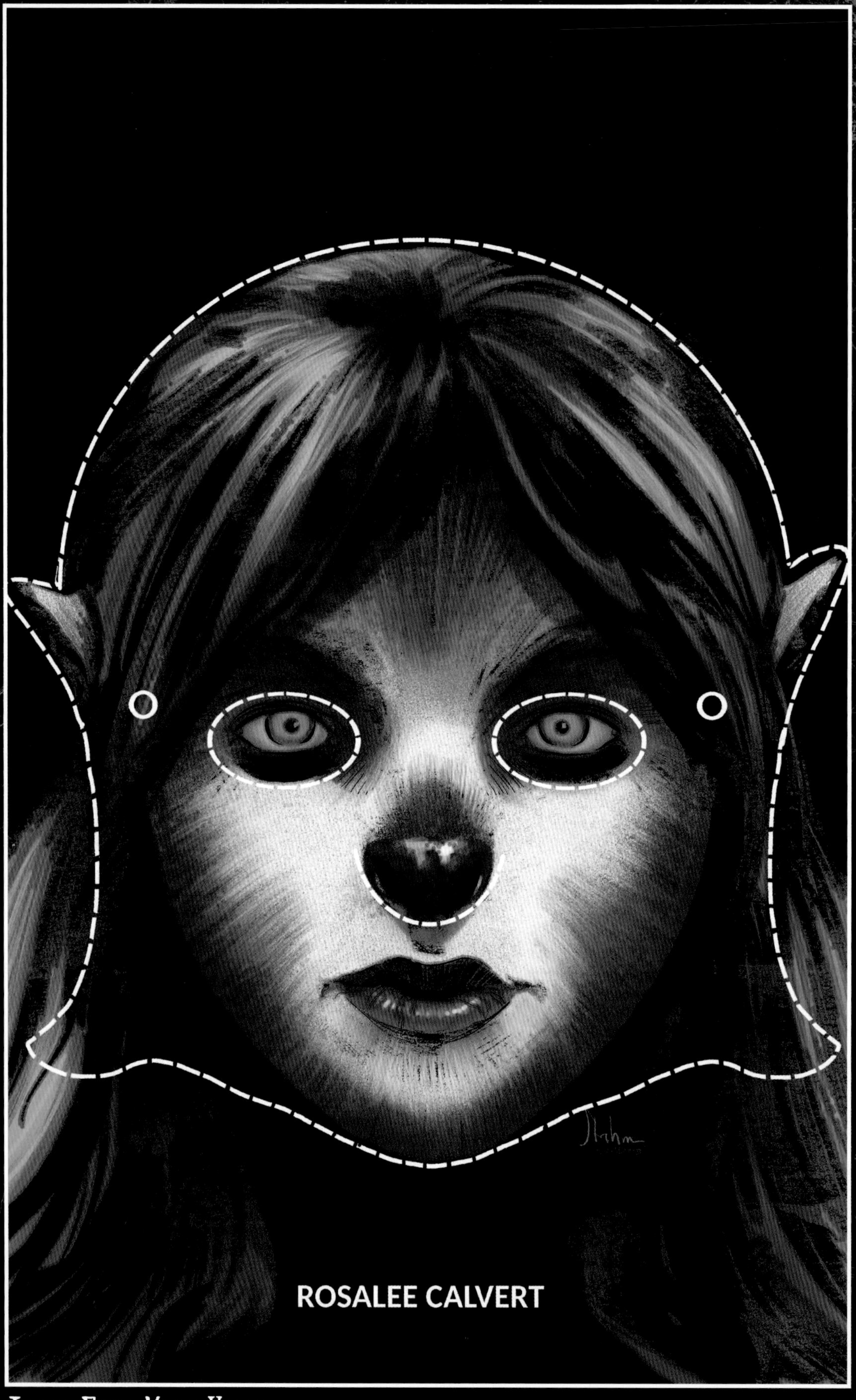
ROSALEE CALVERT

Issue Four Mask Variant
Art by Kyle Strahm | Colors by Greg Smallwood

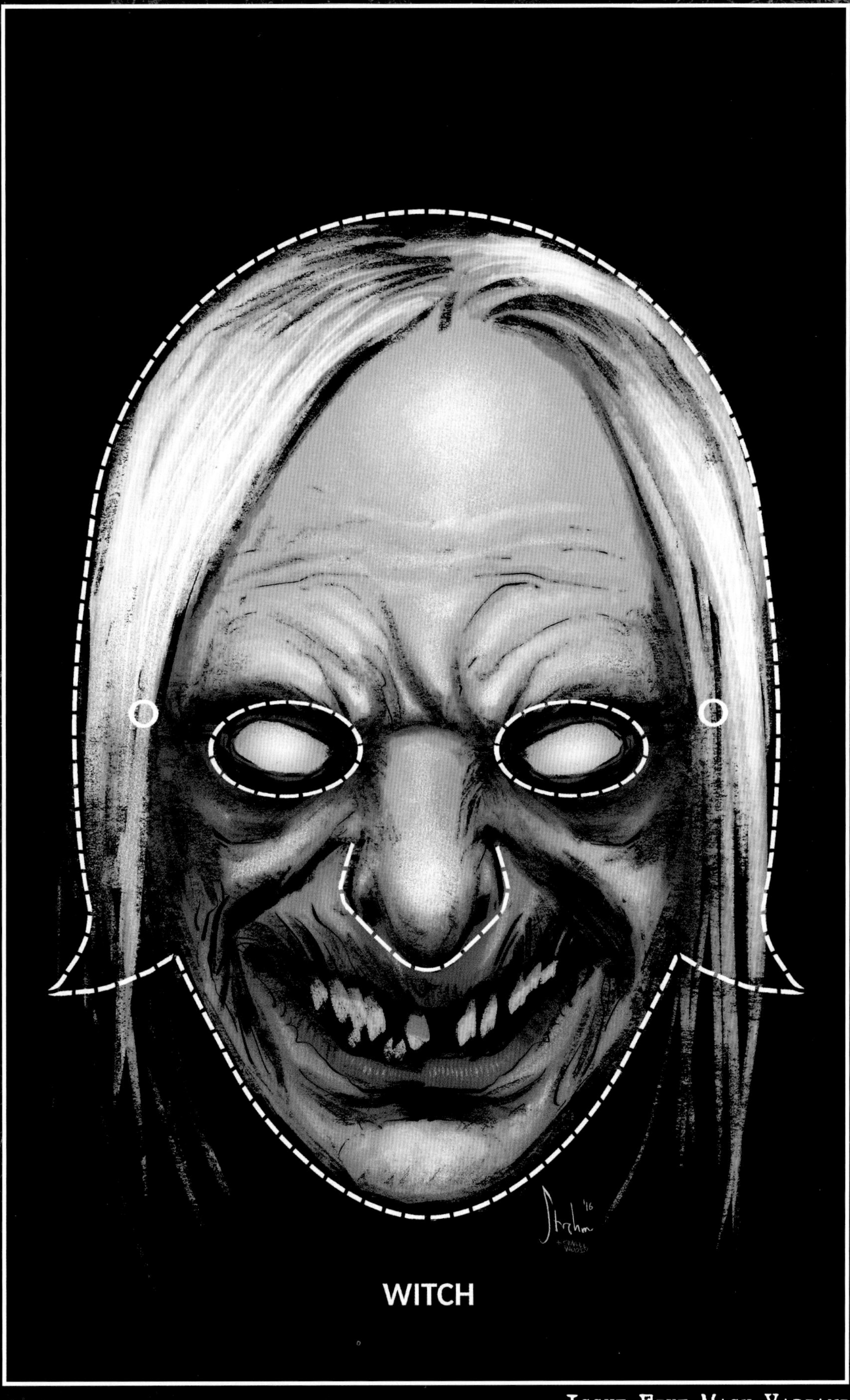
WITCH

Issue Five Mask Variant

Art by Kyle Strahm | Colors by Greg Smallwood

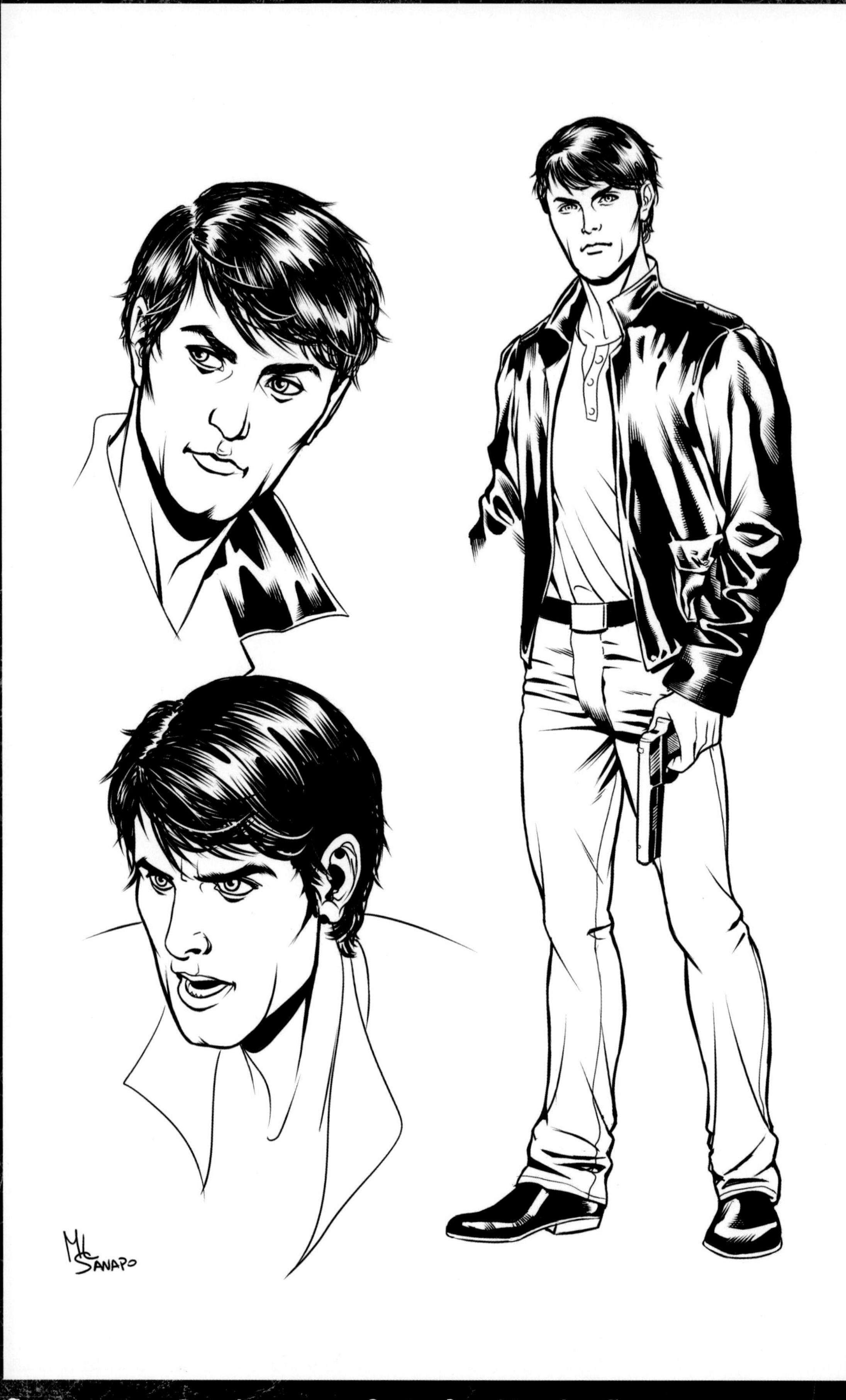

ML SANAPO

Character Design Try-Outs by Maria Sanapo

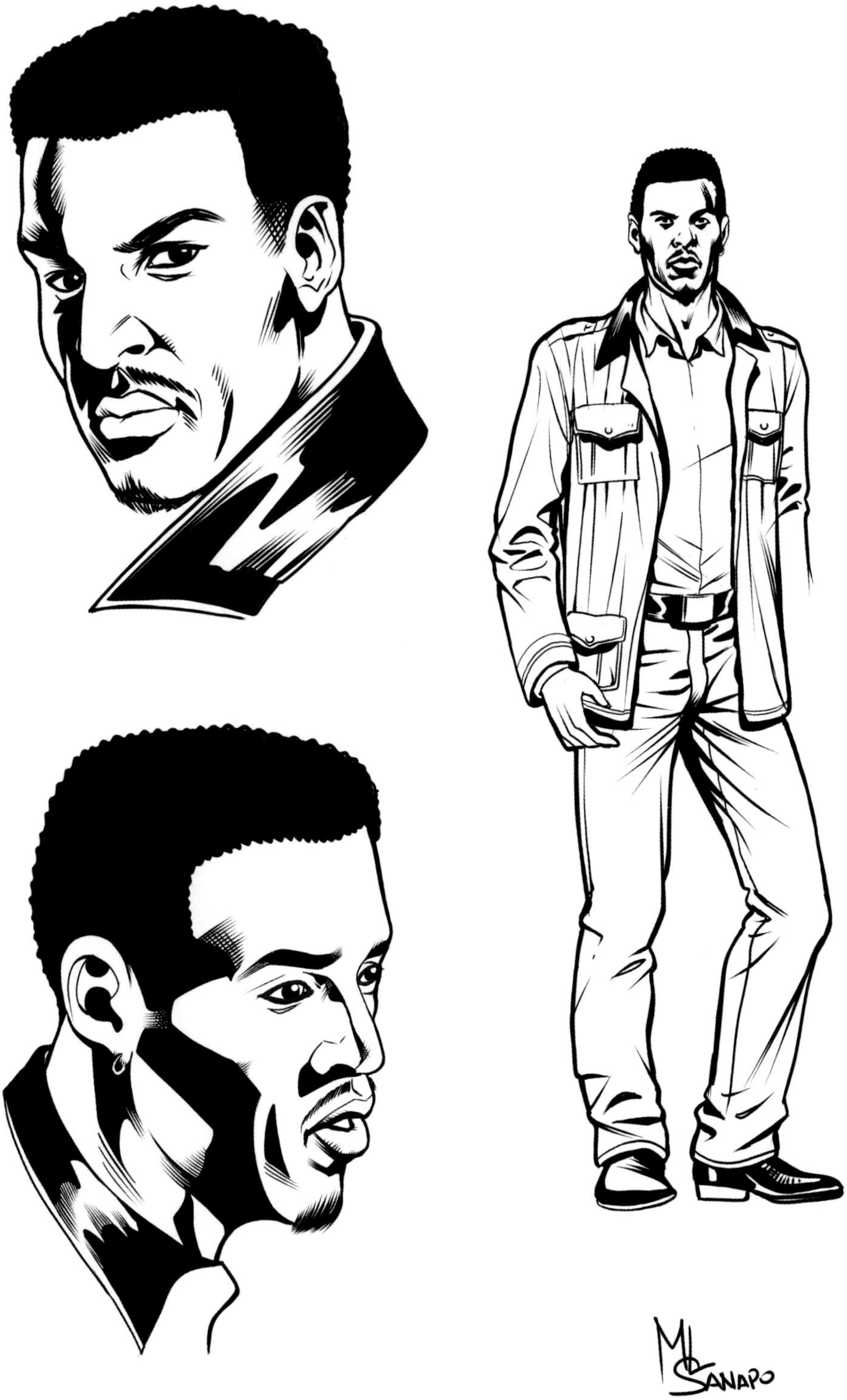

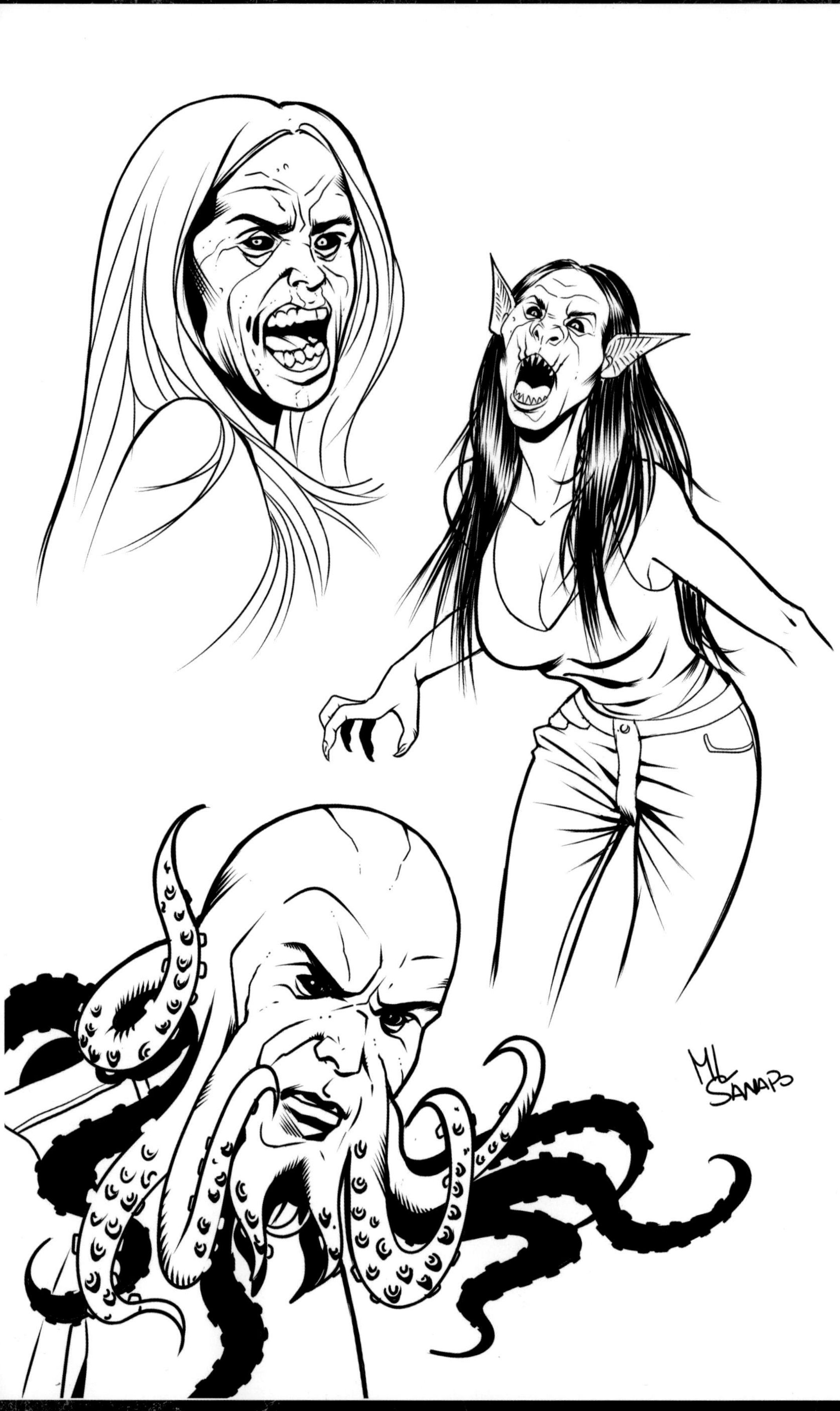
ML SANAPO

Character Design Try-Outs by Maria Sanapo

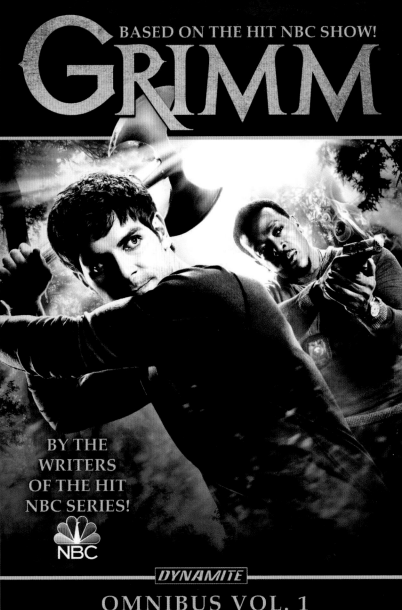 

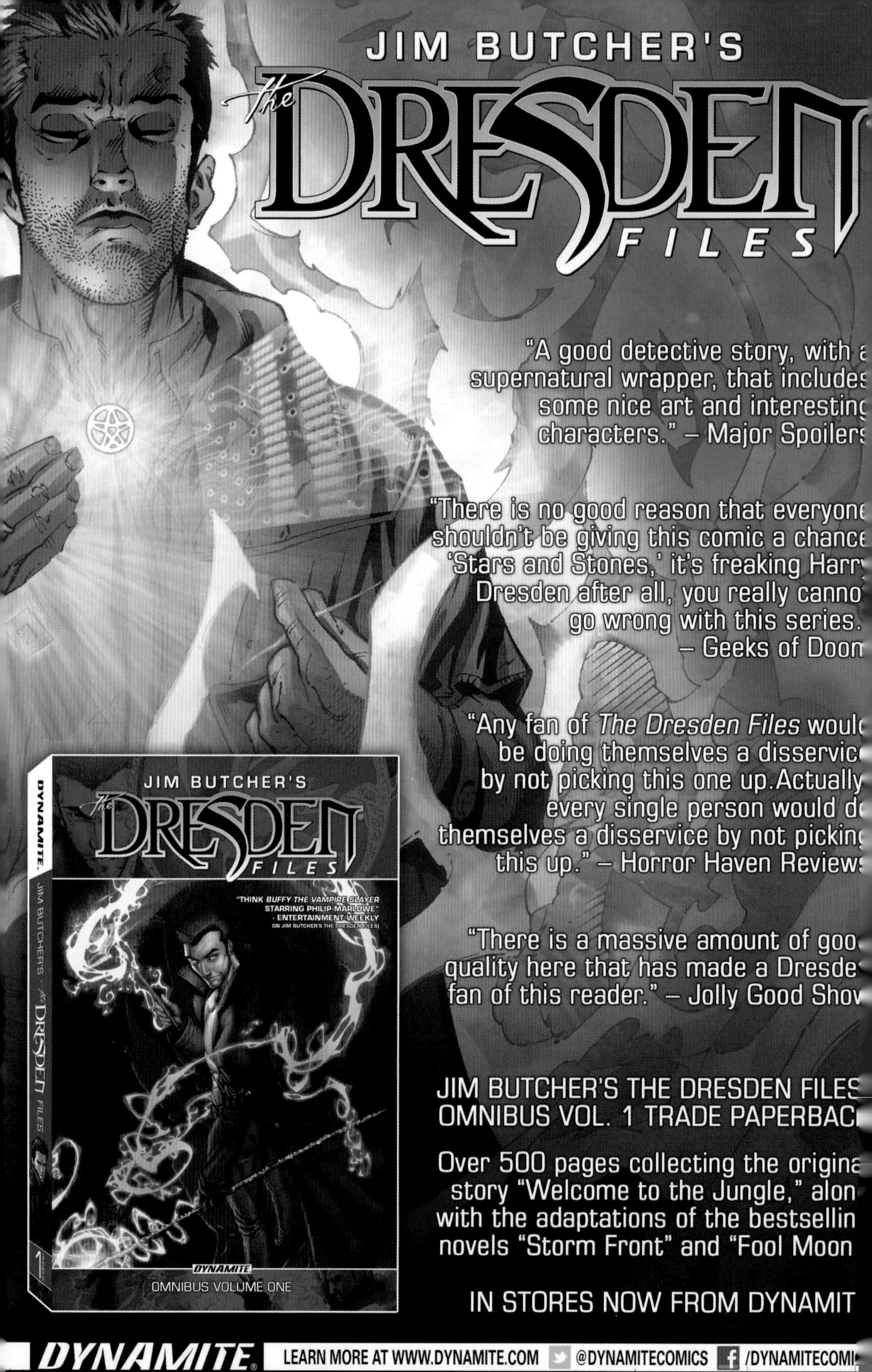
JIM BUTCHER'S
The DRESDEN FILES
"A good detective story, with a supernatural wrapper, that includes some nice art and interesting characters." – Major Spoilers
"There is no good reason that everyone shouldn't be giving this comic a chance 'Stars and Stones,' it's freaking Harry Dresden after all, you really cannot go wrong with this series." – Geeks of Doom
"Any fan of The Dresden Files would be doing themselves a disservice by not picking this one up. Actually every single person would do themselves a disservice by not picking this up." – Horror Haven Reviews
"There is a massive amount of good quality here that has made a Dresden fan of this reader." – Jolly Good Show
JIM BUTCHER'S THE DRESDEN FILES OMNIBUS VOL. 1 TRADE PAPERBACK
Over 500 pages collecting the original story "Welcome to the Jungle," along with the adaptations of the bestselling novels "Storm Front" and "Fool Moon"
IN STORES NOW FROM DYNAMITE
JIM BUTCHER'S The DRESDEN FILES
"THINK BUFFY THE VAMPIRE SLAYER STARRING PHILIP MARLOWE" - ENTERTAINMENT WEEKLY ON JIM BUTCHER'S THE DRESDEN FILES
DYNAMITE
OMNIBUS VOLUME ONE
DYNAMITE
LEARN MORE AT WWW.DYNAMITE.COM
@DYNAMITECOMICS
/DYNAMITECOMICS

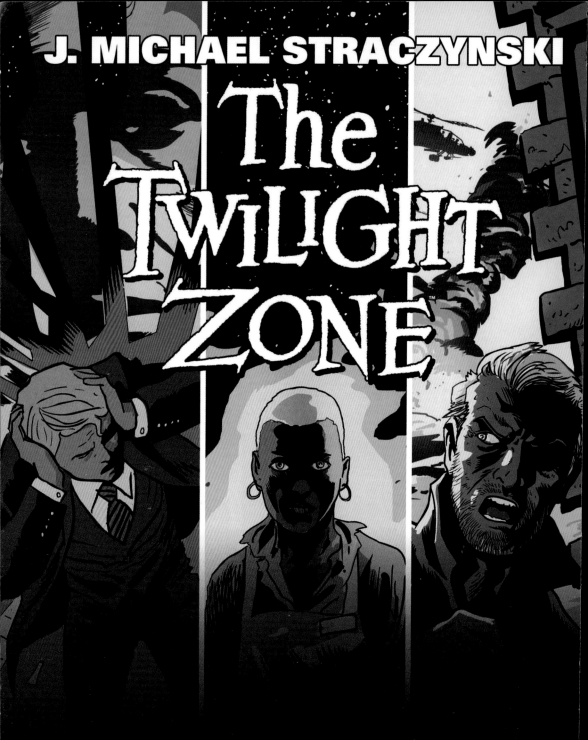

J. MICHAEL STRACZYNSKI

The TWILIGHT ZONE

The Three Volume Series

WRITTEN BY EISNER-AWARD-WINNING WRITER
J. MICHAEL STRACZYNSKI (BATMAN: EARTH ONE)
INTERIOR ART BY **GUIU VILANOVA** (DARK SHADOWS)
COVERS BY EISNER-AWARD-WINNING WRITER
FRANCESCO FRANCAVILLA (THE AFTERLIFE WITH ARCHIE)

In Stores Now